NIGHT NEVER ENDING

EUGENJUSZ ANDREI KOMOROWSKI

with Joseph L. Gilmore

HENRY REGNERY COMPANY—CHICAGO

Library of Congress Cataloging in Publication Data

Komorowski, Eugenjusz Andrei.
  Night never ending.

  1. Katyn Forest Massacre, 1940. 2. World War,
1939-1945—Personal narratives, Polish. 3. Komorowski,
Eugenjusz Andrei. I. Gilmore, Joseph L. 1929-
II. Title.
D804.R9K65   940.54′05′094762   73-19870

Published by Henry Regnery Company
114 West Illinois Street, Chicago, Illinois 60610

Manufactured in the United States of America
International Standard Book Number: 0-8092-9028-6
Library of Congress Catalog Card Number: 73-19870

To my fellow officers and countrymen
who proved that, even though the flesh is vulnerable,
the spirit of freedom
is impregnable.

CONTENTS

viii   Contents

PREFACE

When I was young, and even when I was not so young, I used to dismiss as fanciful self-indulgence the urges of older people to "clear their consciences" before they died. Now I know what they felt, for I am old and, I guess, tired. Not tired of living, of course. I have fought to stay alive too hard for too long simply to give it up now out of weariness. I am tired of hiding, though, and especially of hiding the truth.

We all hide much that is true, sometimes even from ourselves, often from others. But my truth is too big to keep to myself any longer. After all, I *did* literally climb out of the grave in which I had been left for dead. I *have* escaped from both Hitler and Stalin, and while I have been insane for periods up to years, I have surrendered neither my body nor my soul. With my bare hands I have killed men who have tried to send me to my grave to keep me from telling my story.

Now I feel that what my enemies could not do, nature is soon going to do for them—send me to the grave. It was this thought that finally led me to risk discovery of my secret existence in order to set down the story of how one man has survived through a night that has lasted for some 35 years, and to set straight, once and for all, the record of life and death as it concerned the governments of several countries and a Lieutenant-Colonel Eugenjusz Andrei Komorowski, from 1939 to the present day.

Since the outbreak of World War II, *survival* has been my consuming and sole thought. Since that September of 1939 I have been continually looking for ways to hide—from the Germans, the Russians, from death, from madness, from secret agents and informers, from police officials. The game is not played out, but I care less passionately about myself today than I have cared in the past. Now I want to tell my story.

NIGHT
NEVER
ENDING

1: THE FARM

MANY people who cannot remember what they had for dinner last night can recall every detail of some important day in their lives, no matter how long ago it occurred.

It is that way with me. I can't remember where I went three days ago or how I spent my time, but I can remember with painful vividness that September 19, 1939, when we rode toward the Russian lines, hoping to escape the Nazi monster at our heels.

For me, the excitement was tempered by an uneasiness of spirit. The swift, terrible war with the Germans was enough to sever the narrow threads of any man's faith in humanity, even in himself. And although it was good to get away, I was not altogether convinced that it would be better with the Russians. I *hoped* that we would be safe with them, but history was against us.

Dust rose in a swirling tornado at the rear of the staff car as the sergeant drove along the dirt road east of Grodno. General

Boleslaw Olszyna-Wilczynski, a jovial-faced, chunky little man with small, engaging eyes, alternately peered ahead for the Russians and watched the straggling line of beaten Polish soldiers and terrified civilians alongside the road. Beside me, Colonel Kazmierz Dzierzynski, the general's aide, sat like a block of scarcely warm granite. His eyes were riveted on the horizon; his large hands gripped his knees. Sweat ran in rivulets down his thick, strong neck.

It did not occur to me then, but we must truly have looked like three comic knights going out to make peace with the dragon. As usual, even in their jibes, the Germans were right. But then the Germans were always right. Only nineteen days earlier, the German military juggernaut had roared across our borders and moved almost without restraint across Poland, scattering Polish forces and forcing the remnants eastward toward Russia and southward toward Rumania. Indeed, as we rode across the bumpy, dusty road, German shells were battering Grodno from a distance of ten kilometers.

Our desertion of the city—and it was just that—stemmed from our last hope: if the Russians arrived in force, they might prevent Grodno's fall. It was, it is true, a slim chance, for the Russian Army had moved into Poland only on September 17, when it was evident that the country was already lost. Moreover, there were rumors that some Polish cities were fighting Russians. Yes, Russian assistance was a slim hope.

But we had no other. Polish forces were in full flight. I had escaped from Poznan, in northwestern Poland, only the week before. I had been lucky to get out before the Nazi armies encircled the Poznanian Pocket and trapped what became known as Poland's "Lost Army." With my wife, Suzan, I had boarded a train—the last train to leave the city—commandeered by a Polish general. The general, who had stayed in Poznan, had sent out his family, but he had also sent several hundred Polish officers with orders to report to the Grodno Military District commander and to help in the defense of that city against the rapidly moving war machine.

When I had first applied for permission to leave Poznan on the special train, my request had been turned down. There was limited space, and, according to standard procedures, the officers being sent to Grodno were allowed to take their families along. So it was only on the evening before the train was to leave, when a Polish major and his family were blown up in their home by a German shell, that Suzan and I were allocated seats.

With Poland in such disarray—even the government had fled and now was in Rumania—battle with the Germans and dealings with the Russians were matters left to the discretion of individual district commanders. Hence, shortly after the Russians had crossed our borders, claiming they were coming to protect Russian interests and to save Poles of Russian extraction from "continued and deepening harassment from Polish nationals," General Wilczynski had decided, quite on his own, that he would surrender Grodno and the surrounding district to the Russians.

He ordered the men in the district to greet the Russians as friends, even though we had received reports of Red Army atrocities. He believed that, although the Russians might not help fight the Nazis, it was better for the Russians to occupy the district than to have the Nazis destroy it. Our surrender was designed simply to stop the ruthless destruction.

It was an impossible choice for the general. For my part, I shared the opinion of the ranking military figure, Field Marshal Edward Smigly-Rydz, who had been quoted in August as saying, "With Hitler, I run the risk of losing my independence; but with Stalin, I should lose my soul." However, I was glad the decision was not mine.

Furthermore, it seemed as if fate was on my side—personally. My luck was holding out well. On my arrival in Grodno, reporting to headquarters as ordered, I had discovered that General Wilczynski's Russian-speaking interpreter had been killed by a German bomb. I spoke Russian fluently, and, even though I was only a captain and the general's staff consisted mainly of majors and colonels, I had applied for and been given the interpreter's job. The general had anticipated Russian involvement and did not want to be without a fluent interpreter. For several days before the invasion, Stalin had been making noises about "protecting the rights" of Polish-born Russians in eastern Poland. Few believed that he would chance a war with the Germans—no one knew, of course, of the prior agreement made between Molotov and Ribbentrop to split Poland in half and divide the spoils between our historic enemies, Russia and Germany—and the general wanted to be ready for any eventuality and, rather than look further, took me on as his personal interpreter.

The light brown dust flowed like clouds into the car and caught on our eyebrows, eyelashes, and uniforms. General Wilczynski coughed lightly, and I glanced at the short, solidly built man, thinking perhaps he was going to speak. But it was only the dust finding its way to his throat. He had closed his eyes and apparently had slipped into pleasant reverie.

Colonel Dzierzynski patted his thick legs nervously and stared at the horizon. I knew little about him. He rarely spoke, and my attention was constantly focused on the general, whose forceful personality tended to put other men into a kind of shadow. Even with his eyes closed, the general exuded a dynamism that competed with the dust for supremacy of the car's interior. The dust was winning.

We passed innumerable carts filled with belongings. Many were pulled by husbands and wives whose horses had been killed in the shellings and by the daily bombardments of the Luftwaffe. The sun beat upon their backs and on the black top of the staff car. The heat was oppressive, forcing its way into the car with the dust.

As my attention moved back inside the car, I saw that the general had opened his eyes and was gazing at me. From the expression on his face, I speculated that he was feeling pleased that his part in the war was soon to be over. He had made his decision, in the face of great pressure, and he felt at ease. His round, Slavic face was placid, and his dark eyes were bright diamonds in the dust that crusted his eyelids. A half smile crossed his face when I looked at him. He coughed dust from his throat and shifted in the soft seat.

"Captain Komorowski," he said, "we are expecting big things of you today. Your Russian is very good?"

"I think it is good enough, sir," I replied. My stomach became uneasy as I momentarily thought that I might fail the general. Although I spoke five languages, I used Polish almost exclusively; perhaps my Russian would *not* be good enough for the delicate task ahead.

"You are an enterprising officer," he said almost idly. "You escaped from Poznan when escape was virtually impossible."

"I was lucky."

The general studied me for a moment. "Luck and enterprise are closely related," he said, shifting to face me. "To reward the latter and to encourage the former, I am promoting you to major—a field promotion."

He uncrossed his shiny boots and felt in his pocket. He brought out the epaulets of a major and unceremoniously gave them to me.

"This is probably against regulations," he said. "These were taken from an officer who was killed last night by shrapnel. I took them off to send to his widow, but now I need them for more important reasons. I will make it official when we set up administrative offices under the Soviets.

"The Russians are very conscious of rank. No matter what they say about officers being enemies of the people, they still prefer to listen to officers of high rank—the higher the better. If Colonel Dzierzynski had been killed last night, you would be receiving his epaulets."

I glanced quickly at the colonel, but he was still staring directly ahead. He seemed unaffected by the general's comment. Perhaps he was good at hiding his emotions, or perhaps he was merely insensitive to the remark. Perhaps he was a realist.

I thanked the general, removed my captain's insignia, and, in the rolling, rocking car, attached the blood-caked epaulets to my shoulders, hoping that my papers would not be checked before I had time to explain the purpose of our mission. The general's comments only fueled my feelings of uneasiness because my experience was contrary to the general's. I distinctly felt that the Russians had *less* respect for high-ranking officers than for lower-grade officers or ordinary soldiers. Only two days ago, just before the Red Army had crossed our eastern border, small Russian planes had flown over many populated areas of eastern Poland, dropping leaflets. The leaflets proclaimed in large black type:

> In the last few days the Polish army has been finally defeated. The soldiers of the towns of Tarnopol, Halicz, Równe, Dubno, over 6,000 of them, all voluntarily, came over to our side.
>
> Soldiers, what is left to you? What are you fighting for? Against whom are you fighting? Why do you risk your lives? Your resistance is useless. Your officers are light-heartedly driving you to slaughter. They hate you and your families. They shot the negotiators whom you sent to us with a proposal of surrender.*
>
> Do not trust your officers! Your officers and generals are your enemies. They wish your death. Soldiers, turn on your officers and generals! Do not submit to the orders of your officers. Drive them out from your soil. Come to us boldly, to your brothers, to the Red Army. Here you will be cared for, here you will be respected.
>
> Remember that only the Red Army will liberate the Polish people from the fatal war and that, after that, you will be able to begin a new life.
>
> Believe us, the Red Army of the Soviet Union is your only friend.

Many Poles considered the messages another communist ploy, although it was common knowledge that the Russian government considered the military elites in capitalist nations exploiters of the working classes. I thought otherwise. As a teacher of history, I had followed the career of the Bolsheviks closely, from the earliest days of the Russian Revolution. I knew that communist axioms eventually were *made* to come true.

To say the least, I viewed my promotion with mixed emotions,

---

* No rank and file Polish negotiators were ever sent to the Russians.

and I was little comforted by those—General Olszyna-Wilczynski, among them—who suspected that the leaflets, which were signed by Marshal Semyon K. Timoshenko, the highest-ranking Soviet officer, represented a German plot to create dissension in our ranks and that they had been dropped from German planes with Russian markings.

Far ahead of us, dust rose in a tremendous cloud on the horizon. The early afternoon sun streaked through the dirty windscreen and nearly blinded us as we peered at some movement in the distance.

"It's the Russians, sir," the sergeant said disconsolately. "I can see a dozen tanks and several armored vehicles. There are also a lot of trucks and infantry."

Ahead on the right was a small farm clinging to a sloping meadow. The white frame house was coated with dust; the red barn rose high above the dust-covered green grass. In front of the house was a well and a huge oak tree with great spreading branches.

"Pull up at the farm," commanded the general. "We will refresh ourselves with water and wait here for them." He sat up straight in the seat, his eyes carefully following the movements in the distance.

After driving slowly across the smooth lawn in front of the house, the driver stopped in the shade of the oak, and we got out. A grizzled old farmer came warily down the porch steps. His expression was dyspeptic, and he seemed singularly unimpressed with the general's bemedaled chest, polished boots, and erect bearing.

"I suppose you want water like the others," he said. His voice was thick with Russian accent. His grandfather probably had arrived with earlier invaders and had stayed; he was one of the Polish Russians whom other Poles were persecuting, according to Stalin. He was one of the "official" reasons why Russia had violated our eastern border.

"We would like water," the general said quietly.

The old man glanced at the massed Red Army on the horizon and looked disdainfully at the general. His aspect clearly suggested that he felt he could be churlish. He was Russian; the general was "only" a Pole. The farmer nodded toward the well.

"Your kindness is greatly appreciated," the general said, smiling. He moved across the lawn and drew water from the well.

Our stopping seemed to be a signal to the refugees from Grodno. Along the road behind us, everyone halted; ahead the line of people stretching almost to the horizon slowed to a crawl as the refugees confronted the growing army. Ordinary citizens, fleeing from the bombs and shells of the Germans, stopped their carts and found shade under roadside trees or lay in harvested fields. Army units, including many officers, drew up near the farm and waited to see what would happen. The staff car, with the general's insignia, presaged importance.

The general drank from a shiny metal cup and handed it to Colonel Dzierzynski. Then he thanked the sour-faced farmer and got back into the car to wait for the Russians. I took the cup when Colonel Dzierzynski was finished. The water was good, sweet, and it washed the dust out of my throat. I drank more than I needed; the water seemed to calm my nerves.

The Russians came slowly along the road, up and down the undulating countryside. As they drew near, more tanks, artillery, armored vehicles, trucks, and infantrymen appeared on the horizon. The Red Army covered the knolls and then spread out across the horizon like a vast medieval host.

"Ask for the officer in charge," the general instructed me, relaxing in the comfortable seat. "Tell him my name and rank. Tell him also that we are here to surrender Grodno and that we wish to cooperate in order to establish tranquility in the district. Tell him that there will be no more fighting."

I could not imitate the general's calm. Not only was I struck with the realization that Grodno and therefore Suzan—Suzan! —would fall to the Russians if we failed, but also the physical fear that I had felt in Poznan returned as we waited in the farmyard. Without question I was *afraid* of the Russians, afraid of my small part in the task ahead. Little problems nagged me, looming unnecessarily large. Supposing, I mused, the first units were Ukrainian or Georgian or from some other region where difficult dialects were used—what would I do? I spoke Muscovite Russian only.

First to arive was a huge armored vehicle with a red star on its side. It rumbled off the road and stopped near the red barn. A tall, thin lieutenant with a dark thatch of hair and a thin black mustache climbed down. I saluted and asked for the officer in charge; he merely pointed toward the horizon with a small, leather-bound riding crop.

"He will arrive in good time," he said. Another armored car, several trucks, and a tank crunched into the farmyard. The old farmer and his wife smilingly drew water from the well and passed it around to the grinning Russians. "For the moment," the lieutenant continued, taking off thin leather gloves, "*I* am the officer in charge."

"Your name, please?" I asked.

He nodded toward the car, ignoring my question.

"Who is the fat man?"

I couldn't mask the indignation in my voice; it overrode my fear. "That, Lieutenant, is General Boleslaw Olszyna-Wilczynski, Commander of the Military District of . . ."

I got no further. The lieutenant turned to his men and ordered them from their vehicles. Infantrymen surrounded our small force of peace.

"Drag him to the barn," he shouted, his narrow face a study in self-satisfaction.

The incredible happened—far more than I had anticipated. Soldiers dragged General Wilczynski from the car, knocked him to the ground, began to beat him with their fists and rifle butts, and then kicked him with their boots.

What followed is very confused in my mind; things really went too fast for me to register the details. I remember shouting at the top of my voice for the soldiers to stop. Colonel Dzierzynski, a powerfully built man, took a more active role. He dashed into the crowd of soldiers to help the general—only, immediately and unceremoniously, to be knocked unconscious with the butt of a rifle.

"To the barn," the Soviet lieutenant repeatedly shouted. And his men dragged the semi-conscious general from the car over toward the farmer's barn.

The lieutenant turned to me. "Tell your general, Commander of the Military District of . . . what is it?"

"Grodno."

"No matter," the lieutenant said with a leer. "It no longer exists as a military entity. Tell the general to face the barn and to place his hands high on the door."

I protested. "Lieutenant, this is absolutely unnecessary. General Olszyna-Wilczynski made a special point of coming out here to . . ."

"Tell him or I will have all of you shot," the Soviet officer snarled. His arm swept in a semicircle. "Those people, too. They will be chopped up like fodder, all of them." There was a smile on his face, though his voice was strained.

An immature, thoroughly insecure young officer trying to impress his men by manhandling an enemy officer of much superior rank is a dangerous man. I walked toward the general but was stopped by two soldiers. They pushed me back with their rifles. I shouted at the general to turn and place his hands on the door. He looked at me with a puzzled, almost amused expression.

"Tell him again," the lieutenant ordered.

I repeated the order, adding that all of us would be shot if he didn't do as he was told. The general shrugged, permitted himself a smile of derision, and reached high on the barn door. He even stood on tiptoe to emphasize the fact that he was carrying out the ridiculous order to the utmost.

Watching the general's antics, I did not notice that the lieutenant had taken his pistol from his side holster. Suddenly I heard the crack of the pistol and saw the general's stocky body lurch against the red barn door.

"You bastard!" I screamed.

In that moment, madness seemed to break open. Ignoring me, the lieutenant fired at the general again. Simultaneously, there came a withering burst of machine-gun fire from a kneeling Red Army sergeant. The general spun around and fell back against the barn door. His arms went up again, blood mixing with the faded red paint.

The pistol barked again; the machine gun belched unendingly, sputtering with a mania to rip up human flesh. Other soldiers joined in. I was convinced that they would murder us all. Even the old farmer and his fat wife ran to the tenuous safety of their front porch.

General Olszyna-Wilczynski's body twitched and coiled against the barn door as bullets poured into him. His eyes opened wide, and he slid to a sitting position on the bloody grass. Another burst from a machine gun blasted his face into a mass of bone, gristle, and blood. The figure toppled over on the bloody stub that had been a head.

The lieutenant holstered his pistol and turned to me with a satisfied grin, with the look of an artisan who had done a fine piece of work. "Are there any other generals in the Military District of Grodno?" he mocked.

I said in Polish: "To hell with you, you son of a bitch!"

As I turned from the grotesque sight at the barn and knelt over the still unconscious Colonel Dzierzynski, I saw the farmer and his wife standing on the steps. Now that it was all over, their faces were broad with laughter.

2: GRODNO

T HE exodus from Grodno was reversed by the Red Army, which rapidly gathered hundreds of Polish soldiers and civilians into a great, lumbering group. The general's body lay at the barn door; I never found out what happened to it afterward. Colonel Dzierzynski, still unconscious, was thrown into the rear of the staff car, and two Soviet soldiers climbed in as guards. The sergeant turned the car and wove it slowly through the multitude of Polish refugees toward the village between the farm and Grodno. I was taken into the armored vehicle by the Soviet lieutenant.

As we approached the village, the shelling of Grodno stopped, almost eerily, as though some invisible restraining hand had been held up by the Russians and had been heeded by the Germans. We could only guess the reasons. For the moment, we were simply happy that the bombing and shelling had stopped.

We followed the black staff car, leaving the rounding up of fleeing Poles to the Red infantry. The armored vehicle roared right up to the village hall, scattering cars and *droshkas*, frightening horses, and putting the villagers in awe. The mayor, standing on the steps of the village hall, grinned and bowed obsequiously to the upstart officer.

"The Soviets have come to liberate us," I said in Polish, carrying out the lieutenant's orders. "The bastards shot General Wilczynski to death in cold blood."

For a moment, the mayor's face showed a trace of disquiet, but fear quickly brought back his obsequious manner.

"Tell his honor," the lieutenant said officiously, "that we will use his hall as headquarters. His last duty will be to post an order for all men—civilians and military—between the ages of eighteen and sixty to report here at 0700 tomorrow. Failure to do so will result in severe action."

"What type of severe action?" I felt emboldened to ask.

The lieutenant poked the mayor's stomach with his leather crop. "We will find them and kill them on the spot."

I repeated the order to the mayor. He nodded and smiled at Lieutenant Rimsky. "There are. papers I must get from my office," he pleaded.

I informed the lieutenant, who snapped: "Tell the mayor that he needs only to have orders printed and posted. After that, he can go straight to hell. He is no longer mayor. He is nothing."

Colonel Dzierzynski, who had revived during the hot ride from the country, stumbled with me into the village hall, where we were taken to the mayor's office by the insufferable Soviet lieutenant. The colonel still was dazed from the blow to his skull, and he kept rubbing the back of his head with his hand. He muttered obscenities in Polish and answered the lieutenant's questions tersely and bitterly. The Soviet officer ignored the colonel's burning anger.

Shortly after nine o'clock, there was a furor in the streets; a staff car and more armored vehicles had arrived. Russian voices, ringing harshly in the warm night, ordered the confused villagers to clear the streets of their horse-drawn carts.

The clamor, as we soon discovered, signaled the arrival of

Lieutenant General Fyodor Skmorovitch, commander of the Red Army's Fourth Division, of which Lieutenant Rimsky's company was the vanguard. The Soviet general, who also had heard of the ignominious death of General Wilczynski, stormed into the office. For a moment, I was convinced that the stocky, well-built general was really angry. But I also knew—and it would later be confirmed again and again—that many Russians are superb actors. Virtually every human emotion, from fear to anger to kindness to shock, could be summoned instantly to fit any given situation. I have never been able to determine if this is a natural Russian talent or if the Soviet elites were trained to put on such acts virtually on cue, but many Russians had mastered the skills.

"Under whose orders did you execute the Commander of the Military District of Grodno?" the general demanded of the now-erect lieutenant.

"Sir, the leaflets. I . . . "

"Under whose *orders*, Lieutenant?" the general roared, giving us a sidelong glance.

"No orders, sir," the lieutenant said, his voice quavering. "He was an enemy of the people and it is my understanding . . . "

"In the future," the general bellowed, carrying on the verbal charade, "act only on orders. Understand *nothing* except specific orders. Do you understand, Lieutenant?"

"Yes, sir."

"Dismissed!"

The lieutenant quickly gathered up his belongings, cramming his papers haphazardly into his briefcase. He shoved his note pad toward the general and left, a beaten puppy—or so it seemed. The general's face immediately became warm and glowing with friendliness and apology. He began to speak to Colonel Dzierzynski, who watched with morose indifference.

"I am the only one who understands Russian," I told the general. "This is Colonel Kazmierz Dzierzynski, the general's aide and now the superior Polish officer in the district. I am Major Eugenjusz Komorowski."

The Soviet general eased his bulk into the mayor's comfortable chair, which was accustomed to heavy weight and therefore did not even squeak in opposition, and gazed at us. His eyes became warm, mellow. I made a mental note: Act Two of this evening's play was commencing.

"I cannot find sufficient words for apology," he said, his voice deepening and wavering like a talented undertaker's. "This has been a terrible misfortune. A terrible misunderstanding."

"But no orders?" I queried.

General Skmorovitch looked deeply into my eyes, searching for irony or sarcasm, and shook his undertaker's head sadly.

"No orders. Rest assured, Citizens, the men responsible for this terrible misfortune will be punished. Please, Major Komorowski, explain my sentiments to the colonel."

I interpreted the general's words. Colonel Dzierzynski merely rubbed his head and glared at the Soviet commander, his hard blue eyes seeking to penetrate the protective shroud of the general's thick eyebrows. The general shifted uneasily in the mayor's chair, which still issued no protesting squeak.

"Tell Colonel Dzierzynski that I will be most honored to work with him toward a peaceful resolution of the situation," the general said, returning the colonel's stare. "Tell him that we wish no reprisals for your commander's death. Grodno must surrender."

"With your permission, sir," I ventured, "we were on our way to surrender Grodno when the so-called terrible misfortune occurred. It was General Wilczynski's desire to surrender. He went out in peace to meet your army."

"So I have been informed," the general said. "I have also been told that news of the Polish commander's death has spread and has excited the people. The garrison in the city is preparing to fight, not to surrender. I wish only to clear the air, Citizens. Grodno *must* surrender, without delay and without resistance."

I interpreted, but Colonel Dzierzynski remained silent, his eyes never leaving the general's. I found myself glancing from one to the other, looking for signs of incipient violence. Nothing

happened, and this moment passed. The Soviet general arose
—the mayor's chair let out a small squeak, possibly of relief—and
said softly, his eyes moving from me to the colonel: "Have a good
sleep in your quarters. I trust you on your officer's honor to
return here at 0700."

"Ask the bastard what will happen at 0700," Colonel Dzierzynski said in a strangely magnified voice, as though he were
speaking through a microphone. "Ask the bastard what the
Russians plan to do with our people, civilians as well as military."

The mantle of leadership had fallen on the colonel, and he was
going to wear that mantle with authority. I looked at him with a
new interest and growing respect and began to feel a flow of
hope, hope that had left me when the general had been murdered. I repeated his questions, discreetly leaving out the
epithet. The general, toying with the mayor's letter opener,
remained standing. He smiled and replied evasively: "We shall
see—at 0700 tomorrow. Good night, Citizens."

But Colonel Dzierzynski wasn't satisfied. He sat like a stone in
the chair and glowered at the general. "Tell the bastard that we
are staying until he gives us a satisfactory answer—unless he
wants that fucking lieutenant to throw me up against a barn door
and blast *me* to pieces!"

I softened the colonel's words. The general did not move.
Sliding the letter opener through stubby fingers, he said, "When
Grodno surrenders, we will arrange for your military people to
escape into Rumania. As for the civilians, they are workers.
Commerce will continue—under Soviet rules, of course. Your
soldiers may leave and fight the Nazis in another place, or they
may stay and work for the good of all. The choice belongs to
them."

The news stunned me. After all, we *were* prisoners, and
though I had never articulated my fear, I had expected to suffer
the fate of all prisoners taken by the Russians: banishment to
Siberia, at least. Colonel Dzierzynski also seemed surprised,
perhaps even a little shocked, by the general's promise. But
almost at once, a glimmer of disbelief crossed his face.

"What of the officers? Ask the bastard what he will do with the officers," he demanded.

I thought the question peculiar at first. Although the meaning of the leaflets was quite different, the Soviet general's promise had included *all* Polish military personnel. Would the Russians eliminate officers or would they treat all Polish military alike?

When I interpreted Colonel Dzierzynski's question, the general merely stared at me with an unreadable expression. He leaned forward and deliberately scratched the shiny top of the mayor's expensive desk with the letter opener. "Special arrangements are always made for special people," he said cryptically. "Polish officers will receive special treatment."

The general sat down with a smile of dismissal. I stood waiting for Colonel Dzierzynski to rise, but he merely gripped his knees and leaned toward the desk. "Sit down, Komorowski," he said with a level, controlled voice. "Tell the bastard I have more questions. I won't be dismissed like a fucking servant."

Sweat began to seep out of the pores of my forehead and palms. Wiping my hands on my tunic and swallowing hard, I took my seat and looked at General Skmorovitch.

"I would like to know if we are under arrest," the colonel said, his eyes still on the general. "Are we prisoners of an undeclared war?"

"Prisoners?" the general replied with a broad smile when I interpreted. "Let us just say that you are being released to your quarters for tonight. We will discuss the future when everyone is assembled here in the morning."

"Ask him why we can't go to garrison headquarters to bring about the surrender he says he wants." The colonel's voice was clear and sharp, as though he were the victor and the general the prisoner.

"Tell the colonel," the general said with exaggerated patience, "that the inner perimeter of the city has been turned into a virtual fortress. The Poles in the main sector have thrown up barricades to keep out the friendly visitors from Russia." A quick, derisive grin flickered over his thick lips. "Naturally, we have had to post guard details near these barricades to keep Polish soldiers from entering or leaving the city."

"That still doesn't explain why we can't go into the city," Colonel Dzierzynski retorted after I had translated.

The general sighed. I felt a wave of weariness flood over me from translating the strained, guarded words of the two adversaries. As I translated, I tried to remove the heat with which Colonel Dzierzynski spoke, but the Soviet general was not fooled. He could almost smell the colonel's anger and indignation.

"The colonel is slow to understand," he said, rocking gently. "If I were to send you into the city, what assurance would I have that you would not join the rebellious forces and stir them up even more?"

Colonel Dzierzynski studied the question for a moment, then replied: "The bastard says he wants Grodno to surrender. I am the senior officer of record; yet the garrison is now under the command of Lieutenant Colonel Hugo Mijakowski, who apparently presumes me dead along with General Wilczynski. I wish no bloodshed. If I can go to the garrison, I can bring about the surrender—just as General Wilczynski ordered."

The Soviet general took some time to study this reply. Then he smiled and waved his hands helplessly.

"Words make fine sounds," he said, "but I am powerless to let you enter the garrison. I would be taking too large a chance. If you surrendered the garrison, I would be considered a hero. But if. once you were in, you decided to fight our army of liberation, I could be shot as a traitor."

"Typical Russian logic," Colonel Dzierzynski muttered. Then, without taking his eyes from the general, he returned to one of his first questions: What would happen to our officers when the Soviets rounded up everyone in the village square tomorrow morning?

Again General Skmorovitch hedged. Colonel Dzierzynski fired question after question at him. Except for brief flares of impatience in his expression, the general accepted the questioning as the colonel's right. And Colonel Dzierzynski kept it up until almost midnight; then he gave in. Nothing of note was accomplished, and I left the village hall with an uneasy feeling of despair and approaching disaster.

Threading our way through throngs of Soviet war machinery and boisterous soldiers, I felt near exhaustion. My mind was on Suzan. I tried to blot out thoughts of tomorrow—and of today—and to think only of Suzan and her soft loveliness. In my mind, I could see her waiting in a dark apartment, her hands trembling in her lap, her eyes wide and questioning, her fears turning her lovely body into a quivering mass. But Colonel Dzierzynski's mind apparently was on the Soviet general, on the garrison, and on what might happen at 0700. As we reached a deserted corner two blocks from the square, he took my arm. His grip was unusually tight.

"Do you know Lieutenant Antoni Urban well?" he whispered.

"Fairly well. He lives in the building next to mine. A member of the Third Ulanys, I believe. Brave—perhaps a bit foolhardy, I hear."

The colonel nodded. "Just the man we need. Deliver these to him at his apartment." He took a sealed envelope from his pocket and I asked what was in it. "Orders from General Olszyna-Wilczynski," he said.

"But . . . "

"I know. He's dead. But a good general always expects the worst and drafts alternate plans. These are orders for Lieutenant Colonel Hugo Mijakowski, the garrison commander. They instruct him to fight the Russians."

"How can we fight if we're to be at the village hall in the morning?"

"We won't be here," he said. He looked at his expensive American wristwatch. "It's just midnight now. On my way home, I'll contact a few other officers who live outside the perimeter. We'll all meet in my apartment at 0430. Then we'll move out, gather up as many troops as we can, and try to infiltrate the

Russian ring around the city proper. While the Russians sleep, we must move as many men as possible into the garrison and to the barricades. Tell Urban to stay after he delivers the orders to Mijakowski."

It seemed suicidal. I would have preferred to fetch our wives and strike off toward Rumania. But if the others were to fight for the city, I would fight, too. Having been a coward once, I would not run and be a coward again.

We said goodnight, and I turned to go. His hand shot out and caught my arm in a strong grip.

"Say nothing to Suzan. She must not know that you are leaving her behind. She must not know of any plans."

"I'm sorry, Colonel Dzierzynski," I said, fixing upon his eyes in the semidarkness of the quiet street. "I'm going to take Suzan into the city."

"You can't."

"And I can't leave her, either."

He released his grip and nodded. "I understand. But it cannot be any other way. I know she is terrified of the war, and I know how you must feel about her. But we can't be held back by women. Come alone. That's an order."

Lieutenant Antoni Urban was a handsome, sinewy man with wide shoulders and a perpetual smile. He was a cheerful person, much like a mischievous child, who inspired instant liking. Other officers in the garrison considered him a class clown, but I saw in him—almost from the moment of our first meeting—a serious side. What many took for frivolity, I believed to be a reflection of a deeper thought, perhaps of hurt or of fear of being hurt. His comical comments always seemed to carry a tinge of solid reality and not a little of sarcasm.

Urban had one other quality. His reputation as a clown was equaled by his reputation as an expert with women. A bachelor, the lieutenant seemed far more preoccupied with women than he was with the war, though he had fought the Germans furiously during their initial drive toward Grodno. His Third

Ulanys had been virtually decimated before the survivors of the advance units turned back to Grodno. They had met the Nazis thirty kilometers west of the city and had held them up for three days. The few who returned did so in glory, though many were badly wounded. Antoni Urban, who lived in the apartment building next to mine, had come back with jokes about the Nazis, without a mark on his handsome face or virile frame, and with a reputation for heroism.

As I entered the dark foyer, the image of General Olszyna-Wilczynski's gruesome death passed before me. Trying to purge myself of it, my mind caught on Suzan and did not swerve from her beauty: her long blonde hair, her vivid blue eyes, her delicate face, her ample breasts, her soothing voice. I detested the war for what it was doing to her inner spirit.

Virtually a child, Suzan was the antithesis of my first wife, Radjiga, who had been full of fire and independence—and fight. I had met Radjiga while I still attended the high school at Poznan. She was a strong, muscular girl who might have represented Poland in the Olympics if she had applied herself more to gymnastics and less to her personality. I had recognized no fault in her, loving her too deeply in my youthful way. Although my parents had not approved the marriage, they had not forbidden it, either. In any case, we had married just after my graduation from the University of Cracow and before I had begun my two years of required military duty. Reason didn't matter to us. We were in love; we married. Then came the terrible fights, and only three years after our marriage—her death of cancer of the liver.

At the time, I was beginning my second year of teaching in Poznan's main high school. Dismally unprepared, I taught history, wrestling, and gymnastics. In the academic year following Radjiga's death, I went about as though in a dream world. Mentally, I suppressed the many fights we had endured; I remembered only the good moments, especially the wildly abandoned moments of sex, and I resolved never to marry again.

Through a special scholarship fund set up for foreign studies,

I was able to go abroad to take advanced courses in history and languages. Each summer for ten years, I studied in London; for the following five summers, I studied in Brussels. My parents died during those years, and in 1938 I decided that I had been going abroad long enough. I settled down to give teaching my full attention.

Suzan had graduated in 1937. I had noticed her as a student, of course. In fact, I had realized when she first entered my classroom at the age of fifteen not only that she was very attractive but also that she soon had developed a great deal of affection for me.

Daily contact with Suzan for three years had an intense effect on my subconscious mind. I did not know it—or did not recognize it. But Suzan knew, and she quietly and patiently set her mind to the object of marrying me. Thus, after she graduated, she made frequent visits to the high school to practice gymnastics, which I taught in the evenings.

One evening, following an adult gymnastics class I was teaching, Suzan's patience gave out. It was obvious to her that I was not going to make the natural move. She came up to me and said, "How about a cup of tea?"

That was it. Three months later, following the old tradition, I went to her mother and father and made a formal request for her hand. Her mother was Russian; her father, Polish. Her mother was against the marriage because I had no Russian blood in my veins; her father objected because of my age—he was only three years older than I. But her parents had not reckoned with Suzan's persuasiveness. Within a week, she had broken down all their objections. We were married on June 27, 1938. We spent our honeymoon in Danzig, with moonlight cruises along the Baltic's southern shore.

Now, just over a year later, we were still like newlyweds, still very much in love. As each day passed—and especially since the war had come—I realized more and more that Suzan was peculiarly unsuited to the rough parts of life on this earth. She required more than the normal measure of protection, just as she gave forth more than the normal measure of love. And I knew somehow, no matter what Colonel Dzierzynski said, that I would find a way to get her into the garrison.

Still there was little time to think, only to exist. And I existed now mainly to protect Suzan. Remembering this, I hurried up the steps and down the corridor to Lieutenant Urban's apartment. The sooner I completed my small errand, the sooner I could be with Suzan.

I knocked several times before the lieutenant opened the door. He was wearing only shorts, and in the dimness behind him, I could see the outline of a woman in a sheer nightgown silhouetted against a window. It seemed ludicrous, but the tall, muscular lieutenant with the unruly black hair and mischievous grin stood at rigid attention and gave a sharp salute.

"Captain Komorowski?" he asked, peering at me in the dark corridor. "My God, what are you doing here? I thought you were dead, along with General Wilczynski."

"Not yet, Lieutenant." I gave him the sealed orders and told him what must be done. "You're to leave immediately. After you have given these to Colonel Mijakowski personally, remain there." I looked past him at the shapely girl. "Sorry if this interrupts anything."

He grinned. "No problem, sir. I was merely saying good-bye to an old friend before the Russians confiscate her."

I fumbled for a reply. "I apologize for—for cutting it short."

"You didn't," he said. "Hell, we've been saying good-bye for almost four hours." He suddenly snapped back to attention and saluted again. "Sir, may I be among the first to offer congratulations."

"For what?"

He slapped a bare, hairy shoulder, and I remembered the epaulets of the dead major. I grinned and glanced again at the buxom girl near the window.

"Congratulations to you too, Lieutenant. You have fine friends."

Exhaustion seemed to peel away from my body as I ran down the street and up into my own apartment building. Suzan was

waiting for me in the dark apartment; she would be waiting
—even if it took days for me to return. But she was, as usual, very
cautious. Her voice came, frightened, through the door.

"Who is it? Who is there?"

"Open up, silly girl. It's your husband."

The door opened swiftly, and Suzan, tears streaking down her
cheeks, fell into my arms. I guided her inside and closed the
door. I kissed away the tears and calmed her sobs with caresses.

"Why all the tears, precious?" I asked. "Are they tears of
happiness at seeing me or tears of sorrow that I wasn't killed?"
This was a private joke between us. Since she had practically
proposed to me initially, I always teased her about making the
wrong choice and gently accused her of wishing that I would go
out someday and not return.

"On the radio," she said, indicating the cathedral-shaped box
near the window, "they told about the general." Her voice qua-
vered like a child's after punishment. "I thought you all were
dead. And . . . "

"And what?"

She clung tightly to me and buried her face in my shoulder.
Her body gave a great, involuntary shudder.

"Russian soldiers came," she said in a hoarse whisper.

"Did you open the door?" I asked. My voice was tight and I was
scared—mostly of what her answer might be.

"No," she blurted, sobbing again. "They threatened to break
down the door, but the janitor got them to leave. I thought I was
going to be . . . to be . . . "

"Raped?" I said, finishing her sentence. I was so relieved that I
almost laughed.

"Yes."

I pulled her head back. "Such a prize those pigs don't deserve," I said, smoothing her golden hair from her tear-stained
face. Some strands were wet and stuck to her cheeks. Even in the
darkness, I could see the sparkling eyes, the small, triangular
nose, the full, sensuous lips. I could feel her heavy breasts
expanding with her sobbing breath against my chest. "My poor
darling," I whispered. "You had a lot to worry about today."

Even in my relief, I felt a slight trembling inside. Apparently, the Russians who had come to the apartment were not very sure of themselves; they were probably disobeying orders by venturing so close to the city proper. But there was no reason to worry further. I would leave the apartment in less than three hours, and I would take Suzan with me.

Suzan hugged me tightly, flattening her body against me. "Oh, Andrei," she said, "I thought you would never come back. I was so frightened. Please never leave me again. Never."

Suzan was the only person who called me Andrei, my father's first name. The custom in Russia is for the son to take his father's first name as his own middle name. Since Suzan was part Russian, and since she did not like the name Eugenjusz, she began to call me Andrei the first week of our courtship. I liked it.

"I won't ever leave you again," I said. The weariness waned as I held her in my arms.

"You must promise," she said. Her lips were close to my ear, and her clear voice was musical.

"I promise," I replied, pulling back her head and kissing away a new tear.

Her cheek touched the new epaulet, and she drew back, staring at the emblems in the darkness. I explained about my promotion. For the first time she smiled, and the room seemed to brighten.

"They go well with your wide shoulders," she said, touching the epaulets, not knowing that they were caked with blood. "I'll bet you even frightened their generals with your great physique and piercing blue eyes." She touched my chin with a slender finger. "And your strong chin with its dimple. Did you frighten their generals?"

"They quivered in their drawers," I said, drawing her close again.

With Suzan in my arms and the scent of her perfume heady in my brain, I forgot the war and the 0430 meeting. I led my wife through the dark parlor to the large bedroom. As my mind fought again with the war—I must find a way to accomplish the impossible: to serve my country and to keep Suzan with me—we curled warmly on the bed, and her smooth thigh slid up between my legs. I thrust the impossible problem from my mind and buried myself in a growing passion that brought tired muscles and a defeated spirit to life again.

Suzan, her fears abated and her body soft in the soothing afterglow of lovemaking, slept immediately. I lay beside her, sensing her vital breath. Life was precious; yet I had seen it fall from men like leaves from trees. I tried to philosophize about life and death and war, but the more immediate problem kept returning: how could I keep Suzan with me and still fight the Russians?

I slipped from the bed and went into the parlor. Lighting a cigarette, I sat down near the window that looked out at the quiet, tree-lined street. The sighs of a gentle September breeze competed with the distant rumble of war machinery. The city was quiet; some sleeping, others watching and waiting.

When I was thoroughly comfortable and my thoughts were becoming optimistic—perhaps the Germans and Russians would wipe each other out—everything collapsed with a heavy knock at the door.

I leaped to the door before the knocking awoke Suzan and opened it to face the tall, thin lieutenant with the black mustache. Flanking him were two soldiers with rifles.

"Major Komorowski," Lieutenant Rimsky said crisply, "your presence is required at the village hall. Immediately."

I looked at my wristwatch. In just over two hours, I was to be at Colonel Dzierzynski's quarters.

"May I ask why?"

He didn't answer.

I went quietly into the bedroom and got my uniform, which had been draped casually over a chair. The lieutenant stood in the doorway and peered into the darkness. I prayed that Suzan would not awaken. I took my clothes back to the parlor to dress. If Suzan awoke, she would surely begin to scream and God only knew what that might lead to. When I was dressed, the lieutenant looked at me for a long moment.

"You're a very big man," he mused. "Probably quite strong. Most Poles are strong as oxen. But I don't think you are so tough that you won't need your coat and rucksack."

I looked at his face, seeking an answer to the quick fear that leaped into my brain. He had given the impression that I was needed at the village hall for a meeting. But one didn't need a coat and rucksack for a meeting. Was I being placed under arrest again? And what about Colonel Dzierzynski? Had they arrested him, too?

Something—instinct, perhaps—told me that I would never return to my comfortable flat on the quiet, tree-lined street. More, I would never again see Suzan.

The car, with a Red Army sergeant at the wheel, entered the village I had left only a few hours earlier. In that moment, there was a distant rumble, much like thunder. Guns on the opposite side of Grodno had opened up. The deafening crashes rent the air as the guns directly behind us fired. The whistling of shells was followed by a shuddering explosion and bright flashes. Tank guns opened up point-blank at the inadequate barricades. The battle for Grodno had begun.

"*Bekarci!*" I swore in Polish. "All of you are bastards!"

There was chaos in the village and at the village hall. The square was filled with Polish soldiers sitting on the grass. Russian soldiers with automatic rifles surrounded them. From the rooftops, portable floodlights blazed night into day. New groups of Polish soldiers, their hands clasped to the tops of their heads, were being herded onto the crowded grass and made to sit. Officers were being singled out and taken into shops with windows broken by Russian looters, and into the town hall itself.

I was taken from the car a block from the village hall. The slim lieutenant removed his pistol from his holster and poked it into my back.

"You are privileged," he said haughtily. "Instead of spending the remainder of the night outdoors on the grass, you have the honor of comfortable quarters in the mayor's building."

They marched me through a cordon of Soviet soldiers, past the growing mass of Polish soldiers in the square, and directly into the town hall. Here, the lieutenant held back, and the two guards pushed me with their weapons toward the stairs leading to the basement. "You live down there, Polish pig," one of them said. He gave me a shove and I stumbled and nearly fell on the stairs. Both guards stood at the top of the stairs, grinning at me.

The wide corridor was filled with the slumped bodies of Polish officers. Many were badly wounded, and all lay on the cement floor, covered by their greatcoats, their rucksacks under their heads. As I moved among them, stepping over outstretched legs, I heard a loud moan. A young lieutenant who had had his ear blown off—along with a substantial portion of his temple—was crying and complaining that his toes hurt. I looked at his feet. His boots were intact, his feet unharmed. I started to tell the officer that his feet were just fine when I heard a strange whine in his throat. He was dead.

There was no more room in the corridor, so I moved along the hallway, which was lit by two small bulbs in wire cages. Passing offices, I saw officers lying on the floors, on desks, and even squatting in corners. Then as I passed an open doorway, I heard my name.

"Komorowski! In here. The tax commissioner's office."

I went into the office. Colonel Kazmierz Dzierzynski was stretched out on the commissioner's desk, using a folded desk blotter for a pillow. His coat and rucksack were beside him. There were only two other officers in the room, and they were asleep.

"Everything went sour," the colonel said, his face red from frustration and anger. There was a large welt on his right cheek; his lower lip was split, making it difficult for him to talk. "We had begun to organize troops to move into the garrison, but the Reds found out."

"What about Lieutenant Urban?" I asked.

"They followed him after you gave him the orders from General Wilczynski and caught him a hundred meters this side of the barricades."

"So the garrison never received the orders."

"No," the colonel said, "but they will fight. They know what happened to the general. They are fighting now, I suppose. The bastards are shelling the city, right?"

"Yes. And moving in with tanks."

Soon wearied of conversation about matters over which we no longer had control—as if we had ever had control—Colonel Dzierzynski lay back on the desk, covered himself with his great-coat, and went to sleep. Nearly overwhelmed with exhaustion myself, I found a clean, dry corner in the office. Adjusting the hard implements in my rucksack so that I could use it for a pillow, I settled on the floor.

The moans of the wounded officers in the basement came to me between the shattering, thundering sounds of war. More tanks rumbled through the village—on the way to the city? Then the shelling seemed to grow more intense; there came the drone and buzz of airplanes. Even at a distance of more than six kilometers, we could hear the explosions of individual bombs and shells, the firing of cannon, the rumble of tanks, the chatter of automatic weapons. Thankfully, we could not hear the screams of the victims of the terrible assault on the city.

Life in the village hall basement was safe, but that was its only good point. On the first night, the toilet clogged up and spilled its putrid contents over the floor of the tiny bathroom at the end of the main corridor. Men sleeping on the floor near the bathroom soon were compelled to move.

The stink of the toilet spread throughout the building and mixed with the odor of sweat and fear, and the situation was made worse by the constant arrival of new prisoners. By the time we received the word of Grodno's fall—and the air outside was silent again—the tax commissioner's room, which had held only Colonel Dzierzynski and two others when I arrived, contained two dozen men.

One shared the desk top with Colonel Dzierzynski. Others lay on the cement floor, on the metal filing cabinets, even on the high windowsill that looked out at the alley beside the town hall. There was little sleep for any of us. By the morning of the second day, the effluence from the toilet had reached our door and the stench in the room was sickening.

We talked little. Men squatted and stared at invisible points before their eyes, each silent with his own thoughts, his own worries, his own fears. I rarely slept, and when I did, I was tortured by nightmares in which Soviet soldiers with drooling mouths poured into our comfortable apartment, turning it into a torture chamber for my already terrified wife.

On the morning of the third day, a wild rumor flashed through the mass of officers in the stinking basement: Grodno had not only fallen, but the Russians had murdered the officers in the garrison as "enemies of the people" for fighting and killing Red soldiers.

Such an incredible war, I thought. The Russians had punished us for being weak and falling so quickly to the Germans. Now they were murdering our officers for fighting with spirit—if the rumor was true.

3: FREEDOM

We faced the relative silence that followed the battle for Grodno in shock. Grodno never could have held out; yet the news of its fall, combined with the privations of living in the crowded basement, ravaged our hopes and emotions. The worst of it all was the uncertainty—everything was open to question.

For our part, we believed nothing and everything, depending on the rumor we heard. We put aside our distrust long enough to believe in the more persistent rumors: the Russians were formulating a plan to send Polish military people out of Poland so that they could fight against the Nazis; the Polish government was already in Rumania and was planning to move to Paris; and Polish forces were assembling in England and in Syria. The latter two rumors, we learned later, were facts. We were able to assay the truth of the first rumor ourselves.

As the days passed, we fell into a state of almost total apathy. Our curiosity about what was going on outside diminished as the trials of living in the jammed basement became our paramount problem. The routine was deadening and unalterable. Each morning, Polish villagers brought in large black pots of tepid lentil soup—no Russian guard would venture into our squalid hole. It was scarcely worth the effort to get out our mess kits for the small ladle of the thin soup we received. In the afternoon, we were brought warm and murky water; obviously it was being drawn from a nearby creek and not from the fountain of clear water in the square.

On the fifth day, the bodies of eight dead Polish officers were taken from the basement. We had thought that the stench had been caused, in part, by the decomposition of the dead. But if so, we discovered that it would have taken a highly discriminating nose to tell the difference; the air did not seem to improve with the removal of the bodies.

Finally, on Wednesday morning, September 27, after we had spent a full week in the cramped basement, the Russian guards shouted at us to come out. A great cheer went up among the dirty, spiritless officers, but movement up the stairs was slow. Our joints and muscles were stiff and aching from inactivity and from our sleeping in the hard, cold, wet quarters.

A bright sun hit us as we reached the porch, and several men staggered and nearly fell. Squinting into the blinding glare, I stood with Colonel Dzierzynski on the porch and looked across the square. Several thousand—later we estimated the number at more than six thousand—Polish soldiers were sitting on the grass and on the pedestal of a statue of a long-forgotten Polish hero. Rolls of barbed wire surrounded them. From nearby shops, other officers were being brought out and herded through a gate in the barbed-wire enclosure. From the windows of apartments, somber-faced Polish citizens listlessly waved Russian flags.

We walked idly among the throng of haggard soldiers while the Russians ran in and out of the village hall like squirrels preparing for winter. Lieutenant Antoni Urban spotted us from a point near the fence and began to thread his way over toward us through the sea of sprawling arms and legs. Reaching us, he stopped, saluted, and then sat down. He crossed his long legs and regarded his cavalry boots, no longer shining brilliantly.

"I'm sorry," he said, gazing at the ground. "The bastards were waiting for me. They knew exactly where I was going—and why."

"I know," Colonel Dzierzynski said, putting a hand on Urban's thick shoulder. The last time I had seen Antoni, that shoulder had been bare. It seemed aeons ago.

We waited and the sun began to dry the water and urine on our uniforms. Then after a considerable delay, the village hall doors opened, and Lieutenant General Fyodor Skmorovitch came outside. Two men wearing the telltale crimson caps and blue armbands of the Russian secret police, the *Narodniy Kommissariat Vnutrennoch Del* (National Commissariat of Internal Affairs), flanked him.

"Jesus Christ," Antoni said. "What are the secret police doing here? Did somebody piss on a Russian boot?"

Colonel Dzierzynski stared at the two NKVD men, one a colonel, the other a captain. His neck muscles twitched nervously, and he spoke in a kind of hissing whisper. "The bastards have been sent here to give us our 'freedom.' God help the man who asks for it."

A few soldiers near us laughed nervously, but the laughter and conversation were cut short when the guards began to shout: *"Vnimaniye! Vnimaniye! Vnimaniye!"*

"What in the hell are they saying?" Colonel Dzierzynski asked. "What do the bastards want now?"

"They're telling us to stand at attention," I said, getting up. I opened my mouth to shout the instruction in Polish, but several men in the square understood Russian.

We all began to shout: "Stand at attention!"

The response was phenomenal. As one man, the six thousand Poles arose. There was a sharp and insulting clicking of heels, then laughter.

General Skmorovitch, ignoring the gesture, smiled and

leaned sideways to speak to the NKVD colonel. The subsequent announcement was brief: we were to be marched to the railroad system, to be shipped—where?

We waited two hours in the hot sun, while the Russians organized the march into the city, and left late in the afternoon, our bellies empty, our bodies aching. Only a few remained behind.

As we straggled toward Krasinski Boulevard, the Russians prodded us with their rifles, yelling a word we all soon would know well: "*Bestreye!*"

"What are the bastards saying now?" the colonel asked.

"It means, 'Hurry up,' " I said. " 'Go faster.' "

"How do you say, 'Kiss my ass, I'm going as fast as I can?' "

As we approached our own street, Lieutenant Antoni Urban began to scan the crowds lining the sidewalks and cheering us.

"Looking for a blonde in a sheer nightgown?" I asked.

He grinned. "You saw that much of her?"

"Yes, silhouetted against the window."

"Some woman, eh?" he said, winking. "Maybe she'll come out and blow me a kiss good-bye."

I was laughing at his childish hopes when my heart shrank into a knot. Suzan's golden head appeared, and she shouted my name. "For God's sake," I muttered, "don't come any closer!"

She pushed through the throng and ran toward the column shouting: "Andrei! Andrei! Are you there? Andrei, take me with you!"

A burly soldier crossed his rifle in front of her. She struggled with him and tried to push past. Another guard grabbed her hair and yanked her backward. Seeing her fall, I started to leave the ranks. I felt a steel grip on my arm.

"You can't help her," Colonel Dzierzynski said calmly. "Keep moving. For Christ's sake, *bestreye*."

Had the colonel not restrained me, I would have broken ranks to help Suzan, and probably both of us would have been killed. Instead, I walked on, tired of spirit and body. I remembered a time in Danzig when I had had to leave Suzan to buy tobacco. As she stood on the sidewalk, a large and persistent German wearing a homburg and carrying an umbrella accosted her. When I came out of the shop, Suzan was beating him on the head with her purse and shouting obscenities I had no idea she even knew.

"You were a regular jungle beast," I said when the German had fled into the darkness. "I couldn't have done a better job myself."

She was fuming with anger and indignity. "I can't stand to have men paw me," she said hotly.

And now she was being held by Russian guards. The last I saw of Suzan was a pair of pink legs flashing in the sunlight, striking out at her captors.

Grodno was a shambles. It seemed as though a discriminating tornado had moved through the streets, whisking away one building, demolishing another, and leaving the next unharmed. Soviet flags, banners, and slogans were everywhere.

The railway station was pandemonium. Russian guards were everywhere. Soldiers and civilians alike swarmed together until it seemed that it would be impossible to separate them. But the Russians had organized activities at the main station, and they soon managed to snake out the military. We were herded through the mass of humanity to the huge main concourse.

The concourse was packed, and shattered glass from the skylights and shopwindows was underfoot everywhere. We shuffled through the mess in a long, thick line, working our way inexorably to appointed gates.

Guards herded people in every conceivable direction. Civilians were turned away, almost automatically, and soldiers were shifted into special lines, which led, presumably, to trains. From the signs of destruction, we doubted that any trains were running anywhere.

We were kept apart from the others at first; then we were split into smaller groups. The officers were separated from the main group and led to specific gates. It was all done carefully. Only later would we learn that it was done so carefully because the

Russians had already made plans to deal, once and for all, with certain problem groups. For the moment it seemed that General Skmorovitch had been right: special arrangements had been made for special people.

At each gate, an NKVD guard with an automatic rifle slung over his shoulder stood beside a Soviet officer with a clipboard and a pad of paper. The officer was the interpreter, and it was immediately apparent that the Russians were separating officers from enlisted men, and that regular career officers were being separated from reserve officers who had a higher level of education. Why? Then, too, each guard was an NKVD man. Again, why? NKVD men—even sergeants—were far more important in the Soviet hierarchy than regular officers, and yet they were being "wasted" on this trivial task, or so it seemed.

None of it made any sense.

"Name, please?" the interpreter asked in Polish. He was a smallish lieutenant with large, black, searching eyes.

I looked at the NKVD sergeant and said in Russian: "My name is Major Eugenjusz Komorowski."

The subsequent interrogation took forty minutes. I looked at the mass of people in the concourse and estimated that it would take the Russians five years to process all of us.

"Go to Gate 7," the NKVD man finally said, lowering his rifle and looking at Colonel Dzierzynski behind me.

"I would like to stay with my friend here," I said, turning to the colonel.

The lieutenant gave me a shove and the guard spat.

"Gate 7! Next!"

I glanced at Colonel Dzierzynski, who shrugged good-naturedly; I nodded. As I passed back along the line, I clapped Antoni Urban on the shoulder, thinking that I probably would not see him again. At Gate 7 I stood patiently, silently, for three hours, only at the end to be asked the same questions by another NKVD sergeant. After he had finished with me, I expected to be shuttled to another gate, but the sergeant stood aside and nodded for me to enter. The ramps between each set of tracks were jammed with men, though, of course, there was not a single train in the terminal.

Russian guards walked along the empty tracks between the ramps, only their heads, shoulders, and rifles visible to the men squatting and lying on the cement ramps. They kept yelling *"Sadis!"* as new men arrived. A major looked up, then pointed to an open space beside him.

"They want you to sit down," he said in a soft, mellow voice.

"I suppose so," I said, smiling and squatting beside him. "All the others are sitting or lying down."

"If they weren't," the major said, pointing to the guards, "they'd probably be dead. These Russians mean business. When they tell us to sit, we sit. When they tell us to stand, we stand. If they told us to crap our pants, I'm sure we would all do it—or break our assholes trying."

The major was a tall man with unusually long legs and arms, almost skeletal in their thinness. His face, with a hawk nose and a cratered surface, was ugly and handsome all at once. Small black eyes, set wide apart under a broad white brow, could twinkle with amusement or glow with a friendly warmth almost at the same time.

His name was Josef Konopka—an engineer from Bialystok, a city forty kilometers southwest of Grodno. When it had been overrun by the Germans, Major Konopka and many in his company had escaped to the eastern provinces.

I kept watching the entrance gate for Colonel Dzierzynski. Perhaps he had blown up at the NKVD. Would they shoot him on the spot, imprison him in Grodno, or put him on a train for Siberia? The possibilities were endless—all of them frightening.

"You're waiting for your mistress?" Major Konopka suggested with a laugh.

"No, my commanding officer." I had no idea I was being so obvious.

Occasionally, I looked toward the open end of the terminal, listening for trains. But there was only the familiar September breeze—no clicking of metal wheels on metal tracks, no lonesome shriek of a whistle. Although I was surrounded by thousands of my own people, I felt alone.

My thoughts, which had never been completely away from her, returned to Suzan. The image was painful. I saw her as she had been during our honeymoon, standing on the deck of the cruise ship in the Baltic. The image was so clear, so real, that I could almost hear the gentle throb of the ship's engines, the enchanting whine of the wind, even Suzan's breathing. I could almost feel her body against mine, almost smell the fragrance of her perfume.

The image was abruptly shattered as I inhaled the reeking stench of my own uniform, caked in human feces and soaked in urine. The odor came from the others as well, Major Konopka smelling like a newly fertilized farmer's field.

My thoughts broken, I glanced toward the gate again, hoping to see Colonel Dzierzynski. The view was blocked by a tall, thin officer springing over the outstretched limbs of other officers. The figure stopped, not five meters away, and called my name.

I raised myself to my knees, watching a nearby Russian guard with care, to see who had called my name. Lieutenant Antoni Urban stood illuminated by the skylight.

"Antoni," I called out. "Over here."

The Russian guard stopped near me and fairly spat his order into my face: "*Sadis!*"

Smiling at the guard, I turned to Antoni and said in Polish: "To hell with the son of a bitch. He wouldn't dare shoot us. We'd massacre him."

My momentary brazenness—and that was all it was—was encouraged by a round of low cheers from others on the ramps. Antoni threaded his way to me, and officers shifted their rucksacks to make room.

I introduced Major Konopka to Lieutenant Urban. They took to each other immediately. Both were swift with quips, yet both were deeply serious; their jokes were pregnant with satire. To entertain the ghost-eyed men who sat around us, the two men launched a series of jokes about the war, the Russians, and our projected fate.

We knew that we were only fooling ourselves—not very successfully, at that—with our silly jokes. But our group was fortunate. We had endured only the hardships of captivity. Many of the other men on the crowded ramps were badly wounded; some were dead. In any case, the joking went on, even as guards pulled dead bodies from nearby ramps and carried them to the entrance gates.

After full darkness had fallen, we heard a commotion near the gates. Dozens of Polish civilians came into the terminal carrying buckets of soup and baskets of bread. The cheer that went up was quickly silenced by the guards, who rushed along the tracks shouting and waving their weapons.

Buckets of thin, rotten pea soup were distributed by the Polish civilians. Some of the Poles were station porters; others had probably been recruited off the streets. They walked along the tracks and lifted the soup and bread onto the ramps. As they passed, they warned us: "There is enough in each ration for only eight men. Spread it among twenty or some of you will go hungry."

As the meager repast was coming to an end, we heard the distant squeal of train whistles. Everyone sat up and peered toward the far end of the terminal. Bright yellow lights came into view, and we could hear the chugging labors of locomotives as they moved slowly toward the terminal. I counted six trains in the first group.

"Christ," Antoni Urban said happily, "we're getting a train. What luck. Only six trains and one of them is for us."

Train crewmen, hanging from steel ladders on the cars, carried lanterns, which cast eerie shadows among the huddled mass of soldiers. On the top of each car rode a Russian guard with an automatic weapon. The cars, built for transporting cattle, were made of wooden slats set far enough apart so that wind and rain could stream into the cars. The trip to freedom would be a cold one.

Several officers complained about the prospect of riding in cattle cars. A guard who overheard them replied to their comments, in Russian. I translated for the officers who didn't understand. "What's good enough for cows and pigs is good enough for fucking Poles!"

When the trains stopped, the wooden doors of the cars were opened, and the guards began to order everyone on the ramp to board. When men balked, the guards prodded them with bayonets.

Antoni, Major Konopka, and I tried to wait for Colonel Dzierzynski, but the guards forced us inside, where the stench of dung mingled with that of the sweat and filth of our own bodies and uniforms. When the cars were full, the officers still on the ramp—hundreds of them—realizing that we were at least going somewhere, anywhere, began to beat on the slats, demanding to be taken aboard. But the guards pushed them back.

Suddenly I heard a sharp, commanding, and familiar voice: "Let me through, damn you! My brother is on this train." It was Colonel Dzierzynski.

The guard could not understand, of course, so I called out through the slats. "He is my brother," I said in Russian. "We can make room."

The guard hesitated. He didn't believe us, but, perhaps afraid to test the validity of my claim, he gave the word to a brakeman, who unlocked the door. Colonel Dzierzynski came into the car, supporting an exhausted man.

The door slammed shut; the lock clicked. Colonel Dzierzynski lowered Lieutenant Colonel Hugo Mijakowski, commander of the Grodno garrison during the terrible two-day battle, to a corner where the straw was thicker. Two officers moved to make room. Colonel Mijakowski, holding his side with a blood-covered hand, sighed deeply.

Our car held sixty-two men. I had tried to count the cars but had lost count at fifteen. I estimated twenty cars, which meant that more than a thousand Polish officers had been herded onto a single train. Officers only?

We slept on the floor of the cattle car. At dawn, the exodus from Grodno began. A tremendous cheer went up, so loud that glass from the broken skylight sprinkled on the helmets of the guards sitting on the tops of the cars. We all laughed. Lieutenant Antoni Urban was the first to make a move. He squirmed on the hard floor and moaned.

"I'm certainly glad I chose freedom," he said. "I pity those poor bastards who are sleeping in soft beds this morning."

Our train moved slowly out into the brightening dawn. Mist hung over the railroad yards; the sun was as red as blood, indicating miserable weather for our journey. Through a slat, I saw that the Soviet flag flew from the pole on the dome of St. Nicolaus Cathedral. The Polish patriots were all gone—the flag would stay.

As the train gathered speed and the chill dawn air swirled the mist between the slats of the car, I turned up the collar of my greatcoat and hoped that the train would soon turn south —toward Rumania. What else could they do with us but take us to Rumania and to freedom?

That was the promise. We would go to freedom in Rumania and then we would be on our own. How we would cross that country and reach Syria was up to us. But the train never turned south. It picked up speed and chugged eastward, into the blood-red sun.

4: CAPTIVITY

THE rain came before noon, a slicing, sleeting rain that cut into the skin and chilled the bone. The train had run for only a few minutes, getting us clear of Grodno, and then had pulled onto a siding.

We were fed in the afternoon, but the sparse ration of dry bread and tiny chunks of cheese did little to ease our hunger. When night came, we were still on the siding, and I fell asleep with vivid thoughts of Suzan running through my mind.

I awoke at dawn; the train was moving. The guard on the swaying, clacking car whistled above the rush of wind, and I recognized the tune: *"Moskva Moya"* ("My Moscow"). The sound of the whistling reached my senses even before the clatter of the train or the aches in my bones.

Peering through the slats, I realized that we still were traveling eastward. My God, I thought, stirring on the small patch of straw, are we going to *Moscow*? Moscow was due east and the guard on top of the car was whistling a favorite Moscow tune. Were we going to Moscow and not Rumania—and if so, why?

The sun was beaming virtually into our eyes, and golden rays slipped between the slats, warming and drying us. I groaned, stretched, and worked myself up into a sitting position. We had been on the train for nearly thirty-six hours, but I had no idea where we were.

Lieutenant Antoni Urban had fallen asleep near me in the night, but he was gone now. I looked around and saw his dark, handsome, laughing face at the opposite end of the car. Turning suddenly, he began hopping across the sprawled legs and arms of sleeping officers.

"We've been having a guessing game in the men's room," Antoni said with a chuckle. The men's room was a corner in the car where a large horn, much like a Gramophone speaker, served as a commode. It emptied directly onto the tracks.

"Guessing what?" I asked, rubbing sleep from my eyes and wincing at the odors.

"Guessing where we're going," Antoni said, turning somber at his knowledge that said that we were not going to freedom.

"Where are we going?"

"According to the various guards we have heard," Antoni said, squatting beside me on the thin straw, "we're going to Rumania, Bulgaria, Germany, Sweden, Switzerland, France, Hungary, and Greece."

"You mean they're going to split us up?"

"No." He grinned. "We're staying together."

"And going to all those places?"

"Of course. With Russians, nothing is impossible." Then he grew serious again. "Some of us have been checking the villages we pass. We're only about fifty kilometers east of Grodno."

"Only *fifty*? It should be five hundred!"

"I know, but we made several long stops on sidings. You slept through most of them, Major Komorowski. Trains went past us in the night, heading west. Russians moving in force to occupy eastern Poland, we guess."

"*Bekarci*," I muttered.

Almost as he spoke, the train slowed and pulled onto another siding. Others in the car awoke and began to flex sore muscles. Doctors on other cars had passed the word advising us to get as much exercise as possible, even though it was difficult in the cramped cattle cars.

After an hour, guards brought in small buckets of barley soup much in need of barley—two buckets and three loaves of black bread for each car. Enough for a dozen men, it had to serve sixty. We got out mess kits, but it was not worth the effort. I managed a crumb of bread and two spoons of soup.

After the meal, while others grumbled or rested, I leaned against the hard slats of the car and tried to make my mind blank, to convince myself that there are no happier moments in time of trouble than those in which the mind is free of thought. I failed, but it didn't matter. If I had found a happy moment, it would have been brutally short. The guards returned, unlocked the doors, and began to scream at us to get out.

As we assembled on the gravel bank alongside the train, several men began to exercise. The familiar order came: "*Sadis!*"

A fat sergeant ran along the ranks of dirty, haggard Polish officers, repeating the order. He screamed at us and at the guards, berating them for not hurrying us sufficiently. Several officers defied the rule and milled around as the sergeant ran, yelled, and grew red in the face.

"That fat bastard will die of a heart attack before this is over," Colonel Dzierzynski muttered.

"No such luck," Lieutenant Urban said. "You know, all my life I've wanted to see a Russian sergeant fall over dead of a heart attack. It has been one of my fondest . . . "

A guard advanced toward Antoni, jabbing his bayonet at the lieutenant's face and shouting.

"What did he say?" Antoni asked me.

"He wants you to shut up and sit down."

Antoni blew the guard a kiss. "Tell him I want him to stand up and kiss my ass." But the jabbing bayonet glinted close, and the young lieutenant sat on the gravel and was quiet.

When we all were seated, the sergeant still paced the embankment, watching us, snapping at his men, and looking up and down the tracks into the empty distance. The reason for his nervousness became clear to me when I overheard the sergeant say to one of his guards: "The NKVD will be here any minute. We're lucky, Comrade, that they weren't already here to see how badly we organized these Poles."

The Red Army was turning us over to the NKVD, Russia's dreaded secret police? Surely, the army was capable of escorting us to the Rumanian border. I said nothing, hoping not to alarm others. But many understood Russian. They whispered the news to companions, and the knowledge traveled up and down the line. Colonel Dzierzynski leaned close and whispered to me: "Is this true? Is the NKVD coming?"

"That's what the sergeant said," I told him.

"Did he say anything else? Did he say why?"

"No, sir. Nothing else."

The silence among our ranks, strung out alongside the tracks in the shadow of the train, was ominous and biting.

We waited all day for the NKVD, without food or water. Their arrival was heralded at dusk by the barking of Alsatian and German shepherd dogs on long leashes—a hundred men with submachine guns, twenty dogs. They had probably come in trucks to the village we had just passed through. There was no road leading to the remote siding, so the elite NKVD had had to march. They arrived short of temper.

The NKVD leader was a short, stocky lieutenant who spoke with the Red Army sergeant in what seemed to us to be terse, explosive words. They were too far away for me to hear, but word filtered along that the lieutenant was berating the sergeant for not having fed us. This came as a surprise, as did the buckets of cold soup and pieces of soggy bread.

It was dark when we finished eating, and my blood ran cold when I heard the sergeant order his men aboard the train. The old pessimistic streak in me told me that something highly unpleasant was coming.

The Red soldiers climbed into the empty *tieplooshka*, and, to

our great consternation, the train began to move. Several Polish
officers whooped and leaped for the cars, but they were forced
back by the NKVD guards and by the snarling dogs. Ordered to
sit again, we watched with aching hearts as the train clattered
away into the black night. And then the order came from the
lieutenant: we were to sleep on the ground.

At dawn, we were formed into ranks of four and marched
along the tracks for perhaps ten kilometers. We marched slowly
because we were weak, and the wounded had to be helped.
Colonel Dzierzynski, Major Konopka, Lieutenant Urban, and I
took turns helping Colonel Mijakowski. At times, two of us had
to support him. We were afraid the NKVD would shoot any of
the wounded we left behind.

We stopped at noon on a dirt road that crossed the tracks in a
north-south direction. The guards ordered us to sit on the road
while they ate bread, cheese, and canned meat from their rucksacks. We were not fed. Colonel Dzierzynski came out of his
lethargy and told me to ask the NKVD lieutenant about medical
aid for our wounded. I turned to a guard near me and asked,
politely, if I might speak to the commander.

"What for?"

"We have doctors among us," I said. "Our wounded need
medical attention. Even without supplies, something can be
done."

The guard merely shook his head. Colonel Dzierzynski nearly
exploded. His face reddened, and he cursed the guard. When he
started to rise, it was my turn to grip his arm in restraint.

"It won't do any good," I said. "They may want the wounded
to die. They're slowing down the movement."

"Bastards," he muttered. But he remained seated.

When the Russians had finished eating, we began a slow
march southward on the dirt road—toward Rumania, though
few were optimistic that we even would arrive. Without food,
and with our sick and wounded, we could not survive a march of
seven hundred kilometers to the border.

Darkness came, and still we marched. We had gone some twenty-five kilometers without food. We waited for the guards to tell us to stop, but no such order came. Then around midnight, we reached a small village, where we were split into smaller units and taken to barns. Where the farmers or the animals had gone, no one knew, but the barns were empty. The barn in which I was taken with Colonel Dzierzynski, Colonel Mijakowski, Major Konopka, and Lieutenant Urban was so crowded that we lay almost shoulder to shoulder. More than two hundred men were jammed into the structure.

In the morning, we were fed raw fish, black bread, and bits of charred pork fat. We drank all we wanted from the farm's horse trough. Rain came hard during the second night, and crowded as we were, we welcomed the warm protection of the barn.

The stalls and the barn loft were full of officers in filthy, stinking uniforms. Some of them formed small groups, and a few had even brought out playing cards. For the first time since leaving Grodno, we didn't have guards virtually on top of us, and some spirit returned.

But conditions in the barn degenerated. In addition to the smell of cow and horse manure, plus our filthy uniforms and unwashed bodies, there was the odor of our own human wastes. One stall was set aside for toilet uses, and many of the men had diarrhea from bad water, nerves, and lack of proper food.

Colonel Dzierzynski had been like a ticking bomb ever since the NKVD lieutenant had refused to let our doctors treat the wounded. About noon on the third day, he came out of the toilet stall wiping filth from his boots. As he stepped over the legs of sleeping officers to the stall we shared with twenty men, his face was grim, and his strong jaw worked back and forth as he ground his teeth. He sat on a pile of straw and cow manure and put his head in his big hands. He looked up at me, his eyes red and glazed.

"I can't take much more," he said bitterly. "If we don't move out of here soon, I'll go crazy."

"The guards are getting lax," I said. "The last men who

brought in water said many of them were sleeping in other farm buildings and in farmhouses. It's still raining, and they don't care to be out in it."

"Escape? If you're ready, I am, too. We can make it. You, me, Antoni, Major Konopka, and Hugo. All right?"

"All right," I said, getting carried along because the colonel was showing renewed spirit. I was so miserable that I didn't even care if we were caught. I was worried about Suzan and about never seeing her again. Perhaps escape was the answer. Once free, anything was possible, even return to Grodno. "I don't think the Russians will free us anyway," I said.

"Where do you think they're taking us?" the colonel asked. The gleam in his eye told me that we were thinking the same thing.

"To Russia," I said.

"I agree. But why?"

I shook my head. "History tells us that the Russians want our land. It's an obsession with them. We're the kind of men who might stop them, who might try to take it back. If we go into Russia, I don't think we'll ever see Poland again—or anyplace but Russia."

"No," he said, shaking his head. "We will see Poland. We'll take it back. When France and England throw out the Germans, we'll throw out the Russians."

I said nothing. I didn't know the answer to the curious riddle of this "special treatment" from the Russians. One thing I did know: most of the men in our large group not only were officers but also had a high degree of education. A few were bright young cadets; some were doctors, lawyers, journalists, engineers, dentists, teachers. Most were reserve officers, not career men.

A vague pattern of possible Russian intentions was forming in my mind. I thought of the Stalin purges and knew that he had no hesitation about eliminating every man who might be of harm to him. Every dictator fears the person who is intelligent, highly educated, imaginative. Every man in our group fit into this composite category—and they wanted to be free. We might be considered dangerous to Stalin because Stalin wanted Poland.

But the similarity ended there. In 1937 there was no war and no world attention on Russia. Stalin had murdered his victims without publicity until the deed reached immense proportions. Could he murder Polish prisoners of war—an undeclared war—without world reprisal? No. Of course not.

Yet there were the intimidating leaflets that the Soviets had dropped on the day of their invasion. They had separated highly skilled and educated Polish officers from their men and from other officers. I could not reconcile the treatment we were receiving with the promise of freedom given by General Skmorovitch.

Colonel Dzierzynski looked at his wristwatch and broke me from my reverie.

"According to this instrument"—he was very proud of his U.S.-made watch and often referred to it—"it is exactly noon. Dark will come at about 6:20. If the fucking Russkies haven't made a change in our situation by then, we'll loosen up a couple of boards and get out of here. All right, Eugenjusz?"

"Yes, sir."

He polled the others. Even Hugo Mijakowski agreed, although he was in such pain that he could hardly move. A young doctor in the barn with us had taken a look at the wound and pronounced it untreatable without proper facilities, though the wound was not badly infected and Mijakowski's natural antibodies were keeping his condition stable.

We planned to slip away into the night, heading west. It was a plan based on luck, not on shrewdness. We would have done it, but at 2:00 P.M. the barn doors were swung open, and we were ordered outside.

The rain had stopped. Escape impossible for a while, we marched until dusk, when we came to an east-west railway. A ragged cheer went up; at least the interminable marching would end.

We walked in a long, unbroken chain along the tracks, heading directly east. Another cheer went up from the men. The guards began to yell and the dogs to bark, but some of the Polish officers broke into a run. The reason for their exuberance soon became obvious: ahead at a turn in the tracks was a dim red light of a train caboose.

It took two hours for the Russians to load us aboard the cattle cars and to bring us rancid soup of an unknown genre, but at last the train began to move. The ride was much like our first train excursion. We would run for perhaps thirty minutes, then stop on a siding for four or five hours while westbound trains sped past us. The process would then be repeated.

At dawn the next day, we made a happy discovery. The train was heading south! We no longer stopped on sidings for long periods of time, and the engine seemed intent on pulling us all the way to the Black Sea. However, we had been fooled before, so we held back on the cheers until we were certain that we would not head east again.

We traveled all day. But then the train veered eastward. Our hopes diminished but were not dashed. We were hopelessly lost and had no idea if we were even in Poland. We didn't even know how long we had traveled east before turning south.

On the afternoon of October 4, the train made its last huffing plunge into the unknown—and stopped cold. There was no siding, so we knew that we had reached some kind of destination. Peering through the slats, we could see nothing but open fields and small patches of woods. After an afternoon and a night stalled on the tracks, I heard guards discussing the relative merits of marching us through "the city" in the daylight and taking a chance on the Polish citizens' becoming aroused at our emaciated condition, or at night, when some of us might escape into the many cracks and crevices that any city has in abundance.

Whatever the decision, we were unloaded and made to sit on the embankment while the train chugged on into the city. When it was gone, we could see the buildings of a large town in the distance. Antoni Urban peered into the morning sun at the station sign, far down the tracks.

"Tarnopol!" he shouted. "My God, we're still in Poland!"

Ultimately, to our disappointment, the guards did not march us through Tarnopol, deciding, we supposed, that it was safer to march us over the circuitous country roads south of the city. In any case, after a morning's march, we came to the southeastern outskirts of the city, where the Russians had recently built a concentration camp.

Tangles of barbed wire were stretched between telegraph poles along roads and through fields. Tall wooden towers, "storks," stood at the camp's corners and at fifty-meter intervals. A large gate constructed of wooden planks and strands of barbed wire led into the camp. There was a wooden gatehouse for the guards, tents and crude buildings for the Polish prisoners.

The fields had been stomped flat by the feet of many captives. Evidence of previous prisoners was everywhere. Names and ranks of men were carved in the rough-sawn wood of the buildings and the latrines. Most were those of officers from distant points in Poland. Apparently, Tarnopol was a collecting point.

I searched the sea of faces in the camp for someone I knew —someone from Poznan, perhaps even an old university classmate. But I saw no one I knew, and neither did any of my immediate friends. Some officers, however, were reunited with old comrades, and there was some laughing and joking as we settled into our new quarters.

Life in the camp was not unbearable, but we knew with grim finality that we were not going to Rumania. Tarnopol was fairly close to the border—about a hundred kilometers—but there was too much evidence that the Russians were preparing a different route for us.

For one thing, there was a main rail line running from Tarnopol to Kharkov, deep inside western Russia. For another, messages scrawled on the insides of the wooden buildings at the newly erected camp hinted that the previous occupants had not gone to Rumania. One unsigned message in chalk, strangely not erased by the Russians, said: "Leaving today, October 1. Guard said will be given tour of Moscow if all goes well. Great treat!"

The camp also was plastered with Soviet slogans that

indicated—to me at least—that the Russians were trying to indoctrinate us into believing that Russia was heaven on earth. Above the main gate was a huge banner in Polish: LONG LIVE THE BROTHERLY RED LABORER AND PEASANT ARMY THAT LIBERATE THE WORLD FROM CAPITALISM.

The sign told everything. We were capitalists, and we were being liberated, not freed. In the Soviet sense, liberated meant what it had meant to Estonia. We would probably be taken into a protectorate situation in Russia. But we were not workers and peasants; we were highly educated officers and capitalists. We were enemies of Russia.

The sign hinted strongly that we would not see the kind of freedom that we had been promised. But it did not tell us that our captivity would have a unique quality, especially suited to "enemies of Russia."

Two days after our arrival at the Tarnopol camp, another large group of Polish officers was brought in. Among them was a woman, Lieutenant Janina Lewandowski of the Polish Air Force.

Lieutenant Lewandowski was a tall, lithe woman in her late twenties. She moved gracefully when she walked, but she wore an over-sized man's uniform, and the ill-fitting garments concealed whatever contours her body had. Although she was not beautiful, she obviously was good looking. Thus she took pains to make herself look unattractive. Her long face, which could have been pretty with proper attention, was smudged with the dirt of travel, and she didn't bother to wash it when she came to Tarnopol. Her warm brown eyes were wide and fluid, but she seemed deliberately to squint to make them seem cold and haughty. She wore her long brown hair in the tight bun of the matron.

The word of her arrival spread through the camp quickly. Antoni Urban was at the gate even before her group had been processed and shown to quarters. He stared at her as she stood at attention before the camp commander—a rangy, hawk-nosed

NKVD captain—and answered the usual questions. Antoni's careful, practiced eye examined every inch of Janina Lewandowski's frame; then he gave his professional opinion: "With a bath, a tight dress, and a hint of French perfume, she might be worth the marvelous dream I'm going to have about her. But, Jesus, I just wish I could tell if she has any tits."

The NKVD, in an act of uncommon decency, set up a separate tent for Janina—and stationed guards to keep out amorous officers of either Polish or Russian nationality.

"The bastards," Lieutenant Urban groused. He considered it an act of barbarism, not of decency. "They will keep us away from that delectable prize, but guess who will be sneaking into the tent."

"Not the Russians," Major Konopka said, grinning. "One of the men in her group just told me that she put a Red soldier in the hospital when he accosted her on the train. She broke his jaw."

"That delicate thing?" Antoni asked.

"She's not so delicate," Josef Konopka said. "I hear she's an expert gymnast and a prize-winning wrestler."

Antoni brooded for a moment, then brightened. "Good. I'll wrestle with her. Even if she wins, think of the fun! She can break my jaw if she wants to. Christ, I'd even let her *knee* me right now!"

It was good to be around the young Ulany officer—he was good for the spirit. Without humor, even grim battlefield humor, we were lost, and we relied upon him.

Antoni had attracted quite a retinue of friends since our arrival at the camp. Throughout the camp, there were small groups of friends, hastily made for the most part, who not only lived together but also spent all their time together, roaming inside the barbed wire enclosure in a group. It was a virtual necessity to belong to such a small group. Otherwise, you might go insane from loneliness. There were many loners in the camp, but they were alone by choice. In my opinion, these men were already well on the way to insanity.

Although we made many new friends in the temporary camp,

four were to become quite close friends and would remain in our small pack through the months ahead.

One was Captain Henryk Jagiello, a quiet, thin man with a huge, sliver-like nose and a perpetual smile. Jagiello, a desk officer who had been ruled unfit for combat because of an old knee injury, had been a research chemist at the University of Vilno before the Nazis invaded Poland. With his dry sense of humor, he proved to be an excellent straight man for Antoni Urban's continual jokes.

Then there was Captain Vincenty Jankowski, an almost skeletal man with arms and legs longer than Major Konopka's. His enormous head made his lanky body seem even more rangy. He was an extremely friendly man, but we also gravitated to him because we felt that *he* needed us. Without companions to look after him and to respond to his friendly nature, Vincenty Jankowski could easily have become a loner. A professor of economics, he had no understanding of war. None of us did, but we adjusted. Vincenty was unable to adjust to war's ridiculousness.

A third new friend was Lieutenant Leo Bednarek, a dentist from Bialystok. A thick, heavy-set man with massive arms that could yank a head, much less a tooth, Leo Bednarek was one of Antoni's friendly competitors in the realm of humor. He could switch from straight man to comic in the flash of a smile. In a crucial situation, Leo Bednarek was the one man I would want near me. He was calm, good humored, and strong. Yet in his soft blue eyes I could see the germ of a stern and perhaps vicious fighting spirit.

The last man among our new friends was perhaps the most valuable, Captain Rudolf Kochloffel. His giggling and his wide eyes, seemingly signs of fatuity, were perfect masks for the expertise that lay within the core of this little man, a doctor with a private practice in Lublin, in eastern Poland. He was walking proof that appearances should mean nothing in the valuation of a man and his abilities. It was difficult to keep his abilities in mind, not only because of his pudginess and his giggling but also because he had one long wisp of black hair on the top of an otherwise bald head. He combed that wisp in all directions of the compass, attempting to cover his pate.

Captain Rudolf Kochloffel was to prove his worth shortly after his entry into our little group. And Antoni Urban was to prove that he could do more than make jokes to raise our spirits.

On our sixth day at Tarnopol, Lieutenant Colonel Hugo Mijakowski collapsed near the fence while we were walking together. Rudolf Kochloffel had already taken several looks at the wound and had judged that the shrapnel inside the colonel's body had apparently been surrounded by protective tissue. Although Mijakowski had continued to suffer pain, it had become bearable and his temperature had decreased. In consequence, Dr. Kochloffel had ruled against an operation under such primitive conditions, unless it were an absolute necessity.

It seemed that the absolute necessity was at hand. Mijakowski suddenly clutched his side, let out a short, almost stifled scream, and tumbled to the ground. A guard saw him fall and rushed over. Hugo was writhing on the ground, and the guard, his rifle unslung and his suspicions high, gazed down at him.

"*Bolnaya?*" he asked brusquely, although I could detect a note of concern. "Are you sick?"

"He isn't sick," I told the guard. "He's been wounded. He has shrapnel in his side. Please, isn't there a camp doctor?"

The guard shook his head, looked down at the groaning officer, and turned to walk away. I looked around helplessly and was about to ask another Polish officer to help me get Hugo to our quarters when Antoni Urban appeared out of the circle of staring men. We carried Hugo's slight, emaciated body to our quarters and placed him on his bunk. Antoni opened the colonel's tunic, and we both gasped. There was a swollen, festering lump on his side, the size of an orange. I put my hand to his forehead; he was burning up with fever.

"Get Rudolf," I said. "I don't know where he is."

"Don't worry," Antoni replied, already on his way. "I'll find him."

They were back in less than a minute. Rudolf Kochloffel probed the area around the swollen lump, and Hugo let out a scream that would have curdled milk. Rudolf looked up at us.

"The shrapnel has broken through the protective tissue, or the tissue has rotted. The infection is bad; it's all through his system. He'll die without an operation." His eyes seemed to be asking us what to do.

"Can you operate?" I asked.

"With what?" The doctor held out his hands. "My fingernails? We have to do something, but I have no tools. No medicine. I don't even have a knife! Will the Russians help?"

I shook my head. Mijakowski writhed on his cot. Small yelps escaped from his throat from time to time. He was making every effort to keep from screaming, but it was obvious that the pain had become too intense.

"Why is the pain so bad now?" I asked Rudolf. "A few minutes ago we were walking along, and he seemed normal."

"He's not the type to complain," the doctor said. "He's probably been in severe pain for several hours. This couldn't have broken loose just now or he wouldn't have such a fever."

Antoni suddenly pressed forward. We had not noticed him go, but while we'd stood helplessly by, watching Hugo squirm in pain, Antoni had been busy gathering up the necessary implements for an operation. In ten minutes, he had collected three sharp penknives of various sizes, a curved upholstery needle, medicinal salve, silk thread, cotton bandages, and a half-liter of vodka.

"Where in Christ's name did you get these?" Dr. Kochloffel asked.

Antoni grinned. "I have ways."

His "ways," he told us as Rudolf fed vodka to Hugo, included some ingenious devices. For example, he had made friends with an NKVD sergeant at the gatehouse. He knew the sergeant had a ravenous appetite for women, and Antoni had promised to arrange for him to spend a night with Janina Lewandowski if he supplied certain items.

The guard's lust and Antoni's ingenious perfidy worked for Hugo Mijakowski's salvation. Dr. Kochloffel worked swiftly and expertly. He opened the lump with one cut of a penknife blade. Pus rolled out in a thick mass. Within an hour the shrapnel—a piece the size of a boot heel—was lying on the dirty floor, the wound was sewed up and bandaged, and Lieutenant Colonel Hugo Mijakowski was in seventh heaven, drunk on only half the available vodka. We finished what he didn't need and went outside for fresh air.

"Good work, Antoni," Rudolf said. "Now, how are you going to pay off your debt to the NKVD man?"

For a moment Antoni seemed nonplussed. His handsome face darkened, and he gazed at the ground. His smile returned as suddenly as it had gone away.

"I'll tell him I discovered that Janina is a man with long hair," he blurted. "Christ, for all I can tell, maybe she *is!*"

Treatment in the camp was not brutal or even bad. We were there ten days. New arrivals came each day until there were more than ten thousand officers and enlisted men guarded by two hundred NKVD men and fifty dogs. There was little intercourse between the Poles and the Russians, except that we cursed them in Polish and they cursed us in Russian—each side gaining an education in profanity.

The worst part, except for the abominable food—mostly fish gut soup—was the idleness. There was nothing to do—except talk. Rumors flew.

Then on the morning of October 16 trucks with canvas tops arrived. A virtual river of excitement ran through the camp. The NKVD commander announced over the loudspeaker that a thousand men would be taken by truck to the Rumanian border.

The sun was bright, almost blinding, that morning. We stood in a great throng near the gatehouse and listened to names being read by an NKVD sergeant. A thousand men were chosen, all of them officers, including all seventy full colonels in the camp.

There was much rejoicing, but no one was more exuberant

than the men in our small group. All of us, including Colonel
Mijakowski, were chosen to leave. And much to Antoni Urban's
delight, Lieutenant Janina Lewandowski's name was read over
the loudspeaker.

"Thank God," he shouted as he gathered up his belongings.
"I've been hiding from the fucking NKVD sergeant who gave
me the stuff for Hugo's operation. Not only do I escape from
him, but I may yet find out if that woman has any tits."

"Even so," Leo Bednarek chided him, "you'll still talk about
them."

"Christ, yes!" Antoni exulted. "It's better than talking about
fish gut soup."

Colonel Mijakowski refused help in walking to the main gate
and boarding his assigned truck. We all climbed happily aboard,
trying to keep our group together. Vincenty Jankowski and Dr.
Kochloffel lagged behind and were put into another truck, but
we knew we would see them in Rumania—*if* we were going to
Rumania.

When we were on the trucks, the canvas flaps were dropped
and locked. Steel poles had been sewn into the seams of the flaps,
and the poles clanked into holes at the back of the truck. Why
was it necessary to lock us into trucks that were supposed to be
taking us to freedom?

But if we were truly captives—and we were—not even the
locks could dissipate our happiness at leaving or erase the words
of the NKVD commander who said that we were being taken to
freedom.

5: "The Wrong Way to Rumania"

W e froze at night, even though we were packed tightly in the truck—thirty in a truck designed for twenty—and sweated by day. But it didn't matter, of course. In a slow, convoluting convoy, the chain of vehicles rumbled and stopped over southern Poland and western Russia. For an unfathomable reason, the trucks stayed on back country roads and ran for only a few hours each day for three days and nights—although the Rumanian border was only a hundred kilometers from Tarnopol and Russia was even closer.

Antoni cut a tiny slit in the canvas of our truck with one of the penknives we had used to operate on Colonel Mijakowski. Peering through the hole, he became our navigator, or so he claimed.

"We're crossing a river," he would say. It was hardly news, since we could hear and feel the rumbling of the truck over a wooden bridge.

"Which river?" someone would ask.

"Who can tell a river?" Antoni would reply, with his eye to the tiny hole. "It's dirty, and it runs north and south. I suppose we're heading east."

"Rumania is south!" Colonel Dzierzynski would say. "This is the wrong way to Rumania!"

We all knew now—even though few of us admitted it openly —that we would wind up in the Soviet Union, in spite of the promises of freedom.

We were fed like hogs each afternoon, and it was the only time we saw daylight. The canvas flaps were unlocked, and guards tossed in a bucket of tepid fish gut soup. Then the flaps were closed. In the darkness we tried to be civilized about eating, but it was difficult. Someone remarked about how well we behaved when there was not nearly enough food for thirty men near starvation.

"How else *can* we behave?" the colonel snapped. "Who in the world would fight over fish gut soup?"

"Only a Russian culinary expert," Antoni quipped.

It seemed as if we might have gone on forever. Stop. Go. But mostly stop. However, late on the third night, when, as usual, the trucks had stopped, new sounds came: the chugging of a locomotive and the slow clacking of wheels.

The guards unlocked the flap, and almost at once we were revived by the cool autumn air. By contrast, the odor from the truck whooshed out, stupifying the guards so that they staggered back.

"Out! Out!" they yelled in Russian. "*Bestreye!*"

The last command was superfluous. We nearly killed each other scrambling for fresh air.

Putting our overcoats on to protect us from the cold, we were led to the train. After much confusion, the NKVD found the empty freight cars set aside for us and herded us in at bayonet point. Lieutenant Antoni Urban immediately stretched out on the floor, tucked his rucksack under his head, and sighed: "Wake me when we get to Rumania."

I squinted at Colonel Dzierzynski in the darkness and waited for his usual comment, but he said nothing. Had he ceased caring?

"Perhaps this time," I said by way of consolation, "the Russians will find Rumania. They can't be wrong *all* the time."

The colonel grunted. "For your information, Major Komorowski, we crossed the Russian border three rivers back."

Just before dark, he explained, Antoni had spotted a small village. When we were boarding the train, the colonel had overheard a man from another truck saying that the village was a hundred kilometers from Poland.

A hundred kilometers inside Russia! As long as we had been in Poland, my mind held to Suzan, but now that closeness was shattered by the knowledge that I was so far into enemy land.

In that dark night as we lay aboard the train, I resolved that I *would* return. I suppose every other man in the group made the same resolution, but something deep inside my soul told me that *I* at least would return.

We took turns staring out at the countryside through the four tiny, barred windows of each railroad car as the train moved deeper into Russia. A chill crept into our bloodstreams with the knowledge of where we were.

As before, the train stopped frequently. Most of the stops were made to allow military trains to pass, but there also were frequent stops for the guards to inspect, to make certain we hadn't loosened floorboards to escape—an increasingly ludicrous routine in view of the fact that we were moving ever farther into Russia.

We were fed only when the train pulled onto a siding, and then not always. Our menu varied, although it was never a gourmet's delight. Sometimes there would be a steaming kettle of thick, rich pea soup with good biscuits; sometimes raw fish, unscaled and ungutted, with hard, moldy biscuits. Occasionally we received sugar cubes, but never enough for everyone.

The trip seemed endless. The cars were full of lice, bedbugs, and cockroaches. Mice and rats skittered over us at night. Some freight cars didn't have Gramophone toilets, and in them the men used buckets. When the train stopped, Polish officers emptied the buckets in nearby fields, making a small Polish contribution to Russian agriculture.

"I'm glad we have a toilet," Major Konopka said one day as we sat on a siding. "Sometimes, I imagine I hear music coming from it, as though I am home with my wife and children."

"I also hear music," Antoni Urban said with a wicked smile, "but, alas, it's only gas."

Everyone roared with laughter. The guards peered in, wondering what in the world we had to laugh about. But it was easily explained: hysteria was coming ever closer to the surface in many of us—and with it, thoughts of escape.

But they were only thoughts. In our car there was a ladder at one end leading to an escape hatch for use in an emergency, but it was folly to think of using this hatch. Sitting beside it on top of the train was an NKVD guard with a machine gun. All we could do was pray for low tunnels.

Several times during the first days of the journey east, the train took on other cars loaded with Polish officers. The train also took on cars loaded with Russian guards. As the number of prisoners grew, the contingent of guards enlarged until there were three guards on top of each car. When the train stopped for our daily meal, we could see guards by the hundreds walking beside the cars, exercising cramped muscles.

During a long, agonizing day of being shuttled and banged back and forth, we could see some design in the confusion. The Russians were splitting the long train into three segments. We heard that the force of Polish prisoners had grown to more than fifteen thousand. We were sick that so many Polish soldiers —mostly officers—had been captured by the Russians, but we also felt safety in such large numbers.

Using what we considered common sense, we assumed that the Russians would not want to keep so many prisoners. The country was already poor, and it would be expensive to feed, clothe, and house us. It would make more sense, we reasoned, to let us go free. But were the Russians reasonable? We tried desperately to believe they were.

At dark, the task of splitting the train and adding new cars —and of loading new prisoners—was completed. Engines wheezed and whistles shrieked away the evening calm. The trains began to move.

"Still heading east," Colonel Dzierzynski said, gazing at the bright North Star.

We slept fitfully, awakening to the clacking of the train wheels and the huffing of the laboring engines. At dawn, the trains slowed. Kiev! The big sign at the near end of the huge rail yards sent a ripple of excitement and anxiety through the mass of prisoners on the three trains.

For the first time since leaving Tarnopol, we knew where we were—but where we were was more than two hundred kilometers inside Russia. The Rumanian border was far behind us. It was Antoni who spoke what was perhaps in all our minds.

"Gentlemen and citizens," he said, loud enough for everyone in the car to hear, "I certainly hope none of you strained your minds trying to learn Rumanian. You should have been studying you-know-what. Where we're going, Russian will be of much greater value."

"*Bolnaya?*" Colonel Mijakowski asked with a wry smile, imitating the NKVD guard at Tarnopol.

"Of course I'm sick," Antoni retorted. "I'm sick in the mind, but I know when to stop dreaming and to face reality."

Hugo Mijakowski peered through the small, barred window at the gray morning over Kiev. His wound was healing well, but his body was still weak from the arduous journey and the inadequate diet.

"I will never stop dreaming," he said in a low, throaty voice that was almost choked back by tears. "Never."

"*Polska bedzie!*" Antoni said. But there was not much spirit in his claim that "Poland will be." We were all beginning to face the same reality.

In a few moments, we heard the low, mumbling voice of a priest who was in our car, Father Kantak. He prayed louder as the train picked up speed east of Kiev. We joined him in the prayer, an ancient Polish plea to St. Stanislas, our patron, asking the saint to give us understanding when it was difficult to understand what was happening to us. The prayer originated during the dark days following the Partitions, when the Poles could not understand why their land was occupied and why the enemy tried so desperately to stamp out all signs of Polish nationalism and thought.

Onward went the trains, like three laboring serpents playing "follow the leader" over the vastness of Russia. Our train was in the middle, and as the tracks turned through rolling hills and followed curving streams, we could see the train ahead and the one behind. For some reason, this sight brought comfort.

We moved swiftly now, slowing only when the trains came to a rise. In the evening we stopped at Kharkov—five hundred kilometers from Poland, three hundred from the Black Sea, and just over five hundred south of Moscow!

Such statistics became even more dismal when we discovered that our train was alone, heading north toward Moscow. It was Vincenty Jankowski who made this discovery.

"God in heaven," he said to the others in the car. "One train has stopped and the other is going off toward the east!"

Our train picked up speed, and the wheels clattered over the badly laid tracks. We had no idea where the other trains were going or why we had been split up. I watched as the train wound through deep passes and thundered into tunnels. I kept looking back, hoping to see the familiar headlight of a train behind us.

There was nothing but the black of night. We were truly alone now, deep inside Russia—and going deeper.

There were just under five thousand prisoners on our train, similar numbers on the other two. Messages came down along the train on our reliable car-to-car vocal communications system. The messages were no longer rumors; they were an assessment of our current status.

There were four generals and an admiral aboard our train: General Henryk Minkiewicz, the highest in rank; General Miecyslaw Smorawinski, who recently had become famous for defying the NKVD to get his men food and water; General Bronislaw Bohaterewicz; General George Wolkowicki; and Admiral Xavery Czernicki.

Except for a few military cadets, civilian specialists, and provincial police, all the other men were also officers. Many were of high rank—from major to colonel—and all highly educated. There were some from noble families, and many were solid members of the Polish intelligentsia. Among our ranks were doctors, dentists, priests, rabbis, ministers, teachers and professors, lawyers, writers, artists, journalists, radio announcers, scientists, businessmen—a very large share of Poland's educated class.

Our physical condition was reasonably good, in spite of inadequate food, lack of medicines, harsh conditions, and wounds. More than one thousand had war wounds, but only a fraction were serious, and the doctors aboard the various cars were doing everything possible to treat the wounded.

There had been no way of counting deaths since the roundup of prisoners began. We had seen many men carried from the cattle cars and dumped into fields during the early part of our journey. Apparently, the law of survival of the fittest applied: there were no deaths during the journey north from Kharkov.

Late in the afternoon of October 22, the train stopped at a tiny railway station in the central part of western Russia. Antoni, our unofficial navigator, placed us only a few kilometers from Moscow. Colonel Dzierzynski, who had been watching the stars and was, before the war, a professor at the University of Bialystok, believed that we were about midway between Moscow and Smolensk.

Soon, the message came back along the train: "We're at Kozelsk."

"Kozelsk?" Vincenty Jankowski asked. "Where in the hell is that?"

"It isn't in Rumania," Colonel Dzierzynski muttered.

We heard guards running alongside the train and then the familiar order: *"Sadis! Sadis!"*

The doors of our car rumbled open, and bright sunlight poured in. Guards ordered us outside. As we streamed from the car, the guards herded us off the train embankment to a muddy ditch, yelling: *"Sadis! Sadis!"*

Since we had left Tarnopol, we had taken great pains to keep our uniforms and boots clean. When the NKVD began to herd men into the mud, insisting that they sit down in it, there was very nearly a riot. Men refused to sit, and guards waved bayonets dangerously close to their chests. The bayonet is very persuasive. We sat in the mud and grumbled. I gazed at the village behind the station and saw a tremendous white limestone statue of Lenin. It made the station seem infinitesimal.

Kozelsk was like all the other small Russian villages we had seen on our journey. The houses were dilapidated and in need of paint. Some had never been painted. The gardens behind the homes were choked with weeds; nobody had tended them during the summer just past. Around us were undulating fields, equally untended, and patches of evergreens, white birches, and oaks.

After an hour the train left, and the Russians brought us to our feet. Formed into ranks ten abreast, we were marched down the wide main street of the village. As we sloshed through mudholes, we noticed that the village seemed empty of human habitation, although occasionally I thought I saw curtains ripple in dirty windows. The townspeople probably had strict orders to stay out of sight. The only signs of life, besides us and the guards, were the scrawny dogs yapping at our heels.

The generals were at the head of the ranks, slogging along in the mud, setting a slow pace, for which we were grateful. After so much riding in trains and trucks, our legs were rubbery. Even slow walking brought painful cramps. Our exercise program had not helped greatly, except that we would have been in worse shape without it.

The guards, in contrast, seemed in a panic to get us through the town. They kept shouting for us to go faster and looking at the shops and houses to make certain that no Russian citizen witnessed the passing of almost five thousand Polish officers. Uncanny naïveté! To believe that such a large contingent of prisoners could be marched through a village unobserved. Or perhaps the NKVD was simply so feared that when they said, "Don't look," no one looked.

Beyond the town, past a deep valley with a sluggish brown stream, was a thin stand of birch and evergreen trees. Beyond the woods, at the top of a knoll, we glimpsed ruined walls. I tried to gauge the distance, but the valley was deceiving. All I know is that the sun was bright when we left the village, and it was dusk when we reached the bottom of the valley and waded across the stream.

Ahead of us the column was disappearing into the dark protection of the trees. It was difficult for me to see the front of the column, and I knew that it would be difficult for the Russians to see if one or two of us slipped into the trees and hid until the column had passed.

I had only a short time to decide. The column moved swiftly, and I was nearing the trees. Sweat beaded on my forehead. I knew that my chances would be slim, that even if I got away, I would have to travel over many kilometers of Russian soil before reaching even a semblance of freedom.

I don't know why the thought of escaping came so strongly to me then. But I had seen the walled area above the woods when we had come to the edge of Kozelsk village, and I suspected that the walled encampment, if that was what it was, was our destination, perhaps our final destination.

I thought of Suzan. I had promised her that I would return. Surely flight couldn't be worse than captivity.

The moment came and passed. I entered the dark woods; fear took control; I stayed in the ranks. The guards were everywhere. If I ran, there might be shooting. I didn't want to be shot, and I certainly didn't want one of my friends to be accidentally killed in the shooting that might ensue if I tried to escape.

I decided to wait. I didn't know for certain if this strange place on top of the hill was our final destination, but it didn't matter. It would never be *my* final destination. I would escape from any place they put me. I *would* find my way back to Suzan.

We emerged from the woods beside a high stone wall with barbed wire at its top. At the corner was a huge stone guard tower. Bright lights shone down from the wall, and we walked in this artificial daylight to wooden gates thickly crisscrossed with barbed wire.

The problem at the gates was almost as ridiculous as it had been at the railway station in Grodno. Guards flanked the gates, and one held a clipboard, asking interminable questions.

"These bastards will take all night," Colonel Dzierzynski snarled. With that, he unbuttoned his trousers and began to urinate over the side of the path. It was the signal Antoni Urban and several others had been waiting for. Soon the woods were full of splashing sounds and yelling guards.

"*Nyet! Nyet!*" they shouted as the men relieved themselves. But the men continued. The dogs snapped their jaws and bared their fangs. All they got for their efforts was a soaking in long pent-up urine.

"Ah-h-h-h!" Antoni sighed with relief. "Another life-long dream realized. I've just pissed on a Russian dog!"

In spite of fatigue, low spirits, hunger, and terror of what lay behind the stone wall, the men burst into hysterical laughter.

It took another two hours to get us all inside. The gates were closed, and the lights on the walls were swiveled around to illuminate a large courtyard, about half the size of a football field. It was surrounded by white stone buildings, and we were ordered to face the largest, a three-story monstrosity with a wing on one side.

A wiry, stern-faced man in a crisp, freshly ironed uniform came out onto a stone porch. Standing on top of the three steps leading up to the stoop, the officer towered above us.

"I am Major Koraliev, your commandant," he said in a flat, tinny voice. "There is much to be done, but it is late. I wish to welcome you to our vacation resort, where you will spend some little time. I cannot tell you how long. For the moment we will dispense with plans for processing. That will commence at 0700 tomorrow. Meanwhile, have a good night's sleep."

He spoke rapidly in Russian and disappeared into the building. An NKVD lieutenant translated, but he botched it so badly that few knew what was going on—except that we were hungry and that the guards weren't going to feed us.

We were split into groups of varying sizes and led to other buildings in the compound. Our group stayed close, so as not to be separated. But Colonel Dzierzynski, Lieutenant Colonel Mijakowski, and Major Konopka, because of their rank, were taken with another group of officers. The top-ranking officers were led off into the darkness to a cottage near the main building.

Jagiello, Jankowski, Kochloffel, Bednarek, Urban, and I were taken with several others to Barracks 17. The guards there seemed almost kindly. They even bid us to sleep well as they closed the doors and left us in total darkness.

Immediately, men began to hammer on the doors. The guards opened them and peered at the hungry faces.

"We're starving," an officer boomed out in Polish. "Can't you bastards at least throw us a crumb?"

I moved forward and explained that we had not been fed since yesterday. An NKVD sergeant, whose name, I later found out, was Pavel Borodynsky, smiled apologetically and promised that food would be brought soon.

"I don't understand," he said in a kind voice. "The guards who brought you said you were fed in the village."

Unlike our previous guards, he made good his promise. Within fifteen minutes guards carried in a great kettle of steaming potato soup, fresh white bread, and candles, which were placed in holders around the cracked plaster walls. The sergeant explained that we would have electricity the next day.

"Unfortunately," he added, "all preparations have not been completed, although we have worked three weeks to get ready for you."

The statement, which probably carried no intrinsic malice on Sergeant Borodynsky's part, slammed into my brain like a rushing train.

Three weeks ago, they knew we were coming!

Three weeks ago, we were still being told—repeatedly—that we were going to Rumania, to freedom!

It became simple. The Russians never intended to give us freedom. What they intended to do with us I didn't know. Suspicion of it lay in the deepest recesses of my mind and refused to come out. Those suspicions were too frightening to be examined. In any case, as I lay there watching the others joke and talk and eat like schoolboys, my last shred of hope disappeared. There was not one thought that I would ever see Suzan or Poland, or even freedom. I had come, with my comrades, to the place of my death!

Thanks to Antoni Urban, I didn't fall asleep in that dismal state of mind. He had seen me lying on the cot with a blank stare on my face, and he must have guessed my thoughts.

Antoni walked toward me slowly, carrying a bowl of soup and a chunk of the good-smelling bread. He sat on the cot beside me.

"Eat and be merry, Major Komorowski," he said with a pleasant lilt in his voice. "Colonel Dzierzynski said it was the wrong way to Rumania all along. It could be worse, you know."

"Worse? How could it be worse, Antoni?"

"We could be Russians."

This constant emotional ebb and flow, from certainty of return to bleak despair, constantly plagued us all. My only consolation was the fact that despair always gave way to determination, and with determination came certainty.

6: GORKI'S REST HOME

GOOD morning, good morning, good morning."

The voice was pleasant enough, but it punched unwanted holes through the bliss of sleep. It pulled me into the world of reality: I was a prisoner in some godforsaken spot in Russia where the lice were as ravenous as wolves.

"Welcome to our lovely resort, Citizens," the cheerful voice burbled. "Come, come, wake up. See what a beautiful day is ahead. It will be full of sunshine. You will be reborn on this marvelous day."

Antoni lay on a cot beside me. He opened one eye and grimaced at the honeyed words. The speaker, obviously a Russian, was butchering the Polish language mercilessly.

"He talks about rebirth," Antoni grumbled, "and interrupts a fantastic dream of an *un*immaculate conception. I was with Janina Lewandowski, and she had these enormous . . . "

"Ah, I see that some of you are awake," the unctuous voice said. "Come, come. It is 0600. Our day commences."

71

"I am commencing to hate his guts, whoever he is," Antoni muttered as the man moved off to greet others. "Not even animals should be disturbed this early."

There was nothing to getting up, merely altering the use of our overcoats from blankets to coats. Men stumbled against each other in the dim light until their eyes adjusted. We assembled in a semicircle around the man with the unctuous voice.

"I am Aleksi Alexandrovich," he said with a wide grin. "I am your friend while you are here."

"And just where are we?" a voice demanded.

"You are in a special resort for special persons," Aleksi said amiably. "Where monks and nuns once frolicked in diurnal orgies, you will experience a rebirth under the kind and gentle auspices of Russian love for mankind. Let us go outside. A magnificent breakfast awaits."

The chill of the October morning was less penetrating outside. There was a gentleness to it. As we passed through the doors, the cheerful Aleksi Alexandrovich stood like a minister saying good-bye to his flock, smiling and nodding at each of us. Aleksi was almost a pretty man, with a full head of black, curly hair and wide, dark eyes with thin, womanish eyebrows. His short frame, with just a trace of fatness, gave the impression of youth, with its small bones and graceful movements. If he was a homosexual, I doubt he lacked companionship.

"Methinks yon Aleksi has a lean and hungry look," Antoni whispered. "Who is the bastard, anyway?"

"Yon Aleksi," I answered, "is an NKVD captain."

"Wonderful," he said as we formed ranks. "We're gaining in status. Last night a sergeant, today a captain. Tomorrow —perhaps a general."

With cheerful words and a flashing smile, Aleksi led us slowly past other barracks, from which more men were emerging. At a junction we found a large field kitchen and caught the aroma of cooking food.

"Fill your tins, and we shall return to quarters," the captain said. "While you dine on your morning feast, we shall become better acquainted."

To us, it *was* a feast. Russian cooks piled oatmeal, rice, rolls, and sugar onto our metal plates, and we returned to Barracks 17. Some of the men finished the hot meal before we got inside. The rest of us sat on cots and ate ravenously while Aleksi Alexandrovich chattered.

"I am everything to you," he said as I munched contentedly on a sweet roll and slurped the soupy oatmeal. "Friend, companion, helper, guide, father confessor, mother—everything. You have a problem, bring it to your friendly *polit-rook*."

"What is a *polit-rook?*" Vincenty Jankowski asked.

Aleksi smiled fondly at Vincenty, pursed his lips, and said: "It is a short form of *polititchevskiy rookovoditel*."

"And what does that mean?" Vincenty went on.

"I have told you," the captain said, laughing. "Friend, companion, helper, guide, father confessor, mother—everything."

While he chattered on to anyone who would listen, Rudolf Kochloffel explained in whispers: "He is a political guide. He will scrub your mind of the filth of capitalism and rinse it with the purity of communism. Watch your minds, gentlemen. You might pay dearly for this little taste of Russian kindness."

"I'll never have my mind changed," Leo Bednarek declared, flexing his forearm as he mopped up his oatmeal with the last of his sweet roll. "I hate all of the fucking Communists."

None of us had any great love for Communists because, as a political entity, they were as vicious in attaining their goals as the Nazis were. But Leo Bednarek had a special hatred for Communists. When he was a boy, his parents had owned a hundred-acre farm just inside the Russian border near Polotsk on the Dvina River. His mother, a Russian, had inherited the farm, and the Russians permitted the family to operate it. But in 1919 the Communists confiscated the farm and nearly wiped out the Bednarek family. Two of Leo's older brothers died trying to keep the Bolsheviks from collectivizing the farm.

If we could believe our cheerful *polit-rook*, the future at this great vacation resort for the Russian peasant worker was to be a rosy one. Only the most gullible believed this, and they were soon to be disillusioned. For a start it didn't really matter to many of us where we were assigned. One barracks looked as dilapidated as the next. My only hope was that I would remain with at least *some* of my friends, or that I might be assigned to the same barracks as Colonel Dzierzynski. We had grown to depend upon each other for moral support. I needed his solidity, and I believed that he needed my leavening influence to keep him from doing anything hot-headed.

I had survived my deep depression of the night before, but I was soon to learn that in the camp our moods could not be counted on to last more than a few hours. At one moment we were plunged into deep despair, and at the next, we were elevated to a state of near joy. We were victims of a weird, almost schizophrenic behavior under the careful eyes of the NKVD.

That first day was one of unending confusion. The Russians may have prepared for three weeks for our arrival, but we might as well have been unexpected company. When Aleksi Alexandrovich led us outside, groups of Polish officers were hurrying in every direction, already beginning their indoctrination, which consisted of touring the camp, being questioned at the administration building, being photographed, undergoing a medical examination at the camp dispensary, and, in many cases, being reassigned to other barracks. When we joined the activity and movement in the narrow roads between the barracks, the confusion simply became more frenetic. Groups ran into each other, intermingled; men got lost from their particular groups temporarily, jostled each other playfully, laughed, and eventually found their proper groups.

Aleksi Alexandrovich was unruffled, as though he had gone through this chaos a million times. As he led us to the barber in a small wooden shed near the *banya*, or bathhouse, Aleksi smiled. As we waited to have a grimy peasant shave our heads, Aleksi made small conversation with the men closest to him, smiling, whispering little confidences—even laughing at the disorganization.

From the barber's we walked to the administration building,

where other groups were assembled. As we waited, we gazed around at the eighteenth-century buildings, so rundown that no peasant worker could possibly wish to spend a vacation there.

"Some resort," Antoni snorted, glancing across the courtyard at an old church about to collapse. "Better a man should take a vacation in his toilet."

"It's almost like a village without shops or peasant cottages," Leo Bednarek commented.

"Perhaps it was a university," Vincenty Jankowski offered.

"And perhaps you didn't listen to our wonderful friend, companion, helpmate, and mother," Rudolf Kochloffel said. "Monks and nuns used to have orgies here. This was a monastery."

At the present time, however, it was a prison, a Russian prison. The walls of buildings were covered with typical Soviet slogans and photographs of Marx, Lenin, and Stalin. On huge billboards around the courtyard were articles from the Soviet Constitution, printed in Polish. The men read them and laughed.

"Look at Article 118," someone said. " 'All Citizens of the USSR have the right to work.' Wonderful, but it doesn't say if they have the right to receive pay."

"I prefer Article 122," someone else chimed in. " 'Women in the USSR are accorded equal rights with men.' Why are there no women in the NKVD? If Aleksi were a woman, I might listen to him—her."

The greatest ridicule was reserved for Article 124. It concerned religion: "In order to ensure citizens freedom of conscience, the church is separated from the state, and the school from the church. Freedom of religious worship and freedom of antireligious propaganda are recognized for all citizens."

We knew, of course, that religious practice was virtually nonexistent in the Soviet Union. It probably would be prohibited at Kozelsk.

As we continued to wait for the next step, standing in line at the administration building, we grew sullen and silent. We finally came to the side door of the wing that had been hidden in shadows the night before. About ten o'clock I was led into a small room by a scowling sergeant.

An NKVD lieutenant sat at an old wooden desk. He motioned me to a chair opposite him. The lieutenant opened a brown file with my name on it and read in a sleep-inducing monotone precisely what I had told the guard at Grodno.

Looking around the barren room, I could see only the desk and two chairs, plus an old ticking clock on a side wall. There was one window, and the NKVD sergeant stood in front of it, blocking most of the light. Above the desk was a long electric cord and one small bulb. The walls, like those in the barracks, were lined with cracks.

"So you have studied in Brussels and London?" he asked in the same monotone.

I didn't realize that he was addressing me, so I said nothing. The sergeant, about my size and weight, moved up and gripped my right shoulder. His fingers dug into my flesh, and I squirmed away.

"Answer the lieutenant," the man growled.

"I'm sorry," I said, smiling at the lieutenant. "What did you say?"

"I said you studied in Brussels and London. Is this true?"

"Yes. That's true."

"When you address the lieutenant," the big sergeant snapped, "say, 'Sir.'"

I looked up at the scowling man with the dark, slanted eyes and the full thatch of greasy black hair. His face was dirty and round. His teeth were covered with green and yellow scum. He looked as though he had never owned a toothbrush.

The lieutenant leaned back and laughed lightly. "Don't mind Sergeant Kalanin. I don't believe he approves of treating enemy soldiers with kindness."

"I wasn't aware," I said, still watching the ugly sergeant, "that we were enemy soldiers."

"You are an officer in the Polish Army Reserves?"

"Yes. Yes, sir."

"Then you are an enemy of your people and of *our* people."
He said it with a grim finality and in a crisp, decisive manner. His
hard eyes regarded me as though I had committed some vicious
crime. I squirmed in the chair again, glanced toward the
sergeant, who was glaring at me, and looked up at the lieutenant.

"That's a peculiar kind of logic," I said slowly, choosing my
words carefully. "Isn't it possible to be a member of the Polish
Army Reserves without being an enemy . . . "

"It is not!" the lieutenant snapped. "Your station makes you a
capitalistic pig. You are an exploiter of the peasant worker.
Exploiters are enemies. Thus you are an enemy of your people."
He leaned forward, and I thought I detected the hint of a smile.
"We love the Polish people as we love all common people. We
detest exploiters. Therefore, you are our enemy as well as the
enemy of your own people, *Pan* Komorowski."

When he said *"Pan,"* a title of respect such as "sir," he used the
word as though it were dirty. I didn't bother protesting; there
was really nothing to protest.

"Now," he said, turning a page in my folder and glaring at me,
"as to your so-called studies abroad. What did you study?"

"History," I said. "Isn't it there in the record? I've told all this
before and . . . "

Sergeant Kalanin gripped my shoulder tighter, and pain shot
into my back.

"That will be enough, Sergeant," the lieutenant broke in. "Let
us continue with our discussion, Captain Komorowski."

"Major Komorowski," I corrected.

"Oh, yes. You were caught wearing a major's epaulets. Where
did you steal them?"

Once again I told the story of my field promotion. Sergeant
Kalanin snorted and moved to the window. I followed him with
my eyes; he *was* dangerous.

"I see," the lieutenant said when I had finished. "Now, let us
discuss your spying missions to Brussels and London."

"Spying missions?" I could not keep the incredulity from my
voice.

He leaned forward, his elbows on the table, and smiled crookedly at me. "You were sent by your government to obtain information on the fighting strength of Belgium and England. Do you deny this?"

I laughed; I couldn't help it. I couldn't take the man seriously. I gazed at Sergeant Kalanin. He stood in a half crouch, as though he were ready to pounce on me for such effrontery.

"Come, Captain Komorowski," the lieutenant said. "You were spying for the benefit of the now defunct Polish government. True?"

"That's absurd!"

The lieutenant was nonplussed. He hurriedly consulted the record again and looked up. He repeated part of the record from memory: "Each summer for fifteen years you were sent to Brussels and London. You say you studied history, but I know different. What did you learn of Belgian and British military strength during these spying missions?"

"Oh, I learned a great deal," I said, mockingly. "I learned *all* about the military strength of Great Britain, Belgium, France —even Russia."

"Ah, now we are progressing. And you gave this valuable information to your government?"

"No, sir. I gave it to my students in Poznan."

"I beg your pardon."

"Lieutenant, this is ridiculous." A joke can go too far. "I studied history. I learned about Napoleon and his wars against England and Russia. I can give you details of their military strength from 1810 to 1815. Would you like details on the battle at Borodino? I know them all."

"Captain Komorowski, this is neither the time nor the place for foolish games. I care nothing about history. I want to know what you learned during your spying missions to . . ."

"For Christ's sake, Lieutenant," I blurted. "You can get this information from your files. I studied history. I studied languages. Nothing else."

"You're a liar!"

Literally a shout, the words came, unexpectedly, from Sergeant Kalanin, who was behind me now. His foul breath enveloped me.

"You are a filthy capitalistic liar!" he rasped.

Without looking up and without losing composure, I replied: "And you, Sergeant, are a lunatic."

"Enough!" the lieutenant snapped. "*Pan* Komorowski, concerning your spying missions to London in the summers of . . ."

I shut him out. The lieutenant rattled on about spying missions and military intelligence and secret reports to my government, but I didn't even pretend to listen. The droning of his voice mingled with the ticking of the clock. I looked at my fingernails, which were dirty, and at Kalanin, who was dirtier. I gazed through the small window. Across the courtyard, Article 123 of the Soviet Constitution glared in the sunlight: "Equality of the rights of all citizens, irrespective of their nationality or race, in all spheres of economic, governmental, cultural, political, and other public life, is an indefeasible law."

"Do you deny that?" It was the lieutenant, raising his voice to reach into my consciousness.

"It's too absurd to confirm or deny," I said quietly, unaware of what I was to confirm or deny.

Finally, an hour after he had begun, the lieutenant took off his metal-rimmed spectacles and stood up, exasperated. "That will be all for now. We will have other discussions, and you will, of course, be far more cooperative. Sergeant Kalanin, take the captain out and bring in the next man. Good day, *Pan* Komorowski."

"Good day, Lieutenant . . ."

"Borisovets," he said primly.

The sergeant's hand was on my arm. He pulled me from the room and forced me down the corridor, past the line of Poles awaiting their turn. At the door, the NKVD sergeant pulled me close, giving me full benefit of his reeking breath.

"You will pay for what you said. You will pay dearly."

Leo Bednarek had not had any better luck with his interrogator, a burly lieutenant who had seemed willing to test the
dentist's immense strength, but who wisely had not.

"I've always hated them," Leo muttered as we walked across
the courtyard, "but now I find them even easier to hate."

We left the courtyard and went down a side road past the ruins
of the church. Suddenly a great crash of music boomed across
the camp. It was so loud that the speakers on tall poles and on the
roofs of buildings squealed. The volume was quickly turned
down.

"My God," someone said from the ranks. "That's Paderewsky
playing Chopin's Etude in E Minor."

"Ah, beautiful," another voice chimed.

"Shut up and listen."

Captain Alexandrovich was pleased with our reaction. He
walked beside us, smiling and keeping time with his hands, as
though he were conducting the great pianist. We stopped at a
large building, an exceptional one in that it had few windows
unshattered. Several hundred men had formed long lines in
front.

"Your hospital, gentlemen," Alexandrovich said proudly.
"After a complete physical examination and treatment by our
expert medical staff, you will be inoculated against typhoid. We
must assure you of good health. Of course, we are waiting for
certain medical supplies."

The "expert medical staff" consisted of two burly orderlies
and the ugliest Chinese woman this side of the Great Wall, Dr.
Loo, who, like Alexandrovich, wore a perpetual smile. Her teeth
were huge, yellow, and cluttered with bits of food.

Men with wounds were given aspirin. The more serious
wounds were wrapped in soiled bandages. Shots were given in
the manner of a carpenter nailing shingles on a roof. The "complete physical examination" did not exist. The young and handsome were stripped and checked for hernia, a long and probing

check that caused many erections. I was flattered with a hernia examination, but nothing happened. The unbelievably ugly woman created temporary impotence. Leo Bednarek later told me that he closed his eyes and conjured up a beautiful nurse.

"I almost had a climax," he said as we left the grimy hospital and gathered for the next item on our schedule.

"Wait until Antoni arrives," I said, chuckling. "He'll knock out the only remaining window when that doctor gets her hands on him."

We marched back across the compound to where hundreds of men stood in lines and groups. Antoni, Rudolf Kochloffel, and Henryk Jagiello joined us at the top of a small ravine.

We were at a high point in the camp and could see over the wall. A small biplane was landing at an airport, only a few kilometers away. As we went down steep stone steps into the ravine, we looked at each other. A common thought ran through our minds: escape! The airport presented the perfect outlet for escape.

We were led into a small cottage, where a wild-haired old man in a dirty smock took our photographs with a camera that might have been stolen from Mathew Brady just after the American Civil War. The old man bustled about, knocking over chemicals, exposing film, and generally doing a typically Russian job of photography. When I later saw my photo in the brown file, I wasn't disappointed. The old photographer had not slandered his image.

There was a sparse lunch of potato soup and black bread, then a tour of the camp.

"We call our resort Gorki's Rest Home," Captain Alexandrovich said as he led us between buildings with cracked walls and broken windows. "There are twenty-two hotel-type buildings where you will reside in the same comfort offered to the hard-working peasant who brings his family. And now, to the *banya* and the recreation hall."

The *banya*, or bathhouse, was a filthy building with boards covering cracks in the walls. Inside was a wood-burning stove and a hot water boiler. Iron pipes ran across the ceiling; open pipes pointed downward. Cockroaches skittered about on the stone floor; someone in our group saw a rat.

"We are waiting for pesticides," our *polit-rook* explained. "Before you bathe tomorrow, the vermin will be gone. We Russians are very clean."

The recreation hall was equally disappointing, a one-story building with a huge basement.

Our guide ignored the four stone guard towers, the several wooden storks, and a large old house, its windows boarded up. He said nothing about a barbed-wire gate at one corner of the wall, guarded by NKVD men with machine guns and dogs.

By day's end, we referred to Gorki's Rest Home as Camp Kozelsk, the recreation hall as The Club, and the Russian Constitution as a pack of lies.

We were issued "camp supplies," each of us receiving a tattered blanket, a flat pillow with a greasy cover, some foul-smelling soap, a ragged towel, and sundry items—all of the items, we were told, had to be returned when our vacation ended. Our smiling *polit-rook* didn't say when the vacation would end.

Dinner consisted of fish, properly prepared, with biscuits that were neither moldy nor stale. We each were given two sugar cubes and a cup of weak tea. Though bitter from age, it was the first tea we had drunk in several weeks. Nobody complained.

In the camp we had plenty of time for reflection. One thing was certain: we were going to be there for some time. The camp, stuck away in this remote section of Russia, bore no resemblance to the compound near Tarnopol. The buildings there had been rough and hastily erected; the buildings at Kozelsk, though dilapidated, were permanent. Its remoteness from the village—a distance of perhaps ten kilometers—made it an ideal retreat, and the spartan leanings of the monks had marked our new abode indelibly.

There were many solid, if uncomfortable, buildings to serve the purpose of a group as large as ours. Would we be here for the winter? If so, I hoped they would arrange the dining facilities so that we need not continue to be served at an open field kitchen. The winter! At the thought I felt my depression returning. It was difficult to maintain a good spirit when thoughts of lost freedom and the possibility of oblivion were so much on my mind. And Suzan.

Many men, of course, were fighting a similar mental battle. They too had bitter memories and crushed hopes. Some were soon to let such thoughts overwhelm them; they would become little more than vegetables, lying in their beds staring at cracks in the walls and ceilings, living in a fantasy world. A few had already reached that state. I resolved in that moment not to become one of them.

Just before it came time to blow out the candles, the barracks *korpoosnoy*, or sergeant in charge, Pavel Borodynsky, the man who had brought us food the night before, came to the door and summoned me outside.

"I argued with myself about telling you," he began at once in a low voice, glancing over his shoulder as if to make certain we weren't being watched. "What I am doing is dangerous, but I feel a responsibility to the men in this barracks. I want to warn you."

"Warn me? Warn me about what?"

He looked up and down the dark road between the rows of barracks, then leaned closer.

"One of the instructions we have received from the camp commandant," he whispered, "is that there should be no trouble. The commandant wants everything to run smoothly."

"But . . ."

"You have made a formidable enemy," he said cryptically.

"An enemy? According to Lieutenant Borisovets, we're all enemies. Enemies of our own people as well as of the Russians."

"This is different," Sergeant Borodynsky said, looking up and down the road again. "I speak of Kalanin, a *personal* enemy."

"Oh," I said. "Has he told you what happened?"

"He's telling everyone," the sergeant said. "He is bragging that he will kill you at the first opportunity. Several of the guards have told him that he will get into trouble with higher officials, but he doesn't seem to care."

I laughed, trying to show that I wasn't afraid of Kalanin, that I didn't take his threats seriously. Inside, I felt chilled. "Perhaps he's only making noises," I said lightly. "After all, it was only a small thing. Nothing to make threats about."

Sergeant Borodynsky's eyes narrowed, and the warmth left his expression. He put his hand on my arm, and his voice was cold, hard. "Stand clear of him, Citizen. He is not a man to fool with."

There was no mistaking the fact that he took his message seriously. I could do no less. But I didn't know what to say. At least I couldn't let this Russian know just how frightened I was, no matter how kind he seemed in bringing the information to me. I found my voice and said evenly: "Thank you, Sergeant Borodynsky. I'll remember that."

Pavel Borodynsky nodded, glanced again over his shoulder, and walked away.

I stood on the stoop for several minutes, thinking about the warning. I couldn't believe that Borodynsky had come out of the goodness of his heart. Perhaps he was right about the camp commandant's not wanting trouble. Perhaps again it was merely a method of working his way into my confidence. But if so, what could he or the others want from me—or from any of us—that we had not already told them?

Rudolf Kochloffel's comment about scrubbing the filth of capitalism from our minds and rinsing them with communism came back to me. The signs at Tarnopol, the billboards at Kozelsk—were they all part of a plan to turn us into Communists? Was that why we were brought here and not taken to Rumania?

Were the Russians, in their crude, tentative way, trying to show us that communism meant a better way of life than capitalism? If this were true, they were going about it in the wrong way.

Nothing made any real sense to me then, except two things: Pavel Borodynsky had warned me of Kalanin's intentions for a reason—some reason. Sooner or later he would reveal the reason, and I would be ready.

7: THE CLUB

THE vacation at the old resort ended abruptly, though the Russians did not find out about it for a while. We gave up any pretense that we were guests at the vermin-infested camp the day after our arrival. We were prisoners, but we were also Polish officers bound invisibly to General Minkiewicz and other senior officers.

We received no written orders, but on the third day orders reached us through the camp grapevine, which had begun to spread its tentacles shortly after our arrival.

—we were not to salute Soviet officers, regardless of rank.

—we were to maintain military discipline; infractions would be punishable according to the Polish Military Code.

—we were to resist Russian entreaties to alter our political thinking; any man who became a Communist also became a traitor.

—we were to inform Russian interrogators of our true feelings; we were not even to *pretend* to swallow communist doctrine.

86

—Polish officers of any rank were to extend customary courtesies, including salutes, to superior Polish officers.

—we were to maintain clean bodies and clean minds, when possible.

—we were to continue allegiance to the exiled Polish government.

—religious practice was to continue openly unless forbidden; in such case, it would continue surreptitiously.

—we were duty bound to attempt escape, to refuse aid to the enemy, and to withhold Polish military information.

—any escapee must join the growing Polish Underground or Free Polish fighting units in Syria, France, or England.

We were citizen soldiers, reserve officers who had had virtually nothing to do with the military before the war, with the exception of having served our required two years of military duty as young men. We didn't have the *esprit de corps* of regular army men, at least not as a matter of training. The orders from General Minkiewicz made us feel more like soldiers than we had felt since we had been taken prisoner. Even men who were becoming withdrawn came out of their shells, at least temporarily.

The NKVD had their own grapevine communications system, and news of the general's orders eventually reached the camp commandant. He reacted speedily. In the middle of the third day, a lively Polish mazurka was suddenly interrupted by a booming voice, which pronounced in textbook Polish:

"Citizens, we are all part of the glorious scheme of brotherhood that looks kindly upon all men. We are brothers under the warm sun of Mother Russia, which welcomes you to her compassionate bosom. As brothers, we shall rule the world and spread this benevolent sunshine to the oppressed and downtrodden masses who are slaving away under the heavy yoke of imperialistic criminals who make their crimes against mankind in the guise of false democracy and cruel capitalism. Join with us, brothers. Cast off this ignominious yoke and become truly free. Link arms with us, Citizens, and we shall form a ring of brotherhood to encircle the earth and to bring freedom and abundance to all."

The first time this happened we listened, unbelieving, to the voice. It echoed from building to building. If they didn't hear it in Moscow, they weren't listening.

At the second interruption, during Chopin's Piano Concerto Number One, the men in Barracks 17 stood up and sang "*Jeszcze Polska Ni Zginels*"—the Polish national anthem. Of course it didn't matter. But the interruptions continued, relentlessly.

Except when an officer was called to the administration building for further interrogation, there was little to do in the days following orientation. The NKVD deliberately imposed a life of idleness on us, and it was initially welcome. We were tired from the long journey and the lack of proper food. But the idleness had a tendency to sap our stiff resolve.

Within a few days of our arrival, about four hundred officers were separated from the main group, after extensive interrogations, and billeted in a cluster of buildings located almost a kilometer from the camp, on the opposite side of the village. This area, connected to the walled camp by a path through a woods, had once been a retreat, so we named it the *skit*—which means a place to go and think.

The path was approached from the northeast corner of the camp and was guarded by NKVD men with machine guns and dogs and by huge rolls of barbed wire. Rumors began to circulate immediately. The four hundred were from eastern Poland, and many had parents of Russian descent. Some were badly wounded, and virtually all were physically weak in comparison to others in the camp.

The prevailing rumor was that they were not the strongest of Polish patriots and that they held, or once had held, political beliefs that were less than democratic. They were not Communists, but the NKVD considered them ripe for conversion. We suspected that if any were converted to communism, they would be set loose in the camp to help convert the rest of us.

During the evenings, when depression descended on us, talk of escape became most prevalent. Various plans were discussed at length. Rumors were sorted. For example, in our barracks we heard that men in Colonel Dzierzynski's barracks had a plan to climb the wall with a ladder built with scraps of wood found around the camp. We were not the only ones to note the proximity of planes. Moreover, as General Minkiewicz had pointed out, it was our duty to try to escape.

At the same time, we all agreed—and we didn't agree on much—that escape was virtually impossible. The guards on the towers were equipped with mounted fifty-caliber machine guns, and guards with dogs patrolled on both sides of the stone wall. The wall itself was topped by several strands of barbed wire.

In the second week a new facet of life was opened to us. The NKVD had set aside the former monastery cafeteria as a recreation center. During the first week a special committee of officers was assigned to clean it up. We had already named it the Club.

The Club officially opened on the evening of November 1, 1939. We were allowed to visit it after mealtime, but it had to close ten minutes before curfew. This gave us approximately three hours to meet with men from other barracks in a relaxed atmosphere, to swap gossip and rumors, and to formulate escape plans.

On "opening night" I went with Antoni, Leo, Vincenty, Henryk, and Rudolf. We were amazed at what the committee had accomplished. It had somehow cajoled the electrician from the village into installing power, so there was no need for candles or kerosene lamps. The committee members had also stolen a huge chandelier from the church to light the central part of the hall.

Members of the committee had made several decks of playing cards out of strips from old cardboard boxes, carved crude chess pieces, and painted boards on which to play (the NKVD provided four boards). One enterprising officer had even made some excellent darts, using bits of cloth soaked in glue as feathers. Another officer had made several dart boards to supple-

ment those available, and another had made a small stove from a
kerosene lamp to heat water for tea. Although tea was not
usually on our menu, some quick-witted—and
larcenous—officers had snitched old tea leaves from the NKVD
mess hall. The tea was bitter and weak, but it was tea.

On the main floor were a foyer, a large central hall, small
alcoves enclosed by thick pillars, and a separate room where the
top hierarchy of the monastery apparently had dined. The recreation committee had found rickety wooden tables and chairs
in a storeroom and set them up around the hall. The side room
was used mostly by the dart players. In the basement—formerly
the kitchen and pantry—the committee had set up tables for
chess games. The basement was cool and quiet and had no
loudspeaker. For this reason, many of the more studious officers
chose the basement for their "recreational hours" in spite of the
damp and chill.

Old nail kegs, flour barrels, and wooden crates were set along
the wall of the main hall and around the barrel stove near the
foyer. Some men simply sat on the assortment of makeshift
furniture smoking dried grass in their pipes. Sometimes, they
talked in low voices; generally, they were quiet, pensive, smoking
and watching the makeshift stove. At the tables men played with
the thick, unwieldy cards, though there weren't enough cards
for everyone.

Leo Bednarek and I pulled two tables together in a semidark
alcove behind two pillars and gathered up chairs for our group.
Antoni brought a new friend, a young pilot from Barracks 22,
Stanislaw Kaczmarek.

Shortly afterward, Colonel Dzierzynski, Colonel Mijakowski,
and Major Konopka arrived. Antoni spotted them and leaped
up.

"Over here, Colonel. Hey, right here. We have seats."

Colonel Dzierzynski sat heavily in a wooden chair and looked
around at us. He had lost weight, but this only made the muscles
of his neck and arms stand out more clearly. He was thinner, but
he looked stronger.

Hugo Mijakowski had recuperated splendidly from his shrapnel wound and primitive operation. He exuded vitality as he talked and laughed with those around him.

Major Konopka sat with a beaming smile and twinkling eyes, his great hawk's nose a shield behind which he seemed to hide some of the emotion he felt. Except for the nose and the wide white brow, I might not have recognized him. His black, heavily pomaded hair was missing; his skull, bumpy. And he had lost so much weight that he and Vincenty Jankowski could have been twins.

We had been playing cards, but we stopped, and someone from another table came for them. We didn't even miss them, for Antoni had asked, out of the blue: "Shall we tell them now?" Glancing around to make certain that no guard or *polit-rook* had come inside, Stanislaw Kaczmarek leaned forward conspiratorially and nodded to the colonel.

"Everything is tentative so far," Colonel Dzierzynski began, "but we hope to firm up plans within the next week. We can't possibly hope to make a try before the middle of the month. There are guards to bribe and pilots to check out. And there is the difficult decision as to who will go. We have only one chance. Whether we fail or succeed, no other men will be able to use our method."

"And that is to escape to the airport and fly out in those small planes?" Jagiello asked. It did not take a genius to see that that was the most obvious means.

Colonel Dzierzynski nodded. "Lieutenant Kaczmarek and a couple of his friends have been watching the airport, counting and identifying planes. There are so few and . . . "

"Hold it," Leo Bednarek said suddenly, raising his hand. "The sweetest Commie of them all is here."

We turned toward the door. Aleksi Alexandrovich, his handsome face gleaming in the light, was coming toward our tables.

"Who's he?" Colonel Mijakowski asked. "Your friendly *polit-rook*?"

We nodded. More *polit-rooks* moved into the hall, spreading throughout the Club and joining the other tables. Aleksi Alexandrovich took off his cap as he approached us.

"Ah, Citizens and Comrades," he said in his unctuous tone of voice, "no cards to play with? Too bad. I had so hoped to join you in a hand or two."

We tried to ignore him and did not introduce him to our friends from Barracks 22. He seemed to know their names anyway and wouldn't take the hint. He commandeered a chair from another table and joined us.

"What were we discussing, Comrades?" he asked, smiling at each of us in turn. "Women? Whisky? The war? Don't let *me* stop the conversation. Please continue."

"We were planning a gay weekend in Paris," Antoni said, "but we couldn't decide which hotel to favor with our presence."

Aleksi laughed uproariously. He slapped the table and poked Vincenty Jankowski in the ribs. Vincenty glared at him with an expression that was a mixture of hatred and disgust. There was something peculiar in Vincenty's face, something I had not noticed before. His large eyes seemed glazed with dullness, as though all his thoughts were turning inward. I had seen that look on other men.

Aleksi Alexandrovich stayed until the Club closed, and there was no more discussion that night of escape plans. There were no jokes about the Russians, no more friendly gossip. At first we sat like stones and listened to the Russian babble on, making a fool of himself. Indeed, except for the sound of a few *polit-rooks* the hall was quiet.

Even when conversations started up again among the Polish officers, it was only on "safe" subjects. So when Aleksi Alexandrovich engaged Leo Bednarek, Vincenty Jankowski, and Henryk Jagiello in conversation, Colonel Dzierzynski turned to me.

"How do you like Barracks 17?" he asked.

"I suppose it's no better or worse than any other barracks."

He gazed at the rough table top. "I talked with General Smorawinski," he said slowly, then looked straight at me. "Special permission to see him," he explained. "I asked him to confirm your field promotion to major."

"Thank you, sir," I said. I felt neither elation nor depression at the news, nothing. But I did not want the colonel to think that the promotion meant nothing to me. "Thank you very much," I said again.

"Next week," he continued, "they're going to make permanent barracks assignments. General Smorawinski says we should prepare for a very long internment. You know, the war continues, after a fashion, but there seems to be no chance that the British and French will throw the Nazis out of western Poland."

"I've made another request," he said. "If your promotion is confirmed, I want you moved into Barracks 22. All right?"

Now I did have mixed emotions. As much as I liked Colonel Dzierzynski, I had grown attached to the men in our clique in Barracks 17. I would miss them; particularly I would miss Antoni Urban's humor and spirited uplifting. But I realized that the colonel would not invite me if he did not have a special reason for doing so. So I raised no objection.

"Good," the colonel said. He gripped my arm in a friendly gesture. "You know," he said, "that handsome Aleksi Alexandrovich had better watch his step. In a camp of five thousand men and only one woman, who is unavailable, he could get into a lot of trouble."

I laughed. Colonel Dzierzynski was not a humorist, but neither was he without humor.

8: A YEARNING FOR WINGS

SLEEP did not come easily on the night of Thursday, November 2. My mind buzzed with the new developments. I said nothing to the others about my impending promotion and transfer to Barracks 22, but I knew that I soon would be on the inside of the planning for escape, and that escape meant that I might see Suzan again—very soon. In my last conscious moment, I was already aboard a small plane.

Shortly before midnight I realized anew that I was a prisoner. Two guards awakened me and gestured in the dark for me to follow them. I knew instantly what was going on. Many officers had made middle-of-the-night visits to the administration building for marathon interrogations. Now it was my turn.

One guard snapped: "Lieutenant Borisovets has prepared a banquet for you. Hurry before everything turns cold."

The other guard snickered but said nothing. I heard other men stir in their beds. Some were awake; they knew what was happening.

Lieutenant Borisovets, his slender body efficiently erect and his glasses pushed tightly against the bridge of his nose, was sitting at the same wooden desk in the same room I had visited on the first day in camp. Beside the window Sergeant Kalanin stood scowling. Recalling his threat, I began to feel very uneasy.

"This will take only a little time," Lieutenant Borisovets said in a crisp, almost friendly manner. "We need only to clear up a few points in your story."

"All right." I sat opposite the desk in a straight-back wooden chair and waited. I noticed that something had been added since my previous appearance in the small office. On the cracked wall above and behind the lieutenant was a somber-faced photograph of Josef Stalin, who seemed to be watching my every move. The rest of the room was as bare as it had been before.

For a full hour the lieutenant casually read through my entire file, examining small notations and his own report on our first interrogation. My buttocks began to grow numb on the chair, and I shifted regularly to keep the blood circulating. Each time I shifted, Sergeant Kalanin moved and the lieutenant regarded me sternly through his thick glasses.

There were no points to be cleared up. But as soon as Lieutenant Borisovets began to question me about my alleged spying missions to London and Brussels, I knew that I was in for a long and grueling interrogation.

"You still deny that you were sent there to spy on the British and the Belgians?" the lieutenant asked.

I said nothing, remembering General Minkiewicz's orders to give only name, rank, and military number. Kalanin moved from the window and stood near me.

"Answer the lieutenant!" he snapped.

Kalanin was dangerous, and he *had* threatened to kill me. But I experienced no fear. My old feeling of self-confidence returned.

"Answer him!" Kalanin was almost apoplectic with rage.

"Why don't you tell him about *your* spying missions to Stockholm and Berlin?" I asked with exaggerated politeness.

Sergeant Kalanin raised his machine gun, and I thought he was going to hit me. But the lieutenant made a slight motion, and the sergeant lowered the gun and went back to the window.

"Once again, Citizen," the lieutenant said, his voice friendly again. "Please confirm your spying missions."

I shifted in the chair and let blood flow into my tingling left leg. My whole bottom half was going to sleep, and we were only getting started.

The lieutenant droned on about the "spying missions" to London and Brussels, demanding that I admit that I was a spy. I tired of giving my name, rank, and military number and began to give flippant answers, to yawn—even once to belch. Several times Sergeant Kalanin made a threatening move toward me; each time a flick of the lieutenant's hand sent him back.

Some three hours later the lieutenant, his tie loosened and sweat beads appearing on his forehead, got up to sit on the corner of his desk. The big clock ticked dully in my splitting head.

"Captain Komorowski," he said in a slow, deliberate manner, "are you aware that, no matter what you say, we can shoot you as a spy?"

"I am aware that you can do anything you wish with my body. As for my mind, that's another matter."

He sat up straight and seemed surprised. "What do you mean by that, Citizen?"

"Oh, come, Lieutenant," I said, my voice as tired as the rest of me, "we all know what you're trying to do here."

Lieutenant Borisovets laughed. "Tell me, Captain, just what are we trying to do here?"

The lieutenant sat on the corner of the desk for several minutes more, looking down at me. There was no discernible emotion in his expression. "Surely you don't think your previous life was better than the life we have in the Soviet Union," he said finally.

"I do," I replied firmly. "And you'll never convince me that your way of life is better than the life I had under the Polish government."

He reddened. "There *is no* Polish government!"

"Bullshit," I said calmly.

The blow came so swiftly that I scarcely felt it. There was a numbing sensation, then pain at the back of my neck. I felt and heard a small cracking sound as the room began to spin crazily. I fell to the floor. When I came to, I was looking up at Kalanin.

"Back to the chair," he ordered.

Rubbing my neck, I crawled into the chair. I glanced up at the clock and thought that I had been unconscious for only a few minutes. The lieutenant continued talking as though nothing had happened.

"The Poles have no culture. They never had. I don't see what Germany and Russia want with a country of uneducated, piggish morons. Polish women are ugly and have hair on their faces. Polish men are sullen, ill-mannered brutes or dandified homosexuals. I am supposed to teach you the values of communism, but you have no sense of values. You are all pigs."

Now I felt both fear and anger as well as exhaustion. At dawn, my nerves were raw, and I was snapping irritably at the lieutenant as he continued to degrade the Polish. Each time I made a sound, Kalanin moved behind me and raised his machine gun. I waited for the blow to come—even hoped for it—but he did not strike again that night.

Shortly after dawn Lieutenant Borisovets left the room. In a few minutes, a chubby young lieutenant in a crisp uniform and with a freshly scrubbed face came into the room. Kalanin maintained his post by the window.

"Good morning, Citizen Komorowski," the new lieutenant said cheerfully. "I trust that you had an interesting night."

He didn't introduce himself. I had never seen him before, and I soon ceased to care if I never saw him again. After he'd gone through my file, we played the idiotic game of the spying missions again. Then, the new lieutenant took a different tack.

"I have been to Poland many times," he said, leaning back in the chair and tapping a pencil to his teeth. "I find Warsaw very pleasant in the spring. Tell me, do you think the Germans have destroyed those lovely gardens in Lazienski Park? I hope not. I found them quite marvelous for contemplation. And the old city—what do you call it?"

"*Stare Miasto*," I said almost automatically. "Sir, may I please have some water?"

"Yes, the old city," he continued as though I hadn't asked for anything. "I do hope the Germans haven't destroyed that. It goes back how long? Oh, yes, thirteenth century. Right?"

"May I please have some water?"

The lieutenant, fresh from a night's sleep, continued to praise various cities and landmarks in Poland, then swung into a paean to Polish culture, history, and education. The University of Cracow, he said, was perhaps the finest in the world—outside Russia. He hoped most sincerely that the Germans had not destroyed it.

He praised all Poles, from the common peasant to the greatest leaders in art, music, literature, and government. And our military leaders, he said, had far more expertise than the greatest German military men. It was a pity that Germany had so much more armor to throw against the badly equipped armies of Poland.

Even though I knew his praise was part of the technique, I found myself nodding and smiling at everything he said. Still, I did not quite drop my guard. Thus when he picked up my file and asked, "Have you been a spy in other cities besides London and Brussels?" I was ready.

"Oh, for Christ's sake!" I exclaimed.

I flinched and waited for a blow from Kalanin, but it didn't come. I shifted on the hard chair and toyed with the idea of pretending to faint, just to get some rest on the floor. But I decided against this tactic because Kalanin would probably kick in my ribs while I was down.

The hours crept by. At noon Sergeant Kalanin was replaced by another NKVD sergeant, who simply stood like a robot by the window and seemed to contemplate something far away. My mind became hazy and confused. I tried desperately to make my mind a blank, but it swam with fuzzy images and recollections. Actually, I almost asked them to beat me senseless so that I would not have to sit in the chair and listen to the lieutenant's syrupy voice. I was thirsty, hungry, frightened, and overwhelmingly tired.

After the lieutenant had praised every Pole from Copernicus to Chopin to Madame Curie to Paderewski, he suddenly shot up from his chair and glared at me, hatred emanating from every pore. "All of them," he almost shouted, "are nothing more than a litter dropped by the devil's mistress!"

From that point my memory of the interrogation is extremely hazy. The chubby lieutenant was replaced in mid-afternoon by a tall, gangly lieutenant. And Kalanin returned, after only a two-hour absence. He was either a glutton for punishment or a glutton to witness *my* punishment.

I found it impossible to answer questions. The gangly lieutenant, sounding like a machine gun as he fired questions, quickly became angry that he was receiving no answers. Again and again he flicked his hand. Each time Kalanin swung his machine gun, and I fell to the floor (I had been right about Kalanin—he usually took the opportunity to kick me in the ribs). Then I was jerked upright and pushed back into the chair. My legs were lead, and my ribs, shoulders, and neck were on fire from the blows and kicks.

At dusk the gangly lieutenant was replaced by a burly captain. Kalanin stayed on until late evening. There was little variation in the techniques used by the various interrogators. They alternately damned and praised Poland. Treatment ranged from kindness to brutality.

I was given no water and no food. At midnight, twenty-four hours after I had been brought into the little office, Lieutenant Borisovets returned. He was chipper. He adjusted his glasses and spent a long time rereading my file. Once I thought to use the opportunity to fall asleep, but I had slept for perhaps thirty seconds when Kalanin knocked me off the chair.

Interrogators changed. Kalanin seemed always to be there, but I suspect that actually he left for several two-hour periods. Each time he was replaced by the robot, who stood at attention until the interrogator flicked his hand. Then he hit me, usually knocking me to the floor.

I was hit so many times that I lost track. Lumps raised on my head and face, even on various bones. I felt hands pulling at my tunic, felt myself being lifted, felt myself being hit, felt myself falling. Kind and harsh voices blended into one long, relentless harangue. My tongue was so thick from thirst that I could not have spoken even if I had wanted to.

The ordeal had begun at midnight on Thursday. It ended a few minutes after 2:00 A.M. on Sunday—a fraction over seventy-four hours! During that period I had not slept—except for the few seconds that I had stolen (and paid for)—eaten, or drunk.

I remember a voice saying: "Take him to Barracks 17." Something clicked in my mind, and I glanced through swollen lids at the old clock. It was precisely 2:04.

I awoke from the nightmare Sunday night and found little Father Kantak, the old priest who had been on our *tieplooshka*, kneeling beside my cot. He was muttering prayers.

I had not been very religious for years; I certainly was not what one referred to as a "good Catholic." But the muttered prayers touched something in me that the NKVD had failed to reach.

My lips were swollen, but I managed to speak to the priest. "What time is it, Father?"

Father Kantak raised his head and looked at me. His eyes were old and rheumy, but a fierce compassion burned in them. "It is time for God," he replied.

"Yes," I said, "but what time is it on the clock?"

He had no watch, so he lifted my wrist and stared at my watch in the darkness. I was aware that others were nearby, listening. "It is almost midnight," Father Kantak said. "You had some water and some broth when they brought you back. You have slept since then."

Even before he finished talking, I was falling asleep again.

Although I was not the first from Barracks 17 to undergo extended interrogation, I was the first to experience the NKVD's new wrath. Apparently someone had become impatient with the lack of results stemming from "easy treatment" and had decided to take a stronger, more direct approach to the task of conversion.

Interrogations stepped up throughout the camp. On the day I returned, Leo Bednarek was taken to the administration building. I was just beginning to feel like a human being again when Leo returned—almost seventy hours later. His eyes were swollen shut; his face, purple. Worst of all, for Leo, a front tooth was missing. As a dentist, he felt that this was the greatest of all insults to his body.

Antoni got his chance that night. He was taken at nightfall and returned fifty hours later, a severely beaten man. We had taken bets that he would be smiling. He was.

"What did you tell them?" Leo asked.

"I told them," Antoni said through puffy lips, "that Stalin is the product of a Polish prostitute and a Russian idiot, and that he gets what little intelligence he has from the prostitute."

Even little Father Kantak, who came to our barracks to meet all the men interrogated by the NKVD, stopped reciting the rosary to laugh at Antoni.

We made jokes, at times, about the increase in interrogations, but the new phase of mind-scrubbing was deeply disturbing. Men went to bed with the full expectation of being awakened in the middle of the night and taken to the administration building. Even worse, we realized that we would be beaten no matter what we said to the Russians. Men remained silent—and were beaten. Other men told everything they knew—and were beaten. The NKVD demanded our cooperation and our confessions and beat us whether we complied or resisted. We simply didn't know what they wanted us to say or do.

In our favor, of course, was the large number of prisoners —there were too few interrogators to keep each of us in a state of punishment. Realizing this, the men who had already been extensively interrogated began to feel less uneasy, though the fear never left us completely.

One cold night—Monday, November 13—Sergeant Kalanin came to Barracks 17, burst open the door, and bellowed my name. It was almost midnight; the entire barracks was awakened.

"Komorowski!" he shouted. "Get your ass out here, Komorowski! Hurry up about it. Bring your belongings with you. Bring your mattress unless you want to sleep on wires."

My first thought was that I was going to be interrogated again, with all that that involved. My mind was numb as I thought of a future composed of questioning and beating.

Antoni sat up on his cot beside mine. "I think he's alone," he whispered. "We could kill him and bury him under the barracks. All right?"

"No. They only want to question me. I can take it."

"You don't believe that," Antoni chided. He was so rarely serious that I felt he might know something I didn't. "If you leave with that madman, we'll never see you again."

"Perhaps," I said. "But if we kill him, they might execute everyone in the barracks. I'll go with him." I could hardly believe that I was going so calmly about the business of gathering up my belongings.

"Komorowski!" Kalanin shouted again. "I'm waiting for you!"

I rolled my belongings into the lice-ridden mattress, shook hands with Antoni, and walked to the door, convinced that Antoni was right. Sergeant Kalanin shone the strong beam in my face, then lowered it as I walked past him. At least, to my surprise, Kalanin was alone.

"Where are you taking me?" I asked. My body tensed as I waited for him to make his move. He held his machine gun at the ready and pocketed the flashlight. We stood for a long moment in the dark roadway, and I could hear his raspy breathing.

He didn't answer. Instead, he prodded me with the muzzle of the gun. I walked off down the dark road, carrying my possessions like a fleeing peasant. Would he shoot me there or steer me to some remote place first?

In front of Barracks 22, Colonel Dzierzynski's barracks, Kalanin ordered me to stop. He pushed open the door and brought out his flashlight. As he flicked the beam around the dark room, several men raised themselves up and peered at the light. Finally, Kalanin's beam picked out an empty cot, and he prodded me toward it.

"You will stay here," he said with a kind of unhappy growl, as though he was disappointed that he had not fixed me for good. Then he turned away with his flashlight, leaving me in total darkness. I dropped my rolled mattress onto the cot and fumbled to put my things in order. My nerves were on edge, and I jumped violently when I felt a hand on my shoulder. I turned, ready to fight, afraid for a moment that Kalanin had returned without his flashlight.

"Good to have you here, Eugenjusz."

Colonel Dzierzynski. My fears collapsed like a pricked balloon. As we shook hands, I sensed others around us, and I dimly made out Hugo Mijakowski and Major Konopka, who greeted me in whispers. Colonel Dzierzynski had arranged matters so that there had been an empty cot between his and Mijakowski's.

"Your promotion was approved by the commissar," the colonel whispered. "You are now officially a major."

"When Kalanin came for me," I said, "I thought I was officially a dead man."

"Put him out of your mind, Eugenjusz," the Major said. "We have more important matters to consider."

"I know. Survival."

"And escape," Colonel Dzierzynski said. "That's one of the reasons I pressed for your promotion and got you moved in here. I want you in on the escape we're planning."

"What can I do?"

"For one thing you can speak Russian better than any man I know, except for the Russians. We have men who can speak Russian, but they sound just like Poles.

"Also, you really *want* to escape. I know how you feel about your wife. You're dying to see her again, right?"

"Of course. But lots of men here want to see their wives and their families again."

"Not like you," Colonel Dzierzynski replied. "Look around you, Eugenjusz. Hundreds of men are withdrawing into shells. They've lost their desire to do anything. We can't trust them. Even if we could help everyone escape, we wouldn't want those men along. They'd lie down as soon as they got tired. We need men who have a burning desire to get away, to go back home or to Rumania."

"I certainly want to get out of here," I whispered.

"And I have other reasons," Colonel Dzierzynski added. "As General Wilczynski said, you have enterprise. You call it luck. We need both. I admire the way you held up after the general's murder. I nearly cracked. If I hadn't been knocked unconscious, I would have got myself killed. You were calm, cool, Eugenjusz. We need that. Besides, I've grown to like you."

I was silent. I had nothing to say. I couldn't tell Colonel Dzierzynski that I also had nearly cracked after the general's murder or that I admired him for the way he had stood up to the Russian general. And I couldn't tell him how I had wanted to take Suzan and make a run for the Rumanian border. Touched by his interest and trust in me, I simply felt unworthy.

Although the *polit-rooks* often frequented the Club, they were not there every night. Indeed, once the routine was established, often only two or three turned up, and it became possible for men to discuss almost anything freely, even for priests to hear confessions. The fears we had experienced on the first day gradually dissipated.

Thus on the evening following my move to Barracks 22, I finished my dinner quickly and rushed to the Club to help Major Konopka reserve some tables. With Colonel Dzierzynski's permission I had asked Antoni Urban, Leo Bednarek, Henryk

Jagiello, and Rudolf Kochloffel to come to the unofficial meeting of the escape committee.

We had decided not to include Vincenty Jankowski. We all liked him, of course, but Vincenty was showing strong symptoms of withdrawal. He kept to his bed much of the time, leaving the barracks only at mealtime. Even then, he had to be prodded. And Vincenty had begun to talk strangely, without apparent provocation. As a potential escapee he was a liability. Besides, if he knew of the escape plan and was called for interrogation, he might reveal everything.

Shortly after Major Konopka and I had set up three tables and gathered a dozen chairs, Colonel Dzierzynski, Colonel Mijakowski, and four men from the escape committee entered the Club. Leo, Henryk, Antoni, and Rudolf arrived right behind them. As we huddled around the tables, partially hidden by two large pillars, Colonel Dzierzynski set forth the highlights of the plan.

On the night of November 17, a Friday, a hand-picked group of seventy-two men would leave the camp by climbing over the wall at the northeast corner near the entrance to the *skit*. Guards on the nearest stork had already been bribed and would be looking the other way between midnight and 1:00 A.M.

The destination of the seventy-two men would be the tiny airport we had all spotted a short distance from the monastery. It was estimated to be four kilometers from the camp. The main problem was that a large, open area lay between the woods around the camp and the woods near the airport. We would have to move across this open space—a distance of more than a kilometer—totally exposed.

To avoid premature disclosure of any escape attempt, there would be no attempt to take weapons or to harm guards. Success of the plan hinged on reaching the airport without being detected. Spotters, who had watched the airport for several days, had counted twenty-four small aircraft, including two twin-engine planes. Each of the small aircraft would hold from two to four men; the twin-engine craft would probably hold six each. Since the escape committee could not be assured of the exact number of passengers the planes would hold, the total number had been arbitrarily set at seventy-two, to allow twelve groups of six to go over the wall.

Our major problem was that the committee had not yet found twenty-four pilots to fly the variety of planes that had been seen. Most of our pilots were qualified, but many could not be trusted, either because they were in various stages of withdrawal, or because they simply didn't consider escape possible, or because they still clung to the Russian promise of freedom.

"We'll get the other pilots we need," Colonel Dzierzynski said confidently. "Does anyone have any questions? More specifically, does anyone have suggestions to improve the plan?"

"I have a question," I said. "Is there an alternate plan in case something goes wrong?"

"No alternate plan," Hugo Mijakowski interjected. "We've talked with some groups who are planning to go over the wall and head west on foot. We think they'll be caught the first day out."

"Probably," I agreed. "But as I see it, if even one man is caught going over the wall, our plan goes up in smoke. There's a telephone in the administration building, and there must be one at the airport. If they see us heading toward the airport, a warning will be sent out, the planes will be guarded, and they will round us up in minutes."

"There's risk in any plan," Major Konopka said. "If you have an alternate plan, we're more than willing to listen to it."

"I have no plan, but I think we should discuss it. I think the committee should consider what to do in case things go wrong."

"We have," Colonel Dzierzynski said. "We surrender and hope that the goddamn Russkies don't shoot all of us."

It didn't sound like much of a plan. But I didn't have any alternative to offer, so I shut up.

"Did you say two guards have been bribed?" Henryk Jagiello asked.

"Yes."

"Suppose one of them gets sick and isn't on duty when we start over the wall?"

"We just have to hope that nobody gets sick," the colonel responded.

"What about the guards outside—the ones who patrol with dogs?" Leo Bednarek asked.

"Good question," Colonel Dzierzynski replied. "We chose that particular spot for crossing the wall because guards don't patrol near that tower. The guards from the *skit* approach to within a hundred meters on the north, and those from the main camp stop about fifty meters on the south. It takes a guard about an hour to make a complete circuit. We start over the wall just as both guards begin to turn away from the stork. We'll have a full hour to get over before they return."

For the next hour we discussed the fine points of the escape plan. There was considerable risk. A farmer could spot us going across the open area. The bribed guards could betray us. Another guard, from inside or outside, could see us and sound the alarm. There could be a heavy guard contingent at the airport, although we doubted it. A member of the escape group could accidentally tip off the Russians or have the information forced out of him during interrogation.

Everything had to go precisely right for the plan to work. There *had* to be extra gas available at the airport or we would be forced to land the planes far short of the Rumanian border. And I worried particularly that there was no alternate plan. Once we committed ourselves, we had to follow the plan exactly.

Still, in spite of the risks and the worries, each of us sitting around the tables in the Club felt a sense of excitement, of purpose. We yearned for freedom, and there was only one way to get it. If the Russians would not free us—and there was little sign of that eventuality occurring—we had to make it on our own.

The conversation stopped abruptly when Aleksi Alexandrovich joined our tables.

"Ah, Citizens," he bubbled, "you have no cards." His mouth puckered in a mock pout. "You are reduced to mere conversation."

"Yes," Antoni said with a wicked twinkle in his eyes, "but you should hear what we're talking about."

Aleksi leaned forward, smiling brightly, and put his well-manicured hands on the rough table. "Discussing the days of glory?"

Antoni looked around at the rest of us. "Shall we tell him the truth?" he asked.

For a moment my heart fluttered. Then I remembered it was Antoni—who launched into his favorite topic: women.

"Ah," the *polit-rook* gushed. "Women! A worthy and honorable subject. If we had vodka, we could drink a toast to women."

"But, alas, we have no vodka," Antoni said. "Pity."

"A great pity," Aleksi agreed.

On the evening of Thursday, November 16, there was an electric excitement in the camp. The seventy-two prisoners committed to the escape were the most excited, but others who had heard of the plan shared in that experience. I feared for the security risk, especially when we assembled at the Club and several officers came along to wish us luck and to express regret that they weren't going too. But it was too late to do anything about security problems. We were going.

Several priests moved through the crowded Club, chatting in whispers. When the *polit-rooks* weren't watching, the priests blessed us and made the forbidden sign of the cross.

The weather had been clear all week; we felt that nothing could stop us. Everything was with us: luck, planning, spirit, willingness. Most of the escapees even fooled themselves into thinking that the risks were insignificant.

The intoxication of our emotional drunkenness became a crushing hangover at dawn Friday. I awoke as the first light streaked through the dirty barracks windows. For a moment I lay on the lumpy mattress and thought of Suzan; then the realization of our escape plan came to me and I leaped up.

Colonel Dzierzynski and several others were at the windows, their heads bowed, their shoulders slumped.

"What is it?" I asked. "What's wrong?"

Colonel Dzierzynski turned; his face sagged in defeat. He nodded toward the window, which was frosted with ice. Hugo Mijakowski turned from the window and sat heavily on his bunk, his hands over his face. Major Konopka peered through the glass, his long arms hanging limply at his sides.

I knew without looking what was wrong. The light coming into the barracks had a strange quality to it; it was not the usual gray of dawn. I went to the window, though, and looked out. The ground was piled with snow.

During the night a quiet, thick snow—the first of the season—had fallen over the entire area. Eight inches had fallen. The temperature was twenty degrees Fahrenheit, so there was no chance of its melting.

"We can't go tonight," Colonel Dzierzynski moaned. "We'll be lucky if we can go at all."

9: The Gentleman General

The mood of our group and of the camp as a whole was at its lowest point since our arrival in late October. Virtually everyone except the Russians and the men in the *skit* knew of our aborted escape plan. Condolences were offered to the officers who were to have escaped, but the faces of those trying to give encouragement indicated that they needed condolences themselves.

The snow seemed a bad omen, and it put an end to the escape plans made by other groups. Even on the darkest of nights, the NKVD would have no trouble tracking escapees.

On Friday evening, in the Club, the same priests who had given us their blessings the night before now stopped by to tell us to keep faith. The *polit-rooks* who had observed our high spirits on Thursday night were puzzled anew by our sullen quietness.

A few men played cards and chess with a fury; others slammed homemade darts into the dart boards, as if to exorcise their frustrations. At our tables behind the wooden pillars, the silence and gloom were thick with self-pity.

There was much to make us despondent. Not only had the
escape plan been aborted, but also the bribed guards might turn
us in. A search would turn up the few precious ladders secreted
around the camp. Then there was the possibility of
punishment—not that there was much, in our present frame of
mind, that they could do to make us feel worse than we already
did. Some almost would have welcomed punishment to keep
their minds off the fact that freedom, which had been so near,
had been arbitrarily yanked out of their grasp.

On Saturday morning, November 18, excitement of a different sort ran through the camp. Someone had seen two black staff
cars coming down the hill from the village and had spread the
word while we were doing calisthenics in the snow. By the time
the cars arrived at the camp gates, a great throng of Polish
officers had gathered in the courtyard.

With chains on their rear wheels and shades drawn in the rear,
the limousines rumbled through the gates. The camp commandant, Commissar Koraliev, and a large contingent of NKVD
officers were lined up in front of the administration building to
greet the visitors. Guards formed a cordon to keep us at a
distance.

From the first car emerged a handsome man with the insignia
of a Soviet general. He also wore the NKVD emblem. A general
in the NKVD was virtually equal to a field marshal in the army.
An NKVD colonel got out behind the general. From the second
car three more NKVD colonels emerged. All five officers gazed
at the crowd of Polish prisoners, then turned to Commissar
Koraliev and his staff. The commissar saluted snappily.

"Welcome to our vacation resort, *Kombrig* Zarubin," we heard
the camp commandant gush. "Everything has been made ready
for you."

Kombrig is an abbreviation for *kommandir brigady*, a brigade
commander. *Kombrig* Zarubin was indeed a high-ranking
officer. Why had he come to this relatively insignificant camp?
Or were we really so insignificant? A man of such importance

could receive orders only from Moscow. Perhaps from Stalin himself. But why?

And how had we missed the preparations for this Soviet general and for his four staff colonels? There were no quarters suitable for a man of such rank, so there must have been extensive remodeling. Yet our grapevine communications had brought no news of remodeling or of the coming of this general. In the past we had heard about most developments before we had officially been told of them, but this time the Russians' security system had worked. Why had such care been taken?

The general walked smartly to the porch of the administration building. The colonels and camp officials followed. On the small stoop the *kombrig* turned and looked out over the sea of Polish faces. He raised a hand in greeting, and a fleeting smile crossed his lips. Then he disappeared into the administration building.

His gesture on the porch somehow struck a responsive chord among us. The mocking that had begun when the general had saluted ceased immediately. Everyone stared at the handsome general with the fur cap and long fur coat. His face was round, his cheeks pink from the cold. His large eyes seemed to contain more warmth than we were accustomed to seeing in Russians.

Within the hour the camp grapevine, as though to make up for its glaring failure, passed the word that the new colonels had been trained in a new technique: psychological warfare.

"Psychological warfare?" Leo Bednarek asked.

"It means they won't knock your teeth out while they're rinsing your mind," Rudolf explained, with his customary giggle. "They hit you with a white glove, and you can challenge them to a duel."

"With what weapons?" Leo asked, spreading his big, empty hands.

"Snowballs. What else?" Rudolf retorted.

Through the grapevine we knew of every move that *Kombrig* Zarubin made on his first day in the camp. Immediately after he inspected his quarters in the administration building, he visited our leaders to ask their opinion of our treatment. Needless to say, the Polish generals weren't shy in reporting what they thought and knew, and the *kombrig* promised that favorable changes would be made.

Many cheered the new developments; others maintained a wait-and-see attitude. I myself was convinced that changes would be made. Otherwise, the Soviet general would not have come. Certainly he would not have made the promise if something was not going to change. But what?

In the afternoon the *kombrig* and his four NKVD colonels inspected the camp.

At the bathhouse, *Kombrig* Zarubin reportedly exploded when he saw the scum and filth on the floor, the cracks in the walls, and the vermin skittering about on the wet floors.

"How often do the Poles take showers in this pest hole?" he was reported to have asked Commissar Koraliev.

"They have had one shower so far," the commissar replied. "We have had problems with the boiler and . . . "

"I want no more problems," the *kombrig* stated flatly. "The men must have at least one bath a week. See that they do."

At the camp jailhouse, according to another report, the *kombrig* was appalled when he found four priests, two ministers, and a rabbi sitting in their underwear in cold, empty rooms. The religious men, prisoners for more than a week, had no bedding, and each had to use a corner of his room as a toilet. The odor in the building was stupefying.

"Who are these men and why are they here?" the *kombrig* reportedly demanded.

"They are religious men," the commissar answered. "They're in jail for holding religious services against camp rules."

"Give them their clothes and take them to their quarters," *Kombrig* Zarubin ordered. "We will discuss the matter of religious services at another time."

The priests, ministers, and rabbi were returned to their barracks. In the jail they had received less than half the normal ration of food; they were immediately fed a wholesome meal, including meat—at least we heard that that was what happened, but this last we found difficult to believe.

When our own mealtime came, we became believers. There was a delicious dinner of potatoes, vegetables, and *real beef*! It was our first meat since the fish we had been given on the first day in camp.

Kombrig Zarubin became a hero of the highest order. His changes, though not dramatic or sweeping, raised spirits throughout the camp, and the grapevine fairly crackled with news bulletins. Although we thought many of the rumored changes probably were exaggerations, each came true. For example, while we were eating our fine meal, we heard that we would be allowed to receive news from the outside world.

"I'll believe that when it happens," Colonel Dzierzynski snorted. "How are we supposed to receive this news, by holding our ear to the sky?"

"There is a radio in the commissar's office," Major Konopka said. "The NKVD people listen to all the broadcasts from Moscow. Perhaps they'll link up the radio with the loudspeakers."

"Then we'll have to wait a while longer," the colonel said. "It will take the Russians *months* to link up the radio to loudspeakers—if they can do it at all."

Major Konopka nodded. "You have a point. I just hope they know more about radio than they do about railroads."

Even as we talked—and doubted—the music, which played almost constantly, stopped. At first we paid little attention, expecting the usual propaganda message; but as the delay lengthened, we began to wonder what was up.

Colonel Dzierzynski looked at his wristwatch. "My God, it's six o'clock," he said. "Maybe they really are going to . . . "

A booming voice burst from the loudspeaker, interrupting the colonel: "This is Moscow speaking. It is time for the news."

Cheers went up all around the camp, but the cheers were brief. We didn't want to miss a word of the news. The announcer told of continuing negotiations between Germany and Russia regarding their nonaggression pact, of minor incidents on the high seas between the Germans and the British, and of accomplishments within the Soviet Union.

The news was primarily mundane, but it reestablished a vital link with the outside world. We felt a part of life again. Just hearing the familiar voice that we had heard at Tarnopol eased the ache we all felt at being cut off from the world. We had felt alone and deserted in the remote camp; hearing the voice of Moscow took away some of that sense of separateness.

Even more, the broadcast helped to cement our faith in *Kombrig* Zarubin and gave us reason to believe that he would live up to all his promises. Food *would* be improved and provided in greater quantity; a traveling camp store *would* visit regularly; real efforts *would* be made to eliminate vermin; a more lenient attitude *would* be taken toward religious services; we *would* receive a continual flow of news from the outside; interrogations *would* be shortened; harassment *would* cease; and visits between barracks *would* be permitted.

After hearing the news, in fact, we found it impossible to believe only one rumor: that we would be able to write letters home and to receive mail from our families. This was just too good to be true. If, as we suspected, the NKVD had placed us in this remote camp and had kept us incommunicado so that if they failed to convert us to communism, they would be able to dispose of us without anyone's knowing, they would have to abandon this plan if people knew where we were. The NKVD would not dare destroy us if our condition were widely broadcast. We thus had little expectation that we would be allowed to communicate with our families and friends.

Still we *hoped* the rumor would turn out to be true. It would be marvelous to write to Suzan and to receive a letter from her; but remembering my bitter disappointment over our aborted escape plan, I wouldn't let my hopes be unduly raised by a mere rumor.

However, all other signs looked favorable. Even before our grand dinner, peasants had gone into the bathhouse to clean it up and to fix broken pipes. We had heard the evening broadcast from Moscow. Previously sullen NKVD guards now were smiling at us. The dogs were put into their kennels, and guards stopped patrolling the wall inside the camp.

A sense of freedom and cheerfulness swept through the camp. For the first time in weeks we could hope that, even if we did not attain freedom, at least our imprisonment would be less unacceptable.

After dinner the Club was jammed. Antoni and Stanislaw managed to get to one small table, and our group crowded around it. We talked only of the *kombrig* and the changes that had come—and those that we hoped would come. Nobody talked about the rumor concerning mail, but everyone must have thought about it at some time during the evening—at least *I* did.

Early Monday morning a swarm of villagers swept into the camp to clean up. Extermination chemicals, which camp officials previously had said were unobtainable, suddenly appeared. A steady line of men went through the bathhouse for a hot shower and a dousing of a lice-killing chemical.

Each barracks was thoroughly cleaned and fumigated. Mattresses were taken outside and almost soaked in bug killer. Firewood was cut and stacked near stoves, where hot fires blazed and warmed the normally chilly barracks. And while we bathed, villagers from Kozelsk washed, dried, and pressed our uniforms.

Monday's meal was a rich stew made from the beef, vegetables, and potatoes left over from the two previous meals. We heard news broadcasts five times a day, though we learned nothing earth-shattering. *Govorit Moskva* had little to say about the war but much to say about the growing economic and military might of the Soviet Union.

Thus we were feeling good but uninspired when the best news of all came, late Tuesday at bedtime. Two guards came to Barracks 22 and politely asked for Major Eugenjusz Komorowski. I felt a quick pang of fear, but the guards' smiles eased my fears. I walked slowly forward, and the guards bowed. Someone behind me giggled.

"Major Komorowski?" one guard asked politely.

I nodded.

"Please come with us, sir," the guard said. "Colonel Miranov, aide to *Kombrig* Zarubin, wishes the pleasure of your company."

My heart sank. In spite of their smiles and politeness, I didn't trust the guards. Perhaps Kalanin had sent them, or perhaps their politeness hid the fact that I was to be subjected to another marathon interrogation laced with blows.

I put on my greatcoat and went out into the icy night. The guards led me to the administration building, where perhaps fifty other Polish officers—some of whom I recognized as men who could speak Russian—stood in the corridor of the north wing. We stood in the warm corridor for only a few minutes, and then four of us were taken into separate offices.

I went into the office in which Lieutenant Borisovets had interrogated me, but where the lieutenant had sat an NKVD colonel now stood deferentially. I looked around for Kalanin, but the colonel was alone. In a soft, pleasant voice, he said: "Please be seated, Major Komorowski. This will take only a very few moments of your time." His Russian was pure Muscovite, faultless.

Still suspicious and fearful, I watched the colonel closely but could detect no hostility. He was not handsome, but he exuded good will and friendship.

"My name is Colonel Miranov, Major Komorowski, and I have good news."

"I could use some good news," I replied.

"First, let me put your mind at ease. As *Kombrig* Zarubin has promised, harassment is at an end. Second, we have called you and some of your comrades here for a very special purpose." The colonel sat down and lit a cigarette. I stared at the cigarette, and the colonel hastily extended his package. I took a cigarette—he lit it—and as I drew the smoke into my lungs, I felt a glow of satisfaction. It was my first cigarette in two months.

"Each of you called here tonight." Colonel Miranov said, "can speak Russian fluently. Your Russian certainly is excellent. Where did you learn it?"

"Most of it in school," I said. "My wife is part Russian, and she helped me to improve it."

"Yes, we know of your wife." He took a deep draw on his cigarette and went on. "We have chosen men from each of the barracks in camp because we want you to become emissaries for us."

"Oh?"

"Yes, Major Komorowski. We have momentous news, and we would like you and your fellow officers to announce it to the others."

"Announce what?"

Colonel Miranov opened my brown file and studied it through his bifocals. He smiled again and looked up at me over the rims of his glasses.

"You have a lovely wife. Her name is Suzan. Right?"

"Yes." Then, as a conditioned reflex, I added, "Yes, sir."

"I'm happy to report that Suzan is doing quite well in Grodno. She misses you, of course, and worries about your health and safety. You are fortunate to have such a young, beautiful, and devoted wife."

"How do you know so much about Suzan?" I asked. I didn't like the tack.

"We know everything about her."

"How?"

He took off his glasses. "Some of our people have talked to her in Grodno. In fact, our people have talked with the families of most of the men in this camp. However, none of this is very important. What is, is this, Major Komorowski: would you like to correspond with your wife?"

So it was true! The rumor was *true*! "Colonel Miranov," I said, hiding my excitement, "I don't like bad jokes. I would rather be interrogated and beaten than be toyed with in such a manner. Don't fool with me."

He laughed. It was genuine laughter, without derision or disdain. Then he sighed and twirled his glasses.

"It is very unfortunate that our predecessors created such a bad impression of things Russian. But we are going to show you the true spirit of Soviet brotherhood. I assure you, Major Komorowski, this is not a game. *All* the men in the camp may write to their families. You may write to Suzan if you like."

"Of course I want to!" I said explosively. "But no games!"

"No games," he replied softly.

"Will she be able to write to me in return? Will the other prisoners here be able to receive mail from home?"

"Of course," he said. "Why would one write a letter unless one expected to receive a reply?"

"And you're serious about this? This is what *Kombrig* Zarubin has ordered?"

He nodded. "We are quite serious about this."

"What are the conditions?" There had to be conditions; it was the Russian way. We would not, of course, be able to describe the treatment we were receiving, but perhaps we would have to sign phony confessions. Perhaps I would have to admit that my summers of study in London and Brussels had been spying missions. My suspicious mind convinced me that we would pay a price for the privilege of writing home.

"The men must make no mention of being prisoners," Colonel Miranov said. "They must say that they are receiving good care as guests in a fine Soviet resort. There can be no anti-Communist or anti-Russian statements. And of course we must read all letters before they are sent. I believe that is fair."

"Yes, sir. It is fair. When can we write?"

He took a box of paper and envelopes from a carton beside him and shoved them across to me.

"It might be best to wait until morning, when there is light," he said, smiling broadly. "Please give paper and envelopes to your comrades."

I felt like a child receiving candy from a benevolent doctor. I could hardly wait to get back to the barracks to tell the others.

The two guards escorted me down the corridor, where other barracks representatives were waiting to be told the news. Numb with disbelief, I walked like an automaton to the barracks. The guards said a pleasant good night and disappeared into the twilight.

After I had told the others and had distributed the paper and envelopes, I still felt that it was all a dream. Everyone was stunned. Yet try as we might, we could not find an ulterior motive on the part of the NKVD—unless it was to spread the lie that we were in a vacation resort. But that was a weak reason, and our families had already been exposed to the Russian temperament. They would not believe the lie.

If the decision to let us write home was merely another phase of the overall program to convert us, we didn't see how it could work. It would bring us closer to our families, closer to the life we had known. How could it possibly aid the NKVD in their conversion program?

In any case, we concluded, nothing mattered except the fact that we would be able to let our families know that we were alive. Suzan would be ecstatic. And she would write back to me. The anticipation of receiving a letter from her was so great that ultimately I didn't give a damn about the NKVD's motives.

When we were finally silent and I lay back on my chemical-soaked mattress to sleep, the emotion of the past few days touched something in me. Warm tears ran down my face and onto the rough fabric of my pillow.

At dawn men sat huddled on their beds, their blankets across their shoulders, their heads bent to paper. I don't remember what I said in my letter, though of course I followed Colonel Miranov's instructions. I wasn't going to jeopardize this opportunity. We were allowed only one sheet of paper, so we wrote small and crammed in as much as possible.

After roll call a guard we called "The Kicker"—because he had been fond of kicking officers during interrogations—came into the barracks. "Good morning, Citizens," he said cheerfully. We had never before seen him smile. " If you have your letters written, I will mail them for you."

We were afraid to trust our precious letters to this man, but he had been sent to pick them up. And at least he informed us of our correct address: Maxim Gorki's Winter Resort, Province of Smolensk.

This information provided more than a return address. We knew that we must be fairly close to the city of Smolensk, and it was reassuring to know where we were.

It was excellent therapy just being able to write home. It was a better form of catharsis than confession to a priest or smashing homemade darts into a dartboard. I felt as though I had spent the morning talking to Suzan. For the first time in many weeks, I began to feel as though I really was a human being, an individual, a real person. Writing the letter to Suzan tempered many of the shocks and abuses that had been heaped upon my body and spirit since that day in September when the Russians had arrived.

In a short time, we began to *feel* like guests. The changes were so radical that we began to feel almost complacent—so much so, in fact, that at the end of the first week we received word that General Minkiewicz was having second thoughts about *Kombrig* Zarubin and his great changes. Apparently, our senior commander had compared the situation with previous events and had concluded that this was simply another phase in the plan to convert us.

The order from the general was simple: be on guard. We were not to accept communism; nor were we to pretend to accept communism to obtain better treatment. We were still prisoners in an undeclared war, and we must continue to insist on freedom and to make every effort to escape.

The warning was especially necessary since it was becoming increasingly difficult to consider escape with snow all around us, with the bettering of camp conditions, and with the prospect of receiving replies to our letters. Then conditions improved further.

Early in the second week, the operation of the field kitchen was turned over to a special committee of Polish officers. Several of the cadets among our ranks were given the task of preparing our food, which improved in quality and quantity.

Interrogations continued, but they were mild compared to

those we endured before *Kombrig* Zarubin's arrival. There was no harassment or beatings. True, the four colonels on the *kombrig*'s staff still conducted the interrogations at night, but there were no NKVD sergeants on hand to intimidate us. We were not accused of crimes against the people or of having spied for the Polish government. On the two occasions I was taken to see Colonel Miranov, we merely discussed my life in Poland from the time I was born until the time I was taken captive by the Russians. The colonel had an insatiable desire for detail, so I talked at length. The longest interrogation, however, was six hours, and I was given water when I asked for it.

Shortly after the field kitchen was turned over to the Polish committee, we learned that a traveling camp store, located on the rear of a huge closed truck, was soon to visit the camp. The truck, according to rumor, was loaded with candy, gloves, scarves, pastries, canned meats, and other necessities as well as luxury items. Before the store arrived, a group of civilians from the Soviet Jewelry Exchange appeared, set up a table in the Club, and announced that they would buy valuables such as rings, watches, gold trinkets, and medals. They were especially interested in fountain pens, which were scarce in Russia.

The men from the Jewelry Exchange enjoyed a field day. Some men sold everything they had of value, including military insignia. I sold a gold cigarette case Suzan had given me; despite the sentimental value, cigarettes were nonexistent—and I did receive twelve rubles for the case. I thought of selling my watch, but I used it constantly.

The Jewelry Exchange people had hardly left when the camp store truck chugged and clattered up the hill. It barely made it through the narrow gates. The driver parked on the square and opened the sides to reveal his merchandise.

A throng of officers clustered about the store from the time of its arrival until curfew. I bought six cream-filled pastries, which I promptly consumed. Within a half hour, I was so sick that I lost my half-ruble's worth of treats.

Finally, the truck left with the promise that it would return the following week. If business was good, the driver said, he might make the trip up the hill twice a week. It all depended on us. I knew that the store would come twice a week—business was excellent.

Even with all the changes wrought by *Kombrig* Zarubin, there was still the boredom of having nothing to do. Thus during the long afternoons, I began to spend more time with Pavel Borodynsky, the *korpoosnoy* for Barracks 17. Our friendship had begun on the night he had warned me about Sergeant Kalanin, and we had chatted on a few occasions while I was still in Barracks 17. After I moved to Barracks 22, I rarely saw him. However, when the guards were ordered to be more friendly to us—we presumed that they were merely acting under orders —Pavel began showing up at my barracks.

Pavel was a lonely man who appeared to detest his assignment at Kozelsk, and I welcomed his attention for a variety of reasons. First, he helped me pass time. Second, he was a guard, and if I needed a special favor at some future time, I might be able to call on Pavel. Finally, I learned a lot about many other aspects of camp life from Pavel. Many guards, he told me, thought that *Kombrig* Zarubin was being too soft on us and longed for the old way of doing things. I repeated this information to Colonel Dzierzynski, and it eventually made its way to General Minkiewicz. Clearly, if *Kombrig* Zarubin did not have the full support of his men, we would have to continue to be wary.

Pavel also told me that the men in the *skit* were undergoing severe indoctrination and training in communism, and that several men already had cracked. These men, he said, had accepted communism and might someday be sent to Moscow for additional training. Sergeant Borodynsky did not know what eventual use would be made of these converts, but he suspected that they would be sent to eastern Poland to help operate a communist government. It made sense, so I passed along this information, too, through Colonel Dzierzynski.

There were no strings attached to my friendship with Pavel

Borodynsky, and if he had been assigned to gain my confidence, he failed. I never trusted any Russian, and while I was free with my criticisms of the camp and communism, I said nothing about escape or other officers.

Our friendship deepened one evening. After chatting for a few moments, he got up. He stood with his cap in his hands, shifting from one foot to the other.

"Something on your mind, Pavel?" I asked.

"Yes," he said shyly. "I was wondering if perhaps you might like to spend the next four hours with me."

"What's happening in the next four hours?"

"I have guard duty on the northwest tower," he said. "Since *Kombrig* Zarubin came, we have only one man in each tower. It gets lonely standing duty from eight o'clock until midnight."

"But I would be out after curfew," I said.

"I'll escort you back here. There will be no problem."

I smiled and put my hand on his shoulder. "I would consider it a privilege to spend your guard duty with you."

I waited for his ulterior motive to emerge, but he apparently had none. We talked of everything in the long twilight. Cold wind whistled through the tower, but I didn't mind it. I learned that Pavel had an excellent sense of humor, that he hated Kozelsk, and that he wished only to be home in Kiev.

"Why don't you ask the commissar for a transfer?" I asked.

"Do you want me shot?"

"They can shoot you for merely asking for a transfer?"

"To refuse duty is to reveal a lack of love for your Motherland," he said. "Asking for a transfer is the same as refusing duty."

"That's ridiculous. In Poland we can get a transfer any time we wish. Sometimes we don't even need a good reason."

Pavel smiled and leaned forward. "Tell you what. I'll change my name to Molotov and ask for a transfer. When you hear the news tomorrow, you will learn that Molotov has been shot."

Terror returned the following night. I was on my way to the barracks shortly after eight o'clock.

As I passed the old church, a shadow moved. I was wearing wooden clogs to protect my boots, and the only sounds were those of the clogs and of the howling winter wind. The shadow moved into the roadway. Kalanin! He was pointing his machine gun at me and holding his dog on a short leash.

"Well, Citizen," he snarled, "it seems that you are too important to obey the rules."

"I know it's past curfew," I said, watching the gun, his face, and the dog, "but . . ."

Kalanin prodded my chest with the gun, pushed me into shadows between the church and a barracks, and pressed close. I caught the odor of his breath and turned away.

"I'd like to kill you," he said, "but the ground is frozen, and I couldn't bury your miserable corpse. Besides, we have plans for you filthy Poles."

I saw the gun go up and heard the dog growl. I waited for death. The barrel of the gun thudded against my head, and my breath was expelled in a frosty mist. The church spun crazily, and I sank into unconsciousness in the snow.

I awoke two hours later. My arms and legs could hardly move in the bitter cold, and my face, feet, and hands burned. My God, I thought, I'm freezing to death!

I crawled to my feet and stumbled into the barracks. Once inside I fell on my cot, and in the darkness I lay rubbing my hands and feet to restore the circulation to them. I prayed that nothing had frozen.

The darknesss of the barracks was welcome. I didn't want the others to see me because I didn't want to have to tell them about the incident with Kalanin. To tell someone was to involve him, and I had no wish to involve anyone else in my troubles with the crazy sergeant—not even Colonel Dzierzynski.

Even with my greatcoat and tattered blanket over me, I was still cold. But the coldness was the least of my concerns at that moment. A long time had passed since Kalanin had made his threat on my life, and I had become too much at ease. Perhaps that was what Kalanin had intended: the quarry who feels secure is bound to get careless and become an easier victim.

I *had* been careless, but I would not be careless again. Next time I would be ready; perhaps I would strike first. But how could I strike Kalanin to forestall his threat? I could not kill him. Even if I were not caught, the NKVD would extract its pound of flesh for his death—probably by executing another man, or several men, for the crime.

Could I discredit him in some way? There was no simple way. My one chance was Pavel Borodynsky. But even if I were to plant a lie with Pavel Borodynsky, I had no assurance that Pavel would not take that lie to Kalanin himself. And what lie could I concoct?

What about truth? Suppose I were to tell Pavel about Kalanin's unprovoked attack—what would he do? Indeed, what *could* he do? Kalanin might be reprimanded, in keeping with the *kombrig*'s order against corporal punishment, but that would only make him more vicious, more vengeful.

The problem was too big for my troubled mind to handle that night. I felt sleep coming. The shivering had stopped, and I lay still in the darkness and listened to the snoring of the men around me. There was no one to help. I would have to work it out by myself. The ground would not remain frozen forever.

Friday, November 30, was the most eventful day of the month. We had just finished our morning's calisthenics when the loudspeakers throughout the camp blared into action.

"Your attention, please. Citizens, you are requested to assemble in the courtyard in front of the administration building. Mail from your loved ones at home has arrived. Your attention, please . . . "

The camp erupted into bedlam. The announcement was as shocking and as unexpected as a clap of thunder on a cloudless day. We had written home nine days ago and had not expected replies for at least another week, figuring that if the Russians said that our letters would take five days to reach our homes, they would take seven or eight.

Men ran out into the snow without their greatcoats. Barracks doors slammed all over the camp. All signs of military discipline disappeared, and we became a great, yelping gang of happy, delirious children.

Commissar Koraliev stood on the stoop of the administration building with three canvas sacks of mail beside him. It would take hours to distribute the mail if he simply called out names —there were nearly four thousand men waiting anxiously in the snow.

Inevitably, though, the Russians did it the hard way. Instead of separating the mail and men by barracks, the commissar read out names and NKVD guards scurried back and forth.

It took a full hour before the commissar came to a small, yellow envelope and called out my name. I saw a guard take it and begin to move into the crowd. I yelled and ran toward him.

I took the small envelope and stared at it for a long time, my heart swelling almost to the bursting point. All around me men were ripping open envelopes and reading their mail on the spot, some laughing, some crying. Not me. I clutched the yellow letter in my hand and ran back to the barracks.

Throwing off my coat, I stood staring at the envelope and at Suzan's distinctive handwriting for a long time. Then, slowly, as though I were caressing her face, I opened the letter and read it. I read it over and over until I had memorized it. I shall never forget it:

My Dearest Andrei,
    Your letter frightened me when the mailman brought it. I thought perhaps a cruel trick was being played on me. I've experienced many such tricks, and strange men have come to look and to ask questions. In my mind and heart I knew that you were dead.
    Oh, my precious Andrei, to know that you are alive is to live again myself. I have been dead, but now I come alive when I hear footsteps outside—and die again as they pass by. I miss you so terribly that I could not tell you how much, even if they allowed a thousand pages instead of one.
    You cannot imagine how pleased I was to learn that you are in a fine resort and are receiving excellent care. Are you certain you are not injured? Have you met some beautiful woman and fallen in love

with her? You must love me, Andrei, as I love you. You are my life, my god, my future. Would that I were a poet so that I could say what is in my heart.

Andrei, beg them to let you come to me. Life is not so bad here, but food is scarce. Beg them to let you return. With you I should need no food, no drink. I need only you. Andrei, swallow your pride and fall to your knees in front of the Russians. Beg them, my darling. All that matters is that we be together forever and ever.

I cannot write anymore. There is no room on this paper. There is no more room in my heart for words. My heart is burning for you.

Beg them, Andrei! Come to me. I love you and I need you! Come to me now.

Your Beloved Suzan

Others came into the barracks, laughing and shouting. I turned my face to the wall so that no one would see the tears that fell like raindrops.

10: "MERRY CHRISTMAS, COMRADES"

NEW snow came almost every day. Other groups who had planned to go over the wall and walk to freedom had given up all hope of escape until spring. As for our group, we decided to wait for the first thaw, which we learned normally came in February. In anticipation, we kept the airport under observation.

Despite the boredom, the days were not altogether unpleasant during the first part of December. Everyone in our group had received mail from home, and it was all good news. Colonel Dzierzynski's wife was still in Grodno and, like Suzan, was getting along well. The only one in our group not helped spiritually by the mail was Vincenty Jankowski. He had received a letter from his wife, but he was so far withdrawn that he was unable to read it. Rudolf Kochloffel read it to him, but Vincenty merely stared into space.

I began to spend more time with Pavel Borodynsky. Several of the Polish officers, especially those who could speak Russian, had become friends with guards, and all of us learned that the guards were almost as anxious as we were to leave the camp.

Pavel not only helped to pass away the dragging time, he was almost as pleasant to be with as Antoni, who was spending more time with Janina's crowd, having gained entrée to her circle of fliers through Stanislaw Kaczmarek. Pavel shared Antoni's lecherous feelings toward Janina Lewandowski. Often when I went to visit him on guard duty, we fell into a playful routine. I would go to the base of the stork and call up to him: "Are you there, Pavel?"

"No," he would reply in a deep voice. "This is Comrade Lavrenti Beria." Sometimes, he would be Stalin or Molotov—even Hitler.

"All right, Comrade Beria," I would answer. "May I come up and join you without getting shot in the head?"

"Only if you bring the woman pilot. Comrade Beria has the hots for her. You will be shot unless you bring her up here to me."

We would laugh at our own slim humor, and then I would climb the steep steps. We would talk, often about Janina, sometimes about the war, especially the war with Finland (about which we heard ad nauseam from *Govorit Moskva*), until his duty was over, and he would escort me to my barracks. We became fast friends, though when I asked him when the Russians would let us go home, he would just laugh and avoid giving an answer.

The relatively pleasant days of early December were few. The changes in our routine, and especially the sending and receiving of mail from home, proved to offer only a temporary tonic for lagging spirits. When that feeling expired, a bitter backlash struck the camp. We were like men who had tasted one sip of nectar and now demanded a whole bucket of it.

We were permitted to write home again on December 3, and in my letter to Suzan I used the words "guards" and "high wall" to let her know that we were not guests but prisoners. We were sure that most Poles knew that the soldiers taken to Russia were prisoners, but I wanted to make it even plainer to Suzan

—whatever the risks, to her as well as to me. It was overridingly important that she not misunderstand my reason for not coming to her.

Later, I learned that many men in the camp had tried to figure out ways to let their families know that they were prisoners. There was a general feeling—probably a false hope—that something would be done about our situation if the public in Poland knew what had happened to us. We also were disturbed by Soviet reports that Polish civilians had happily accepted the Russians as liberators. We wanted to let them know that the Russians were liars who would do or say anything to absorb our country.

Then a few days after we had written our letters, several officers were thrown into the camp jail, initially closed by the *kombrig* but now reopened. The men were not charged with anything; they were simply put into the icy building and held for several days. We suspected that the men were imprisoned because of what they had put in their letters. I wondered if perhaps the NKVD might throw me, too, into the jail. But as days passed and nothing happened, I stopped worrying about what I had said in my letter.

I could not, however, help noticing that other unpleasant changes were occurring. At the end of the first week of December, we began to hear of fights among Polish officers. On Saturday, December 9, Major Konopka got into a fierce argument with another officer in Barracks 22. The officer had inadvertently put his boot on the major's cot, and the major blew up. We had to restrain both men from attacking each other, and although the spat lasted only a few minutes, the two glowered at each other for several days. Even close friends had begun to snap at each other; friendships that had existed before the war were shattered in a few seconds of emotional upheaval.

Military discipline also began to break down. Men would turn out for the NKVD roll call but would walk sullenly away when the Polish officers began taking their separate roll. Senior officers were no longer saluted.

Cases of withdrawal became epidemic. Although Vincenty

Jankowski was the only man in our group who had gone into withdrawal, there were hundreds of cases throughout the camp. Some even had to be forced out of the barracks for the daily NKVD roll calls.

On December 11 we learned that the first in a series of films would be shown at the Club four days later. However, the news had no discernible effect on morale. Personally on that same day, December 11, I received two visitors who had no intentions of raising my morale. Two guards came to Barracks 22 and politely asked for me. I got my coat and went to the door.

"Major Komorowski," one of the guards said, "come with us."

"Certainly," I responded. I had no idea that anything was amiss. "Where are we going?"

The guard said: "Colonel Miranov has a special use for you."

I took this to mean that the interrogator wanted to see me, but I was wrong. The guards led me to the camp jail and started up the steps of the ramshackle old building.

"Why are you bringing me here?" I demanded.

The guard who was the spokesman turned to me. "From this point, Major Komorowski, no questions. You will remain silent. Take my advice, Comrade, it will hasten your departure from this rest home."

Inside the foyer was an old stove, the only heat in the big building. A guard sat at a desk near the stove. "Ah, another guest," he said, getting up and grinning. "We'll put him in Room 6. It's the only one that is empty."

A thick door kept the foyer separate from the rest of the building. The guard unlocked the door and led me down a freezing hallway to a room with the number six on it. He opened the door and grinned at me again. "Okay," he said. "Let's have all your clothing except your underwear."

"You're joking," I said. "It's freezing in there."

"You were warned to maintain silence," he said, his grin fading. "You have been sentenced to three days. We will add a full day for each word you utter from this moment on."

I removed my clothing and went into the room. The door was

closed behind me. The room was dark, so I moved around carefully to explore my cell. There was no furniture, and the wooden floor was bare and rough. There was no cot, no mattress. The single window in the room was covered with heavy boards. I stood shivering in the middle of the small room, listening for sounds of others in the jail; but there was an eerie silence in the old building, broken only by the wind howling softly outside the boarded window.

Although I suspected that my imprisonment in this cold, miserable cell stemmed from the faint hints in my letter to Suzan, I was never told so. Even later, when I questioned Colonel Miranov about it, he merely smiled and ignored my question.

For three days and nights I cowered in the room, rolling my body into a fetal position in a vain effort to retain warmth. I had to use a corner of the room as a toilet—and to clean it up once a day when the guard brought me a small cup of foul lentil soup.

At first, incensed by this cruel punishment, I tried to nurture my anger, realizing that anger might keep me from weakening. I would not be reduced to a subhuman and thus be made pliable for conversion. I would remain a man, an officer in the Polish Army Reserves, a human being free in spirit if not in flesh. But the coldness and the loneliness and the uncertainty took their toll. By the end of the second day I was ready to sell my soul for a bed and a blanket. By the third day I reached another plateau: I was numb to most emotions. Not even thoughts of Suzan could arouse me from a kind of torpor that dulled all thought and extinguished all hope.

On the afternoon of December 14 the door was opened, and I was ordered out. I could barely walk, but I struggled into my clothes, and the two guards who had brought me to the jail escorted me back to the barracks.

Colonel Dzierzynski, Colonel Mijakowski, and Major Konopka helped me to my cot and piled their blankets on top of me. They had saved part of their soup, and they heated it on the old steel barrel that served as a barracks stove.

The colonel's face had lost much of its strength, and his eyes were taking on the dull glaze of a man nearing withdrawal. I dreaded seeing it happen to him; I needed someone strong to keep me from giving up, and from the beginning I had found particular sustenance in his strength.

In sharp contrast to the new wave of cruelty, the first scheduled film was shown at the Club on Friday, December 15. The hall at the Club would hold only three hundred men, so we were broken into groups to view the movie. The men from Barracks 22 were among those selected to see the film the first night. I went reluctantly, scarcely recovered from my confinement; many others didn't go at all.

The film was Russian, a long, boring, and depressing story of the Russian Civil War that followed the Revolution of 1917. The hero spouted reams of communist dogma and was killed by anti-Bolsheviks. It seemed a fitting reward. Several men, bored with the film and the bad Polish of the NKVD lieutenant who translated, got up and left.

The following night, we heard, men who got up to leave found that the doors had been locked. They had to stay for the entire film, then were "treated" to a two-hour antireligion speech by an NKVD officer.

On succeeding nights, when few men went to see the film, NKVD guards began to round up "volunteers" to take them to the Club for the film and lecture. Fortunately, I escaped being selected.

As relations between the prisoners and the guards grew worse, I became afraid to visit Pavel Borodynsky on guard duty. But when I met him in the roadway in the third week of December and he asked why I never came to see him, I didn't tell him that I didn't trust him now that relations were worsening between guards and prisoners. "I've been feeling badly since spending three nights in jail," I said.

He stared at the ground. "I heard about that. I'm sorry it happened to you."

"Pavel," I said, looking into his eyes, "what is going on? What is the *kombrig* trying to accomplish?"

"I'm only a sergeant," he said, looking away from me. "Just be patient. In time you'll know. And so will I."

Didn't he know what was happening? Was he lying to me? I decided not to visit him again unless the uneasy climate in the camp improved considerably.

Conditions didn't improve. They got worse. On December 18 I was taken to see Colonel Miranov again. A short, husky guard stood near the window of the small office, and Colonel Miranov's friendly voice had turned stern and crisp.

"Major Komorowski," he said briskly, "there is still the matter of your spying missions to London and Brussels to be resolved. Tell me about them. Everything."

When I was silent, he gestured to the guard, who moved forward and slammed his gun butt against the side of my head.

The interrogation lasted only six hours, yet it was an incredible experience. I was hit a dozen times, but I was not knocked unconscious. Colonel Miranov was a consummate artist, changing, like a schizophrenic, from a friendly, patronizing comrade to a raging, angry beast—then reversing the process and starting again. One moment he would extol the virtues of Polish culture and fighting spirit; the next he would compare Poles with pigs and barbarians.

"Pig! Swine! Idiot!" he would shout, making me jump. "I should have filth like you buried alive, but Russian soil is too precious to waste on such shit!"

Then immediately he would lower his voice and say soothingly: "How can an intelligent man like you not see the error of your ways? Listen to me, Citizen. I want to help you. You have a wealth of culture and knowledge in that handsome head. Be honest and we will put such valuable assets to excellent use."

After six hours the colonel dismissed me with an ugly snort, and the guard shoved me into the corridor. Two guards were waiting to take me back to the barracks.

In striking contrast to the six hours of insanity with Colonel

Miranov, several men were sitting around the stove singing a Christmas carol. We were nearing the birthday of Christ.

The men from the Soviet Jewelry Exchange paid their second visit on December 19, and we were ready this time, having decided to pool our paltry wealth and to buy more healthy foodstuffs. Colonel Dzierzynski took off his gold wristwatch and gave it to the commissary officer to sell.

"It was made in Milwaukee, Wisconsin, U.S.A.," he said. "It should bring a good price." I turned over my own wristwatch and my fountain pen. We kept four pens in the barracks to be shared the next time we were allowed to write home—if we were ever again allowed to write home.

Among the two hundred and fifteen men in Barracks 22, we amassed a virtual fortune, four hundred rubles and thirty-five hundred zlotys. Our commissary officer, a young air force lieutenant who had served in that capacity during the war, assured us that we had enough money to provide supplementary food for all the men in the barracks for at least six months. Comforting though this thought was, it was depressing to think of spending so much time in the miserable camp.

Clubs were started. Hockey enthusiasts built fires to melt snow for a hockey rink. The men who made clogs for us carved out skates. Other groups formed ski clubs, using rough slats for skis on the gentle slopes inside the camp. We had lecturers on every subject; one even spoke about Polish history.

The pace was almost frantic, but still a growing number of men withdrew. They stopped speaking; they did not attend lectures or join clubs; they did not appear at the Club. For the most part they lay on their cots and stared blankly. Not even the priests, ministers, and rabbis could bring them out of their shells.

The days of December passed slowly. I waited for a letter from Suzan, but none came. My mind started slipping into a cruel dream world that not even the thought of Christmas could dispel. New snow came daily, and the peasants from Kozelsk swept it into high banks around the courtyard and buildings.

Major Konopka, *starosta* for our barracks, responsible for keeping it clean and making certain that the men were inside before curfew, discussed my growing despondency with Dr. Kochloffel and then put me in charge of the Cockroach Cavalry, formed to rid the barracks of roaches.

With a kind of grim humor each barracks had its special groups to eliminate vermin. There were the Mouse and Rat Regiments, the Bedbug Brigades, and the Flea and Lice Legions. We waged constant war on vermin, although the Russians claimed that no such problem existed. I played at war with relish, desperately grasping at reality, activity, life. We all had need of help.

A few days before Christmas, word came through the grapevine that *Kombrig* Zarubin, under pressure from Moscow, had told General Minkiewicz that the NKVD could no longer close its eyes to such disgressions as religious services, even at Christmas. Guards would now break up any service.

First to test this rule was Father Jan Ziolkowski, a stocky young priest who seemed to be everywhere in the camp at once. He held mass openly and was promptly thrown into jail. Other priests became more cautious; they held secret masses and walked around with men, pretending to converse while hearing confessions. Even so, everyone felt that the rule from *Kombrig* Zarubin would not be enforced unless violations were blatant. God, how wrong we were!

Preparations for Christmas continued with minor alterations. Masses would be held secretly in dark barracks; sermons would be whispered. Some men had stocked up candy and cakes as gifts for friends. I usually kept a small supply of such luxuries, which I gave periodically to Pavel—not as a bribe, but as a gesture of friendship. Pavel could not afford these items and could not have bought them even if he had the money. He told me that the Communists considered our lust for luxuries proof of our decadence.

Some made sketches, sculptures, chess men, and other items as gifts. Janina's friends bribed a guard to let them have a bottle of vodka for a Christmas party at her cottage. They even managed to sneak a Christmas tree into the cottage, and other men obtained trees for some of the barracks from the old cemetery where the monks were buried, where the Russians never went.

More than anything else I wanted to be with Suzan. Barring that, I wanted a letter from her. We would learn later that the NKVD had received mail for the prisoners at Kozelsk but were keeping it hidden until after Christmas.

On December 24, a bright, sunny Sunday, everyone except the sick and the withdrawn went around wishing others a merry Christmas. Even the guards responded to such good cheer. But they added a predictable touch: "Merry Christmas, *Comrades.*"

Antoni had great fun with guards who greeted him in this manner. He would find one who understood no Polish, flash his wide, disarming smile, and shout: "Merry Christmas, *bekarci!*"

"One of them is going to find out that *bekarci* means bastard," Stanislaw Kaczmarek warned him, "and give you a merry Christmas right up your ass."'

In the afternoon of that Christmas Eve, I went to the guard barracks to deliver a gift to Pavel Borodynsky. I felt uneasy visiting their barracks, but Pavel had assured me several days before that pressure from higher-ranking NKVD men had eased up and that the guards were backing off. Our grapevine sources verified this, and there had been no stories of harsh interrogations for almost a week. Perhaps General Minkiewicz's complaint had been effective. I didn't know. I only knew that many in the camp expected the recent laxity on the part of camp officials to be the traditional lull before the storm.

Pavel came out into the sunshine, and we stood on the steps of the guard barracks and chatted a few moments. There seemed to be a sadness about him, but he said nothing to indicate why he might be sad, and perhaps I only imagined it. Before I left, I thrust the small package into his hand. Wrapped in old cloth and tied with evergreen sprigs were a small cake and a 10-ruble note, the latter for his family.

Pavel Borodynsky gazed at the gift and said nothing, then ran into the barracks as though he was embarrassed by the gesture. I could not understand why, unless it was because the Russians did not exchange Christmas gifts or in any other way acknowledge the birthday of Christ.

In the evening Antoni, Vincenty, Rudolf, Leo, and Henryk came to our barracks, and we sang carols. Everyone sang, even the men who had withdrawn and who had spent weeks staring blankly. We were as happy as men could be under such circumstances, and I was delighted to see Vincenty acting almost normally again.

And then it happened. An air force lieutenant ran into the building just before curfew, shouting: "They're taking away all the priests!"

We ran to the courtyard. There, huddled in a mass, were the priests, ministers, and rabbis. I tried to count them, but the guards were pushing and herding them toward the gate. We heard the rumble of engines. The gates swung open, and we saw the trucks. Colonel Dzierzynski gritted his teeth and swore.

"The stupid bastards," he muttered. "They think they can stop religion by taking away our men of God? Well, they're wrong!"

We watched as the religious leaders were forced through the gates. As they went, they prayed and shouted words of encouragement to us.

Suddenly there was a cry from one point in the crowd. Turning, we saw two NKVD guards dragging sick little Father Camillus Kantak from the infirmary.

"My God," Leo said, "he doesn't even have a coat or a blanket."

Hands reached down to receive him, and we saw a Protestant minister take his own blanket and wrap it around Father Kantak.

I looked around for *Kombrig* Zarubin, or even Commissar Koraliev. Someone had to speak out in defense of these men. But there was no one in authority, and I knew that my objections would not be heeded. We watched helplessly as the trucks prepared to leave.

Then, above our shouts of protest, there came a small, weak voice. One of the priests had begun to sing an ancient Polish hymn, sung in time of great peril: "Under your protection, we call upon Thee, Holy Mother of God."

Soon all the men on the trucks and in the courtyard were

singing. The entire camp rumbled with the power of our voices. Not even the bayonets and dogs could stop us. Even after the gates were closed and the sound of the trucks was gone, the air rang with our thundering litany.

As we sang, guards came running out of several barracks with the scantily decorated Christmas trees. They piled them in the courtyard and set fire to them. We still sang the ancient hymn.

There was not a man in the camp whose life and spirit had not been touched, at least once, by the priests, ministers, and rabbis who were now on their way to God knew where. As we stood there in the cold night singing our old hymn, I began to understand why the Russians had been lenient with us the past few days, why they had let us go ahead with our plans to observe Christmas in the traditional way. And I understood the sadness I had seen in Pavel's eyes when I had gone to wish him merry Christmas and to take my gift to him.

The Russians had been planning for some time to take our religious men away and, with typical cruelty, had timed the action for the holiest of all nights. (The fact that Christmas is not a religious holiday for the Jews did not detract from the sadness the Jews felt at the loss of their rabbis.)

Whatever lay ahead for us would be far more difficult to stand without our men of God to guide us, to hear our complaints and our confessions, to assure us with their words, their deeds, and their presence that God was with us. Only Father Jan Ziolkowski, who was being held in the camp prison and had been overlooked in the roundup, was left to serve as a link with God for most of the men at Kozelsk.

11: WINTER, 1940

A dismal lethargy set in. On Christmas Eve we wanted to kill the guards and to escape across frozen Russia, but on Christmas Day we walked about like automatons programmed for submission.

We had lost more than the priests. With them went our fighting spirit, humor, and hope. Men who had never prayed and who did not even believe in God began to spend quiet moments conversing with whatever superior being might exist, pleading for some relief from the despair that was becoming epidemic. Even the most hopeful saw nothing ahead but misery, discontent, uncertainty, and terror.

A massive storm hit us after Christmas and confined us to the barracks. Twenty inches of snow fell, and the temperatures dropped to forty below zero. The pipes burst in the bathhouse, but few cared. Who would fight snow, ice, and subzero temperatures for the dubious pleasure of a shower in the company of cockroaches and rats?

The weather cleared by the second week in January, and mail was finally distributed. Perhaps it was too late. Colonel Dzierzynski had to nudge me when my name was called.

I received a letter from Suzan, but I simply took it slowly back to the barracks, feeling no elation. Something told me that the letter brought bad news. Suzan wrote that food in Grodno was almost finished, that she had been ill, and that the Russians visited frequently—for reasons I dared not speculate about.

Her hitherto beautiful handwriting was sketchy and stilted. There were words that I could not decipher. I surmised that she was dangerously ill, starving, or going mad. Possibly all three, though Suzan wrote: "Don't worry about me, I am doing well." And I could do *nothing*.

This time, I wept openly. The handwriting, plus what was not said, left much to my imagination.

The NKVD seemed concerned that so many men were becoming withdrawn, especially after the priests, ministers, and rabbis were taken away, and in early January they replaced the dull Soviet films with an American-made musical comedy and promised that no communist lectures would be given following the film. The Club was packed every night for a week, and the film, incredibly, seemed to help morale—but only for those who had not already begun to reject life.

Interrogations became less frequent, involving relatively few officers. *Kombrig* Zarubin also increased his favors by inviting more men to his quarters for what we had begun to call "Tea and Garbage" conversations.

On the evening of January 10, 1940, we were given proof of what the NKVD was trying to accomplish.

An infantry colonel signed a confession stating that he had spied on the Soviet Union for three years prior to the war. The NKVD did not announce the signing of the confession, but word passed around the camp, anyway.

We learned that after having signed a confession, the colonel was being forced by the NKVD to try to induce other officers, especially those of high rank, to do likewise. If he refused, the NKVD threatened to make the confession public in the colonel's home region in Poland as well as in the camp. The man would be branded a traitor, and if the NKVD plan worked, he would not live ten minutes among the inmates of Kozelsk.

When General Minkiewicz heard of the forced confession, he reportedly called the colonel to his quarters, explained that he knew the colonel had signed under duress, and, in effect, exonerated the officer. He also told the colonel to continue to play the NKVD game.

Another NKVD plan backfired. In the presence of his *polit-rook*, the colonel extolled the virtues of communism to officers who knew the whole story. In return, the colonel was exempt from interrogation and harassment—and even received better food.

If the NKVD ever found out that the colonel was working both sides of the street, so to speak, it never let on. But we had had proof positive of the intentions of the NKVD.

There were only three other events of note during that frozen January of 1940.

In the second week of January a new film arrived—another American musical comedy, we were told. Thus the Club was crowded when the new film opened. However, when the lights went out and the opening scene burst upon the cracked wall, which was used as a screen, two nuns and a priest were depicted engaged in an incredibly lewd sexual escapade.

Obviously, the participants were only actors dressed up in Catholic garb, but the results were devastating. The men in the room, including myself and several of my friends from Barracks 17, headed for the doors. Not only were the doors locked, but six burly guards stood there with machine guns to make certain we didn't break them down.

We had to sit through the entire film. Few watched, but we could not shut out the sound of the leering lieutenant who translated as the film progressed. It was the most disgusting material I had ever seen, and it was followed by two hours of even more disgusting live entertainment: the self-styled NKVD theologian with another of his antireligious lectures.

We felt bitterly disillusioned and utterly bewildered, unable to understand the process to which we were being subjected. It was all of a piece, up, then down. But our minds were too tired to handle the emotional stress, which was, of course, exactly as the Russians intended.

Each time we fell into the trap, it became more difficult to avoid doing the same the next time. Later in January when guards came and took me to the administration building, I fell into the trap. I expected long hours of interrogation, possibly even a beating, but instead I was led to the *kombrig*'s quarters.

"Good evening, Major Komorowski," the general said expansively. His slender hand grasped mine as his eyes assessed my condition.

We played a weird charade. He served tea and sweet rolls, then brought out two oranges and handed me one. Oranges were rare in Russia at all times. In January they were collectors' items. But the gift failed to overwhelm me. As he peeled his orange and ate it with relish, I stared at mine. My nostrils savored the nostalgic odor of its freshness.

"Come, Major Komorowski," he said jovially. "You can't imagine the difficulty I have obtaining such delicacies. Please join me."

I ate the orange without tasting it. I listened to the *kombrig* without hearing. My mind flitted from fantasy to fantasy, from an image of Suzan being raped to images of priests being butchered to the blandness of a long, flat country on which nothing grew. Was I going insane?

I thought: How does a man know when he is going crazy? Is it as easily diagnosed as an appendicitis attack, a heart attack, a stroke? Is it as certain as death?

After a half hour the *kombrig* was no longer jolly. He said good-bye stiffly, and I was led to the barracks, where I crawled beneath my blanket and greatcoat. I stared at a meandering crack in the wall. It was the Danube, that crack. It was the Danube coursing through the green hills of southern Europe.

Eventually, Colonel Dzierzynski and Dr. Rudolf Kochloffel decided to take me to task, to challenge me to live. They compared me to those men who had given up on life.

Most of the time I simply lay back and stared at my "Danube." But I finally protested, "Oh, you're making something out of nothing. I'm only depressed about Suzan. I'll get over it."

Rudolf shook his head sadly. Even as I spoke, my voice trailed off and I gazed at the Danube again.

"The Russians have a word for this," Rudolf said. "They call it *dokhadyagha*. It means being on the way to the grave. They laugh at those who lie and stare at walls and say that they have been caught by *dokhadyagha*. The Poles are committing mental suicide, which can be followed only by actual death."

They sounded to me as though they were in another room. I listened lethargically, and then a lucid moment came. I felt tugging at my sleeve, then a familiar grip on my arm. I looked up into the determined face of Colonel Dzierzynski.

"Come with me, Eugenjusz. We're going for a walk."

"You can't do that," Rudolf said. "It's after curfew."

"To hell with curfew," the colonel retorted. "This man needs help. Come, Eugenjusz, on your feet."

I sat up dumbly, and someone slipped my greatcoat and cap on me. Someone else jammed on my boots and tied my wooden clogs in place.

"Where are we going?"

"The colonel is taking you out," Rudolf said.

We walked into the cold night. I shivered in the bitter wind and wanted to return to the safety of my blanket and cot. Colonel Dzierzynski's grip refused me that pleasure.

The colonel led me past the old church and across the courtyard. As we walked, he spoke in a low voice of Poland and Suzan and the hope that we would someday be free. He spoke of the past and of the future, carefully avoiding the present.

His words had no effect. I escaped them, and my mind soared through the vacuum of uncertainty and ignorance. But he kept on trying to draw me back from *dokhadyagha*.

"*You*'re not going with the others, Eugenjusz," he said. "I personally guarantee it. When spring comes, we'll plan another escape, and you'll be a strong link in the chain. Do you understand, Eugenjusz?"

"I understand," I mumbled.

But I understood only that the biting wind was whistling across the hill and swirling the dry snow in the courtyard. I understood that my body was cold and that I wanted to be left alone. I wanted only to return to the small, safe world of my weakened mind.

"You'd better understand, damn you," Colonel Dzierzynski said firmly. "I don't care about the others, the weak ones, but I won't forgive it in the strong. I told you when they took the priests that they couldn't take God. We need God, and we have Him. We need you, and we shall have you. Do you understand what I'm saying?"

"Yes. I understand."

He knew I was lying, but he talked on. We circled the frozen courtyard and turned toward the old church. I shivered, but I was happy. Soon, I would lie on my cot and watch the Danube flow through the beautiful hills and fertile meadows of southern Europe and into the Black Sea.

We passed the church and entered a dark roadway between some barracks and high snowbanks. I was thinking of the glorious moment when we would be in the barracks and he would be silent. I was only vaguely aware that the colonel's grip had tightened on my arm and that we had stopped.

Dumbly, I stood while he peered into the shadows. I started to say something, but he shushed me. Then he pulled me along like a hospital orderly leading an idiot.

The world turned into a jumble of action in that moment. I saw the hulking shadow of the guard and heard the snarl of the dog. And then the shadow was in front of us, and I heard another voice.

"Komorowski, have you forgotten what I said I would do if I caught you out after curfew once more?"

"He's a sick man," the colonel said, trying to pull me around Kalanin. "I'm trying to bring him out of it."

"Sick?" Kalanin laughed. "You mean, Citizen, that he's crazy."

"All right," Colonel Dzierzynski said, still holding my arm, "he's crazy. We've just been walking and talking and . . . "

Kalanin shoved his machine gun into the colonel's stomach; he held his dog at the collar. I felt no fear because I still was not really present, though, too, I was not entirely oblivious to what was happening. A part of my mind was alert to danger.

"Between the buildings!" Kalanin ordered. "You Polish bastards think we make rules for fun. I'll teach you about rules."

"Oh, come now, Sergeant Kalanin," Colonel Dzierzynski said, half placatingly, half severely. "Surely a little walk in the night air won't destroy camp discipline."

"Between the buildings!" Kalanin snarled.

Colonel Dzierzynski argued until Kalanin herded us through a high snowbank into the darkness between two barracks. There Kalanin forced Colonel Dzierzynski against one wall and pushed me against the opposite wall. He posted his dog in front of me and ordered it to sit. The dog obeyed; I was pinned in place.

Light from the courtyard filtered into the snowy alcove, and I vaguely saw Kalanin raise his gun. Then there was a sickening thud, and the colonel let out a muffled cry. His arms flailed out at Kalanin, but the gun thudded again.

Blinding flashes tore through my fuzzy mind. I recalled the night Kalanin had left me to freeze. In a second I seemed to recall every outrage committed by the Soviets, from the brutal murder of General Wilczynski to the removal of the priests. I remembered Suzan's last letter. And I heard the clunk, clunk, clunk of the gun on Colonel Dzierzynski's head.

Then, with a roar, I leaped forward. The dog also leaped, but I caught it in mid-air. The dog squirmed in my grip, and I held it by the neck, and it twisted and turned, trying to bite my arms. Suddenly it was still, and I flung it at Kalanin, striking him in the back. Kalanin let out a guttural roar, and man and dog sprawled on the snow.

The dog ran off, and the machine gun, wet with Colonel Dzierzynski's blood, lay at my feet. The colonel leaned against the barracks, his bloody head swaying from side to side. I looked at the gun and thought of using it on Kalanin. But instead I caught Kalanin as he was getting up. He was usually stronger than I, especially after the months of inadequate diet, but a crazy strength seemed to flood through my body. Perhaps it was the flow of adrenalin that comes to all animals in time of crisis.

I hit the stocky NKVD sergeant in the face and felt warm blood on my fingers. It spurted from his flattened nose and served only to increase my fury. Punching, kicking, gouging, tearing, I fell upon Kalanin. Then my fingers, savoring the new strength that came with rage, tightened and sank into his soft flesh, cutting off his stinking breath.

Kalanin's narrow eyes widened in horror at the death that was descending on him. Then I felt a familiar strong grip on my arm and heard the colonel's soft voice: "For the love of God, don't kill the bastard. Eugenjusz! Let him go!"

A sea of happiness swept over me. I had heard each word distinctly and knew what each word meant. One terrible act of insanity had brought me back to my senses. I loosened my grip on Kalanin's throat and picked up the machine gun, casually ejecting all the cartridges and throwing them as far as I could into the darkness.

Working smoothly, without fear, without dullness of mind, I revived Kalanin to keep him from freezing to death. Coming to, he made no move. Then, when I was certain that he would be able to move on his own, I took the colonel's arm.

"Come on, sir," I said in a calm, steady voice. "I think we've had enough air for one night."

The incident with Kalanin was a vital turning point. It had pulled me from the ranks of *dokhadyagha*, but it also had served to increase my sense of uneasiness. Kalanin would surely attack again, and next time I would not be so lucky. Yet nothing happened. I saw him a number of times, but he ignored me. I wanted to discuss my fears with Pavel Borodynsky but didn't. How would he respond? Casual friendship is one thing; we were still enemies. There was nothing I could do about Kalanin but wait and be on guard against any slip.

So January passed. Discontent was rampant through the camp. Although I had come out of my dangerous state of mind, Vincenty now tipped over into madness.

"He's gone completely bugs," Antoni said one day. "He doesn't just sit and stare like the others who have slipped. He's really crazy.

"Just last night," Antoni went on, "he went outside naked and got a handful of snow. He brought it in and sat on his bunk and watched it melt. Then he cried because it was gone. Jesus, three of us had to keep bringing him new snow to keep him from crying. And he does other wild things, crazy things."

"Can't Rudolf do anything for him?"

"Rudolf has given up. I think maybe he's a little bugs himself. And several NKVD bastards are nuts also. They had to be sent away."

In Barracks 17 we found Vincenty sitting on his cot, completely naked. His torso, so thin that you could count his ribs in a single glance, was bent like a thin tree on a windy plain.

"How are you, Vincenty?" I asked, sitting beside him on the cot.

He held out his hand and spoke in a deep, soulful voice: "You may kiss my ring."

He had no ring. His skinny fingers were empty.

"All right." I took his cold, bony hand and pretended to kiss the nonexistent ring. "Now, will you tell me how you are?"

"I am fine," he replied, his sad eyes gazing at the ceiling, "but I can't hold audience today. Send them all away. Perhaps tomorrow."

I looked at Antoni, who shrugged. "He thinks he's the goddamn Pope."

"But the Pope doesn't sit around naked. He wears robes," I said to Vincenty.

He drew up his lean frame and smoothed invisible cloth across his chest. "And what do you think *I'm* wearing?"

"Robes," Antoni said before I could tell the captain he was naked. "Flowing white robes, Pope Vincenty."

With a flick of his hand Vincenty dismissed me from his cot, which he called his throne, and curled up like a snake, facing the wall. Outside, I asked Antoni how long Vincenty had been this bad.

"Couple of days. But he isn't *all* bats. Sometimes, he's as normal as you and me."

"That's no big reassurance," I said, remembering my days of mental withdrawal. "How about you, Antoni? Are you holding up well?"

"They can't touch me," Antoni said, grinning in his old familiar way. "I have the edge on them."

"In what way?"

"I was crazy the day I was born. Not even the goddamn Russians can drive a crazy man crazy."

We walked in the unusually warm sunshine and discussed the latest rumors. The grapevine reported that "something big" was in the wind. There had been an increase in calls from Moscow. The prevailing rumor was that *Kombrig* Zarubin and his psychologists had failed to convert a significant number of Poles and that Moscow was unhappy.

"Just the other day," Antoni said, "a guard told me that it would soon be over. When the weather breaks, we'll be heading west."

"I'll believe it when it happens."

"I won't believe it even then," he said. "Jesus, the whole camp is crazy with rumors. One day we're going to be set free; the next day we're going to be killed and buried in this fucking camp."

"And what do you think?"

"I try not to think, unless it's about women."

In mid-February, when rumors, fear, and discontent had reached an incredible level, a few of us received startling news concerning a conversation between General Minkiewicz and *Kombrig* Zarubin. Leo Bednarek, who was a friend of General Minkiewicz's aide, brought the news to Colonel Dzierzynski —and naturally to the others in our group.

General Minkiewicz, concerned about the rumors and the

number of men slipping into dream worlds, had gone to the
kombrig and asked point blank what was going to happen to us.
The *kombrig*, after much hesitation, finally had said that the men
would *all* go crazy if they knew what the Russians planned.

Normally, such news would have spread like a smallpox
epidemic. But General Minkiewicz told only a handful of his
close associates. Colonel Dzierzynski swore us to secrecy, so we
lived with the terrible information running through our minds.

Keeping the news of the *kombrig*'s statement secret was
perhaps the most difficult task we faced, and I am not convinced
that we did the right thing. Perhaps many would have gone
mad knowing about the conversation, but it might have been
enough to spur the rest of us to break out, to get away. Many of
us would have survived. But the terrible secret was kept.

As spring approached, I felt a strengthening of my mind.
When mail arrived in late February and there was no letter
from Suzan, I was depressed, but I didn't return to the terrible
shell of fantasy.

In early March an event took place that was to have a great
bearing on our future.

Kombrig Zarubin and three of his colonels, including Colonel
Miranov, quietly left the camp on the night of March 4. Their
departure was a surprise—another failure for our intelligence
corps—and nobody knew why.

I was still friendly with Pavel Borodynsky, so I went to him to
see if he knew anything.

"All I know," Pavel told me as we stood in front of the guard
barracks, "is that Colonel Kutchkov is staying behind to run the
camp with Commissar Koraliev."

"And you don't know why the *kombrig* left? You don't know
what the authorities plan to do with us?"

Pavel did not look at me. "Soon," he said simply, "we'll all be
where we belong. That's all I can say, Eugenjusz. Don't ask
anything more."

Radical changes were implemented in the next few days: interrogations ceased; the men from the *skit* were allowed out of their special area; guards made special visits to the barracks to report "unofficially" that we would be "heading toward home" or "going to the west" or "moving toward Poland."

One guard told the men in Antoni's barracks, "All you *panski* will soon be with your ladies on your fine estates." Another told a group, "Each of you will soon see an end to your agony."

None of us caught the double meaning of the comments. I talked at length with Pavel as we sat on the northwest guard tower and shared a cake I had bought at the camp store. I fished for information.

"Actually," he said, avoiding my questions, "I am Comrade Lenin in disguise. You have nothing to worry about, Comrade. I have ordered Moscow to release you and to pay you for your time."

"Do you think Moscow will obey a man who has been dead for fifteen years?"

"I am Lenin," he boomed, raising his fist into the air. "Even when I speak from the grave, Moscow listens."

"Then speak, Comrade Lenin," I said without smiling. "We need all the help we can get."

The departure of *Kombrig* Zarubin and the radical changes in treatment, plus the hopeful rumors, resulted in a general uplifting, almost imperceptible at first, that grew into a widespread feeling that all would be well. The human spirit is almost indomitable.

Antoni Urban and Stanislaw Kaczmarek apologized to each other, and throughout the camp men who had argued patched up their differences and were friends again. Dyspeptic attitudes seemed to fall away in the warming March sun, which melted the snows and heralded an end to the discontent wrought by a long and bitter winter.

As farmers take stock of their equipment, livestock, and supplies in spring, we took stock of ourselves. Most of us had lost considerable weight. Colonel Dzierzynski no longer appeared strong and stocky, although the muscles of his neck retained some thickness, and Hugo Mijakowski seemed slighter and even shorter. Only Antoni knew for certain how much he had lost in weight; he was the only one brave enough to face Dr. Loo's grinning teeth and clutching hands by going to the dispensary, where there was a scale.

Our recreation center once again became a popular spot and was filled every night with laughing, joking men, hopeful men, trusting men who grasped at the rumors being spread by the NKVD guards. The *polit-rooks*, including Aleksi Alexandrovich, also returned to the Club, but they no longer spouted communist dogma. To the contrary, they encouraged us to believe the rumors that we would soon "head toward home."

It was difficult to feel gloomy when I saw emaciated men walking about or playing at the Club, broad smiles on their pinched faces. And it was difficult to be the devil's advocate while listening to Antoni and Stanislaw joke their way through an evening at the Club. It was good, very good, to see my friends coming out of their lethargy and fear, to hear them talk of home, and to joke about matters which were close to their hearts.

But there was still that nagging worry at the back of my mind. What had *Kombrig* Zarubin meant when he said that we would all go crazy if we knew what the Russians planned to do with us?

12: "WE'LL ALL MEET AGAIN IN PARIS"

Early spring was a waiting game, but not a wholly unpleasant period. Rumors of freedom were so prevalent that even the most suspicious of men in the camp began to accept them as fact. We were merely waiting, we heard, until the NKVD arranged transportation to take us westward, back to Poland. There was no talk of going to Rumania; all the rumors suggested that we would go home.

A spell of unusually good weather followed *Kombrig* Zarubin's departure. On the sunny days men walked about without great-coats, chatting about what they were convinced were the final days of our imprisonment. Peasants from Kozelsk fixed the boiler and replaced the broken pipes in the bathhouse, so we were able to take weekly showers. Strong disinfectants were sprayed in the old bathhouse to kill the vermin. Bathing became one of our greater pleasures.

Talk of escape disappeared entirely in the face of continual promises of freedom. Even Colonel Dzierzynski, who shared my distrust of NKVD promises, realized that we could not put together a successful escape plan. There simply was not enough desire among the men to run the risks of an escape attempt when freedom seemed within our grasp.

"Why should we go to all that trouble to run to the airport and fly those rickety old crates when the Russians will send us a train?" Stanislaw Kaczmarek asked Colonel Dzierzynski one night in the Club. "As for myself, I prefer to wait for the train."

With the young pilot's defection, the other pilots who had continued to discuss escape backed off. The remaining members of the escape committee shared Stanislaw's attitude, and we were left with only a handful of men who would even consider an escape. In short, regardless of our distrust of the NKVD's promise of freedom, we had no choice but to wait.

Then, in the middle of March, the *polit-rooks* left Kozelsk. This further indication of Russian failure was to some another hopeful sign that the camp would be disbanded and that we would be taken home.

Aleksi Alexandrovich, friend, companion, helper, guide, father confessor to Barracks 17, made a special trip to my barracks to say good-bye to me. "For a time," he said with his pretty, open smile, "I thought we might have you on our side, Major Komorowski."

"What makes you say that?"

He pursed his lips and his bright eyes sparkled with good humor. "When I talked, you seemed to listen. You didn't turn off your mind like the others."

"Do you really believe that?"

His smile did not diminish. We had talked on a number of occasions, and he had given the usual version of communist ideology. I had listened, but I had also talked. I had given him my version of communism, which wasn't very favorable, and I had made it clear that I preferred freedom, democracy.

"I always had the feeling that you had an open mind about politics, Comrade," he said.

"Your feeling was wrong, Aleksi," I told him. "I have a closed mind when it comes to communism. Any political ideology that places so much power in the hands of so few people cannot be good, either for the masses or for the authority. It oppresses the one and corrupts the other."

He smiled even more brightly. "You have just described your own country," he said. "But let's not quarrel now. I believe I know what is in your mind. Soon you will be one with us all."

"You have no idea of what was on my mind when we had our little talks about communism," I said.

He laughed and slapped my shoulder. "You were thinking of women, of course."

"Not women. Just one woman."

"Ah, yes, Suzan. I hear that she is a very beautiful young lady. What does she say in her letters? Is she doing well in Grodno?"

"You've done your homework well, Aleksi," I said, "but you missed a point. I haven't had a letter from Suzan since early January."

His eyes fell away for a moment; then he looked directly into my eyes. Perhaps I only imagined it, but I thought the old brightness seemed dulled. He brought back the smile with an effort and slapped my shoulder again.

"Don't worry. The mails are slow. You'll hear from her soon. As a matter of fact, you'll be with her soon. How would you like that, Citizen?"

"I would like it very much."

He shook my hand quickly and seemed eager to get away. He waved to a few acquaintances in the barracks, glanced swiftly back at me, and hurried outside. I distinctly felt that something was wrong. It was impossible to tell if Aleksi Alexandrovich was a pleasant fool or a shrewd manipulator. If he knew so much about Suzan, why hadn't he known that I had not heard from her in more than two months? Or was he just rubbing salt in my wounds?

And why had his eyes lost their brightness when he told me that I would be with Suzan very soon? Indeed, why had he come to the barracks to say good-bye to me? I had been under his political guidance in Barracks 17 for only a few weeks. Surely, he had enough to do just to say good-bye to the men in that barracks.

There were no answers, of course. But I consoled myself —partially, at least—with the thought that there had to be logical reasons for everything—for Aleksi's visit, for Suzan's continued silence, for my feeling of anxious dread. But if so, what were they?

During March we were subjected to no bothersome Soviet propaganda. From morning until night, we heard a variety of music, mostly Polish, interspersed with Russian and American selections. Idleness was still a factor, but an air of expectancy could be felt throughout the camp.

By the middle of the month, nearly half the guard contingent had disappeared. Guards no longer patrolled outside the walls. In contrast, the administration building office seemed to bustle with activity.

Men from the *skit* moved freely through the camp, and we learned of the extensive interrogation they had undergone. We suspected that many of them had signed phony confessions or even had become Communists, but I knew of no cases of men from the *skit* trying to influence officers from the main camp.

It was almost a relief not to have to consider the problem of escape. No new orders concerning escape had come down from General Minkiewicz, and everyone simply waited for the captor to release his grip on the captive.

On the evening of Monday, April 1, Antoni brought moment-ous news: the spies at the administration building reported a sharp increase in telephone calls from Moscow.

"I just came from the administration building," Antoni said as he took a chair at our customary tables at the Club. "Everybody is excited, even the guards."

Colonel Dzierzynski grunted. "So there are calls from Moscow. What does that mean?"

"They're calling with our *names*," Antoni said. "The clerks are taking the names and making lists."

"That doesn't make sense," Major Konopka told him. "They

already have our names. Why would they have to get our names again—and all the way from Moscow?"

"No disrespect intended, Major Konopka," Antoni said, "but even a blind idiot knows the answers. Men on the lists will be set free."

"And you believe this new lie?" the major asked, not daring to believe what he wanted to believe.

"I do. It's simple. We were brought here in one large group, right? Okay. The Russian mind works this way: take prisoners to jail in a large group; release them in small groups."

"There's no logic to that," Hugo Mijakowski interjected.

"Exactly," Antoni said. "That's why the Russians are doing it this way. Jesus Christ, I didn't say their minds were *logical*. They're simple."

"Their minds are as simple as a telephone," Colonel Dzierzynski mused. "It's easy to pick up a telephone and talk to someone miles away. But try to figure out how your voice travels through the wires and a bunch of little parts. Then you will understand how simple the Russian mind is. Don't underestimate them. We underestimated the Germans and look what happened. The Russians are as cunning as the Germans are powerful, and twice as devious."

"You are dead right, Colonel, sir," Antoni said, "but tell me this: After all the stories from the guards about our going home, why would Moscow be calling here and giving lists of names? Since mid-afternoon ten calls have come in from Moscow, and ten lists have been made up."

"*I* can't explain it," Colonel Dzierzynski said, "but apparently, you already have the answer."

"It's simple. The Russians are preparing to take us from the camp in small groups. Our spies say that each list contains from one hundred to more than two hundred names. They're convinced that each list corresponds to a departing group. They'll probably take out one group a day until we're all free of this pest hole."

Colonel Mijakowski shook his head and watched Antoni with a

glum expression. "Why would they do that, Antoni, if they brought us here in one large group? We all came at the same time. Doesn't it seem logical that we would all leave at the same time?"

Antoni spread his hands on the table and hunched his shoulders. His face grinned triumphantly.

"That, sir, is precisely what I've been trying to explain. We're always looking for them to do the logical thing. If they had brought us here in small bands, they would ship us all out in one group. That's the way their minds work."

Colonel Dzierzynski sighed at Antoni's simplification. "All right, Antoni, we'll think of it your way. We can't do anything else, so we might as well. All we can do is wait and see."

"We won't have long to wait," Antoni said gleefully, slapping his palms together. "Jesus, do you realize that we will soon be free?"

Several of us laughed at his naive enthusiasm, but we all began to share in it. The calls from Moscow certainly had a purpose, and Antoni's surmise was as good as anyone's. Once we were able to admit that he could be right, the conversation turned to the possibility of freedom within the next few days.

"I wonder where they'll take us," Henryk Jagiello mused, breaking the silence he had maintained all evening.

"The guards say to Poland," Leo Bednarek said. "Maybe they'll dump us in the camp at Tarnopol and let us find our way home."

"To hell with home," Antoni declared. "There are Russians and Germans crawling up everybody's asses at home. I'm going to Paris." He rolled his eyes with ecstasy. "Jesus, can you imagine it? Paris! When I reach Paris, there won't be a virgin left in the whole city."

"There probably aren't any there now," Josef Konopka muttered.

"If there are," Antoni said, kissing his fingertips in the French fashion, "I'll find them. The city will rock with their cries of delight."

We were all caught up in the daydream now. Even Colonel Dzierzynski spoke as though the Russians would really free us.

"We're all forgetting one thing," Hugo Mijakowski said, bringing us up short. "The Russians never take us where they say they're going to take us. The guards keep talking about heading west, but we still could be taken to Rumania. We might have a chance to fight the Nazis yet."

Leo Bednarek was in favor of that. "I hope they do take us to Rumania. It will be easy to go to Syria from there and join up with Polish forces. When peaces comes again and I go back into dental practice, I don't want to have to tell my patients that I spent the war sitting on my ass in a Russian monastery. I want to do some more fighting."

The discussion continued until curfew, and we were late leaving the Club. It didn't seem to matter. We met several NKVD guards on the way back to our respective barracks, but they only nodded and smiled. I wondered why Kalanin wasn't dogging my trail; I had no doubt that he had been waiting weeks for me to make just such a slip.

That night I lay on my cot and reviewed the talk about impending freedom. I would not let my hopes be built too high, but the possibilities were delicious. One moment I resolved that, no matter where the Russians took me, I would leave that place, find Suzan, and disappear with her to some small farming community along the Vistula. I would never leave Poland again.

The next second I knew that I would go with the others, to Syria or Paris or London, and fight the Germans and, if necessary, the Russians, until Poland was free again. Then I would go with Suzan to live along the Vistula.

On the morning of April 5, a Friday, the rumors emanating from the administration building began to come true. Antoni had been right. Seven trucks arrived, and guards went from barracks to barracks reading names of men who, they said, "constitute the vanguard of many groups of Polish officers to be taken toward home." The trucks would take the men to the railway station in Kozelsk village.

The effect was galvanic. Everyone in the camp turned out in a mob around the courtyard where the 150 men were assembled. We watched with keen jealousy as the men turned in their camp equipment: lice-ridden mattresses and pillows, tattered blankets, towels, and other items.

Most of the men in the first group were colonels, lieutenant colonels, and majors, but they pranced and giggled like children. We had been in the camp five and a half months; away from home almost seven months. None of us standing by blamed them for acting silly; we would have done the same.

Commissar Koraliev came to the stoop and we saw Colonel Kutchkov lurking glumly behind him. Koraliev spoke only briefly.

"We have enjoyed having you as guests of the Soviet Union. I trust that your stay has been enjoyable and that your journey toward home will be very pleasant. We have taken every precaution to assure you a safe journey to your destination. You are the first to go to a long-awaited freedom, but others will follow and you will all be together again. You have been excellent guests, but we must send you away so that once again the valiant peasant workers of Russia may enjoy the delights of this pastoral setting. Good-bye, Citizens, and good luck."

Instead of disappearing inside, the commissar mingled with the departing group, shaking hands, smiling. Once he walked over to a long table that the guards had set up and opened one of the large packages that were being handed to each departing prisoner. Each package, wrapped in expensive white paper, contained herring, bread, butter, and sugar—enough food for a long journey.

"In any other country," Antoni said as he stared enviously at the food, "that would do for two thousand kilometers. In Russia those poor bastards may starve before they leave the railway station."

"No," Hugo said, smacking his lips. "They should move swiftly now."

Josef Konopka snorted. "You think there has been a miracle since we came? Those men would be wise to nibble their food and make it last. They could travel for a month and still be within shouting distance of us."

The men tucked the white parcels into their rucksacks, buttoned their greatcoats against the chill wind, and climbed happily onto the trucks. They needed no bayonet prodding. The engines roared into life, and a great cheer went up from the seven trucks. The huge mob of prisoners moved toward the gate to shout good-bye. The men waved from the trucks and shouted back. Many wept with joy. One officer shouted from the truck: "Good-bye! We'll see you in Paris!"

For a few moments we had vicariously shared the happiness of the 150 who were leaving. With the closing of the gates and the fading rumble of engines, the remoteness of our world closed in on us again.

When the men began to disperse, a mixture of happiness and sadness was discernible. The word had already circulated that no group would leave on the following day. There was to be a kind of farewell dinner for our top officers before more groups would leave.

On Sunday afternoon, when the sun broke through and took the sharp edge off the new chill, I realized that I had not seen Pavel Borodynsky for several days—in fact, since the last week of March—and so decided to take a walk to the guard barracks. In the back of my mind I wondered if he could shed light on where the NKVD was taking us and on why General Wolkowicki and Admiral Czernicki had been slighted at the dinner.

Two NKVD men lounged in front of the barracks, soaking up the sunshine. I asked one of them if he would send word to Sergeant Borodynsky that I would like to speak with him.

"Borodynsky?" the man asked. "I don't think he's here. He left a week ago."

The second man nodded. "Yes, Borodynsky is probably having a good time right now."

Both men laughed, but their laughter did not seem quite normal. I felt the same uneasiness about their laughter that I had felt when Aleksi Alexandrovich had said good-bye and had talked about Suzan. Something was wrong—but what?

"Thank you," I said politely and turned to walk away. I went only a few steps when a thought came to me. If Pavel was gone, what about my old enemy? I turned to the guards.

"Can you tell me if Sergeant Kalanin is here?"

They laughed again. "You can be certain that the wild one is having just as good a time as Borodynsky. They're both gone, Citizen."

I walked away, wishing that I hadn't come. My good mood had dissipated. It was good to know that Kalanin had gone, but Pavel? And why hadn't Pavel come around to say good-bye?

Groups began to depart with regularity. The saddest day for me was April 16, when Colonel Dzierzynski and Lieutenant Colonel Mijakowski left. Antoni, Josef, Leo, and I helped them prepare.

"I've written to my wife telling her that I'll be home soon," Colonel Dzierzynski said with an edge of sadness to his voice. "With luck, I'll be there before the letter arrives."

"I'm certain you will, sir," I said.

He looked at me with a painful expression, and his eyes clouded briefly with tears. He grasped my hand tightly. "Eugenjusz, you've been a good friend," he said. "I really didn't like you when you were assigned to General Wilczynski's staff, but now I consider you my closest friend."

Even indirect compliments embarrass me, and I said nothing. I merely gripped his hands and looked into his face. The rugged lines had sagged, and he seemed smaller. Yet, at that moment, we never felt closer to each other. I didn't allow myself tears until his group had left.

The following day, Major Konopka and Captain Jagiello left with a group that included Admiral Czernicki. A growing sadness overwhelmed me as I lost two more friends and another top officer to the trucks. The admiral smiled as he walked across the courtyard between the rows of assembled officers. He was old and weak, and he wobbled erratically. His strength gave out before he reached the trucks. With it went his dignity. He sobbed with a mixture of shame and joy as two officers virtually carried him along.

One day later Antoni Urban was crushed beyond repair —Janina Lewandowski was chosen by Moscow to go to freedom. Father Ziolkowski was also on the list, causing a number of men great pain.

Antoni cared nothing for the stocky priest; his pain—and it was true pain—lay elsewhere. "I begged to be in her group," he moaned as he sat on my cot with his head in his hands. His voice trembled. "I went to the commissar and begged. I even got on my knees in front of the slimy bastard."

"What did he say?" Leo Bednarek asked.

"He said the lists are made in Moscow. He has no authority to make any changes."

"You should have told him you were a priest," Lieutenant Kaczmarek said bitterly. "He seems happy to get rid of priests."

Antoni glared at Stanislaw, then smiled. "It wouldn't have worked."

"Why not?" I asked.

"I'd already told him that Father Ziolkowski had married me to Janina."

There was a strange silence as the same thought ran through our minds. We asked, almost in unison: "Did he?"

Antoni groaned and rolled his eyes. "Sweet Jesus in heaven, I'd give up my destined place on the Riviera if it were true!"

By the final week in April the camp seemed empty, and it was lonely. Some of the barracks became vacant as the dwindling inmates moved into other barracks for company. Antoni, Stanislaw, Vincenty, Leo, and Rudolf came to Barracks 22. We talked incessantly of where we were going and of what we would do when we got there. As usual the most popular theory was that we would all go to Paris.

On April 25, a large group of three hundred was taken, and I calculated that only about one thousand of the original five thousand remained. It suddenly occurred to me that everyone above the rank of major had left. What remained in the camp were first and second lieutenants, a group of cadets, several civilian engineers and lawyers, a few provincial police, and a smattering of captains and majors.

Then on the evening of April 27, Antoni rushed in with happy excitement on his face.

"I've just found out," he shouted. "We're on the list for tomorrow!"

"What list?" Leo asked, looking up from the worn letter he had received three weeks ago from his wife. "The latrine-cleaner's list?"

"We go tomorrow," Antoni said, glancing happily from face to face. "You are on it, Leo. And you, Eugenjusz. Hey, Stanislaw, you ugly airplane driver, you go to freedom with us elite Ulanys. And Vincenty also."

He sat down beside Vincenty, who that week had been none other than one of Poland's military leaders, Edward Smyglyrydz, a vast comedown from his previous role as Pope. "Vincenty, do you understand? You are going to freedom with us," Antoni said.

Vincenty Jankowski raised his head, struck a dignified pose, pursed his lips, and declaimed: "If Herr Hitler thinks for a moment that he will have an easy day with Poland, as he had with Czechoslovakia, then he is an idiot as well as a whoremongering paperhanger, and his armies will meet disaster one inch inside our borders. But turn your eyes also to the east, gentlemen, because there is a shoemaker's son there who is Hitler's equal, perhaps his mentor, in the realm of trickery and insanity. Given my choice, gentlemen, I choose Hitler, for with him I might lose my life. With Stalin, I should lose my soul. And furthermore . . ."

He preached on to the wall until his voice became soft and then silent. We sat on our cots and contemplated Antoni's news. Were we at the doorway to freedom? A strange elation rose inside me, but I feared to give full rein to my feelings.

Looking up from my reverie, I saw the haggard look on

Rudolf Kochloffel's face. He was staring at Antoni, who quickly
sensed the trouble.

"I'm certain you're on the list, Rudolf," he said. "I didn't stay to
hear all the names, but I know we'll all leave together."

Rudolf paced the rough floor. "I hope so, Antoni, I truly hope
so. It would be unbearable here without friends."

"You will go with us, Rudolf," I said. "I promise it." Why
anyone would believe me, I had no idea. But no one said any
more.

We slept little that night. Even if we had not been excited
about leaving, the storm would have kept us awake. A cloud-
burst, lashed by thunder and lightning, dumped oceans of rain
on the decrepit old buildings of Maxim Gorki's rest home. I
doubt that many slept more than sporadically, and when slanting rays of sunshine aroused me, Antoni and the others had
already rolled up their mattresses and camp equipment. Their
rucksacks sat apart. One pile would go to the camp storeroom;
one would go to freedom.

At ten o'clock two guards came in and read the names of those
who would leave. As each name was called, breath exploded with
relief. In our group, the relief was not total until we heard the
name we all were waiting for. Finally, it came: "Captain Rudolf
Kochloffel, doctor of medicine."

A dam of emotion broke. We laughed and hugged the little
doctor. Antoni danced around the rough board floor with him,
and tears fell from Rudolf's big eyes.

We rushed to the courtyard and turned in our camp equipment. We strapped our rucksacks to our backs, listened to the
usual farewell talk by the commissar, received our food packages, and waited for the rumble of truck engines.

An hour passed, and we sat on the muddy ground under the
warm sunshine. Minutes crept by, and still there was no sound of
trucks. As noon approached, I became convinced that we were
again being made the object of another cruel NKVD joke.

At noon Commissar Koraliev came out onto the stoop and

faced the 161 men who waited in the muddy courtyard. We struggled to our feet and watched the commissar, waiting for the words of doom.

"Gentlemen, I am sorry," he began. "The rain last night has made the road to the village impassable.

"However," the commissar said crisply, interrupting the moan of disappointment, "the train is waiting for you, and we cannot keep a train waiting. Until the road dries each group must march to the railway station. I trust that you will not feel greatly inconvenienced."

Our responding cheer was proof that we felt no inconvenience. Amid shouts of good-bye we marched with a dozen guards through the open gates, laughing, yelping, and clutching our precious food parcels.

And then all happiness was squelched, then and forever!

At the bottom of the hill, on the muddy road near the swollen stream, stood a large group of NKVD guards. As we came out of the woods, the guards unslung their rifles and machine guns and gave their dogs more leash. A grim-faced lieutenant we had never seen before commanded silence. We stood, stricken with disbelief, and stared at the men, the guns, and the dogs.

For a fleeting instant, I had the impression that this brutal welcoming committee had been set up especially for our group; then truth came in a tidal wave of monstrous reality. Every group leaving Kozelsk for the elusive freedom had been met with similar force, probably at the railway station, leaving no doubt that they were under the strong and relentless grip of a determined NKVD.

In that moment a kaleidoscope of emotions gushed through my brain: I felt fear and wanted to run into the woods; I felt defeat and wanted to fall to the ground and let the guards do with me what they wished; I felt anger and wanted to dash at the dogs and guards in a towering rage.

A roll of grumbling cascaded over our ranks and grew into a rumble. The guards moved closer, and the dogs growled deep in their throats. The NKVD lieutenant shouted for silence, then gave a terse, sharp command in Polish: "We will march in orderly fashion to the railway station. Any bastard that tries to escape will be shot. Understood?"

13: Katyn Forest

During our six months at Kozelsk the NKVD had, at times, tried to crush our spirit; at other times they had filled us with hope, even happiness. But they had not succeeded in crushing my spirit—not entirely. In that agonizing moment of confusion and hurt as we were forced into ranks for the march to the village, my spirit was finally crushed.

"Get moving," the harsh voice of the lieutenant commanded. "Hurry. The train is waiting."

"And we can't keep a train waiting in Russia," Antoni mocked. "Jesus Christ, that's all they do is wait."

"Silence, you Polish bastard!" An NKVD sergeant moved close to Antoni as we neared the swollen stream. Hatred blazed from Antoni's black eyes.

When the guard looked away, Antoni whispered: "All my life I've wanted to piss on a Russian. If I get a chance, *he* will be the one."

"All right, you Polish garbage," the Russian lieutenant barked. "Into the stream. Water won't hurt you."

We could hear the men at the front of the column howling as they waded into the fast, cold water. The first time we had forded this stream, it had been barely over our ankles. Now it came to our waists, and we had to fight the strong current. Finally, however, we crawled onto the muddy bank on the opposite side. Antoni had forged ahead, and when I came out, he took my hand and pulled me the last few feet. I was amazed at the strength in his slender body.

We tried to form ranks again, but it was impossible. Even the guards slipped in the muck. We began a straggling march toward the village, walking in deep ruts. The guards had more trouble. The mud was thicker where they were walking, alongside the path.

In a short time we were stretched over a kilometer of mud-choked road. Weaker men fell behind, and we split into several straggling groups. The guards were frantic. Suddenly, one rushed past me toward the rear, and I turned to see why. A little way back, Stanislaw Kaczmarek was struggling with Vincenty, who had stopped to deliver one of his speeches.

Stanislaw argued with the guard, and the guard pushed him. The pilot slid into the ditch, and I saw his face go red as the guard ordered him, at gunpoint, to return to the road. At that precise moment, Vincenty sat down in the mud, raised his great head, and began to bellow like a cow.

Had it not been so sad and perilous, it would have been comical. The guard tried to get one man back on the road and the other on his feet. A second guard went to his aid, and a dog snarled at Vincenty, who just kept on bellowing.

I watched this ludicrous scene without feeling. I was only vaguely aware that my friends were in danger—until the guard pointed his gun at Stanislaw and threatened to shoot. Then something clicked inside my head.

Despair was taking a more positive turn throughout our ranks as men slipped in the mud and guards screamed at them. Ahead, men were yelling back at the guards; dogs were snapping and snarling. Antoni turned toward me and began to run, looking beyond me. Wheeling around, I saw the NKVD guard smash Stanislaw across the back with his gun. The pilot fell on his face in the mud.

Death was near. The guards were losing control. Fear showed on their white faces, the way it had shown on ours when we first came down the hill from the camp and found the detail of guards waiting for us. From somewhere very near, I heard a voice shout in Polish: "Kill the guards! They're planning to murder us all!"

There was no guard near me, but Antoni had reached Vincenty and was wrestling with the guard's big Alsatian dog. Stanislaw had regained his footing on the track and was struggling with the second guard for possession of the machine gun. The guard beside Vincenty had released the leash on his dog, and he held his gun with both hands, the barrel tight against Vincenty's skull.

There was shouting up and down the road. I began to run through the mud, shouting at the guard not to shoot Vincenty. Again, someone screamed at us to kill the guards. There was the chatter of a machine gun behind me, then the firing of rifles. I ran harder, intent on reaching Vincenty. More shouts, angry and painful, rent the air.

Stanislaw finally wrested the machine gun from the guard on the side of the road. Kill the bastard! I thought. But the guard's dog leaped at Stanislaw, who swung toward the animal. The gun went off, and the dog tumbled in a bloody heap into the ditch.

"Kill the guard, Stanislaw," I shouted. "Now! Kill the bastard!"

The guard standing beside Vincenty turned when I shouted. I was within three meters of him and Antoni, who was wrestling on the ground with his dog. Then, nearby, I heard the sound of a machine gun. Stanislaw? I was nearly there when the guard near Vincenty swore loudly and raised his gun. I saw it jerk in his hand. Fire flashed from the muzzle.

A dull blow struck me in the left side, just below the rib cage, spinning me partly around. Incredibly, I did not fall. I kept stumbling through the mud. Stanislaw had not shot his guard; from the corner of my eye, I saw him once again fighting the guard for the gun. Antoni was strangling the dog.

Then the machine gun sounded again, and I was spun around by a blast to my right shoulder and right thigh. I seemed to drop in slow motion, watching Vincenty sitting on the muddy road, his grating voice imitating President Roosevelt's.

The pain rose in an overwhelming tide and took control; the world disappeared into blackness.

There was the clacking of train wheels, a gentle motion from side to side, and the overpowering odor of human feces. Tiny rays of light came from nowhere, but I could see nothing. Warm fluid covered my face; it oozed from above, soaking my hair and streaking down my cheeks. Heaviness lay on top of me; softness surrounded me.

In some dark recess of my mind there was a vague awareness that death had much to do with this strange, soft, fluid world. Then blackness returned.

Again the clacking of train wheels, the gentle side-to-side motion. I opened my eyes. The substance on my face was no longer liquid and warm; it was crusty. My arms were pinned, and I was on my stomach. I tried to turn my head but couldn't. My chin rested on something hard.

My mind not only explored my unknown environment but also searched for memories to explain it. Slowly, I realized that I was in a train. The soft objects around me were the dead bodies of human beings. The heaviness above was a man who had been bleeding. The hardness beneath my chin was a shoulder blade. The odor was explained by the fact that each man, after death, had evacuated his bowels.

The tiny slanting rays of light that came from nowhere were dimming. I lay in a coffin of human flesh. There was air to breathe, but that was all.

As my memory struggled to function, I remembered the

muddy road and the fight. I recalled that someone shouted at us to kill the guards. I saw Stanislaw Kaczmarek shoot a Russian dog, and I saw a guard holding a gun to Vincenty Jankowski's head. Then came red flashes and awful pain.

What had happened? What had *happened*? How long had I been in this dark place with so many dead men?

As I tried to remember, pain overwhelmed my body and clouded my mind, and I sank again into unconsciousness.

Once again there was the clacking of train wheels, a gentle motion from side to side, and the overpowering odor of human feces and rotting flesh. Light penetrated the sprawl of arms, legs, heads, and torsos.

And my mind *knew*.

Methodically, it reconstructed the fight and what must have occurred later. How many had died? How many were carried up that muddy road by tired and spiritless companions who could barely walk? What had we achieved?

There was a window somewhere to let light through. Dawn? We had traveled—how far? Nature's anesthetic had kept me in blackness. When would the blackness become permanent?

The odor of death was putrid. Rays of light flickered as the train plunged past buildings, trees, and telegraph poles. I turned my head, in spite of the hard shoulder blade, which had rubbed my chin raw.

A shudder went through my body as my eyes focused on a pair of highly polished wings and colorful ribbons. Near the ribbons was a dark blood stain. My God, it was the chest of Stanislaw Kaczmarek!

Who else was dead? And why wasn't I dead? Or *was* I dead? Kill the guards? Jesus!

The sight of Stanislaw's chest sickened me. I turned my head to the left, and a ray of light shone on a face. I didn't recognize it at first—it was covered with blood—but, gradually, the features became clear: Antoni! I almost screamed.

His right eye was gone, and a large clot of blood lay on his cheek where the blood had gushed out and dried. His mouth was not a mouth at all. In the dim light I could see lips chopped into a mass of flesh, blood, and broken teeth.

Sweet blackness came again.

Pain moved in waves through my body, and I tried to remember where I had been hit. I remembered the dull ache in my left side, and I prayed that no vital organ had been hit. My right shoulder was on fire, and I was certain that the bullet there had broken bones. It throbbed as though someone were trying to twist my arm off my body. My right leg also hurt, and I traced the pain to my upper thigh. Had I been hit in other places? Was I going to die in that stinking compartment?

Half dreaming, I thought of life, not of death and dying. A crystal image of Antoni's face appeared in the darkness. He was in his apartment with a gorgeous woman behind him. He was grinning as he urinated into a Russian snowbank. His buttocks pushed aside a board so that he could peek into the bathhouse. He was in the Club, his dark eyes and immense charm focused upon Janina Lewandowski.

My mind settled peacefully on the lovely golden hair and beautiful features of Suzan. She sat in the apartment in Grodno and gazed out at the quiet, tree-lined street. She was waiting for me, smiling. Suddenly, her hands covered her face. She was crying!

No, no, Suzan. I'm not dead! I'm coming to you. I have survived, and I'm on my way. Suzan, please don't cry over me!

A voice cut through my fantasy, and Suzan's face disappeared. It was daylight again. "God, we're coming into Smolensk," the voice cried. "What are we doing in Smolensk?"

The voice came from the next compartment. I tried to move, to inspect my surroundings, but I was trapped.

What *were* we doing in Smolensk?

It didn't matter; blackness came again.

The clacking of train wheels slowed, and the gentle motion

stopped. Brakes squealed, voices called harshly, steam hissed
—and then silence.

Muted sound filtered through to the coffin of flesh. Engines
rumbled, and voices of guards crackled in the air. It was cold in
the compartment. I tried to stop shivering, somehow knowing
that my only hope for survival lay in pretending to be dead. It
was a slim hope.

Engines rumbled louder. Doors squeaked. Guards shouted:
"Hurry! Get on the buses!"

Polish voices responded: "Why are we stopping here?"
"Where are you taking us on buses?" "We've come only a few
kilometers from Smolensk. Are we going to prison?"

Next came the shuffling of feet. I heard wooden clogs. The
footsteps continued for some minutes. Again engines rumbled,
doors slammed. There was silence for perhaps a half hour. Then
the cacophony was repeated.

It was late afternoon when the door of my compartment
squeaked open and fresh air gushed in.

"Drag the bastards out. The truck is coming."

I felt the heaviness slide from above me and strong hands grip
my boots. There was a brief argument between two guards.

"These are fine boots. They'll never be missed."

"You asshole. Do you want to be shot?"

"Only one pair of boots? They wouldn't be missed, Comrade."

"Shut up. The boots can't be taken. They're to be buried in
Katyn with boots and papers so that no trace of them is ever
found."

Katyn? Dimly, I dredged my memory for a familiar reference,
and years of study paid off. Katyn was the huge forest that
encircled Smolensk.

The hands tightened, and the pain became intense as I was
pulled roughly from the pile and dragged through the car. I
relaxed my muscles, like a drunk, even when the guard bounced
me down the steps and tossed me like a rag doll onto the ground.
The air was very cold. I "watched" with my ears as others were
dropped near me.

"Where's that fucking truck?" a growling voice complained.

"It'll come. Just one pair of boots, Piotr?"

A darkness covered my eyelids; the sun had gone down or someone was standing close. Minutes crept past, and the pain threatened to knock me out again. I prayed for unconsciousness. It would be easier to play at death.

The truck came slowly, grinding gears.

"All right, throw the swine on the back."

I counted the thuds as we were thrown onto the truck. Fourteen. Fortunately, I was one of the last, so I lay on top. The train whistled and pulled away in hissing steam.

"Do you have a cigarette, Comrade?" It was the truck driver.

"You deserve one, after this," was the reply.

Knowing that the guards would be busy lighting cigarettes, I opened my eyes. Through the slats I could see a village square. Beyond it was a yellow dirt road. I saw small homes and ugly shops with grimy signs. Beyond these was a thick forest. Dying sunlight tipped bare branches and a few budding leaves. There were no people anywhere, although chimneys belched smoke.

"Thank you, Comrade," the truck driver said, slamming the door. "I hope this is the last."

"There will be more," a guard replied. "Perhaps not for your truck, but certainly for the buses."

Another door slammed, and I knew a guard was in the cab. As the truck pulled away, it turned so that I faced the tracks and the station. In the approaching twilight I saw the faded black and white sign: GNEZDOVO.

The truck labored up a small hill and plunged into the forest. The road wound through the trees and then straightened out for a long, bumpy stretch. I closed my eyes against the swirling dust, opening them only periodically.

At last, at the base of a steep hill, the truck stopped. A metal gate was opened, and the truck rumbled through. I could dimly make out a high fence, laced with barbed wire, stretching into the forest from each side of the road. Guards with rifles slung over their shoulders closed the gate.

The truck rumbled up the hill, spitting rocks and gravel. The forest seemed unusually quiet. There was not even the call of a bird. In the cold air a most peculiar odor hung in the woods like a warning. I began to tremble, but I brought the trembling under control as we approached a large wooden lodge.

Through slitted eyelids I watched an NKVD officer approach the truck. Other guards stood on the porch. Beyond the *dacha* was a group of Polish officers. The truck slowed while the officer looked at the bodies on the rear. Then it made a right turn and dipped down a dusty road, deeper into the forest. The odor became thicker.

Turning my head to the right, I could see only trees; but when the truck, with much jostling and bumping, turned to face the lodge and stopped, I was confronted with a horrible sight.

Beside us was a huge pit, twenty meters long and ten wide. The bottom was filled with the bodies of Polish officers, all lying on their stomachs. A mass grave!

Each man was stretched full length; how many there were I could not count. Many had their hands tied behind their backs, their greatcoats pulled over their heads. The cord that tied their hands was looped around their necks and pulled extremely tight. If they had struggled just before the moment of death, the cord would have cut off their wind.

There was no way of knowing how many layers of bodies already were in the huge grave. I could see only the top layer clearly, but an occasional boot or hand protruded from the layer beneath. The officers had been placed in the grave in such a way that it would hold a maximum number of bodies. The feet of one man lay next to the head of the man beside him; this formed the pattern for each long row of bodies.

The full impact of what I saw and of what was happening in this dark forest did not strike me at first, and I regarded the grave and its silent occupants with a peculiar detachment. My body ached, and my mind was dull with the loss of blood and the horror of all that had happened to me since leaving Kozelsk.

Then a sudden realization of what I was seeing spun into my

head, nausea with it. I felt a sickening rumble in my stomach. On the verge of vomiting, I quickly remembered my position —survival truly is a strong instinct in man. Oh, God, my mind shrieked, *don't let me throw up!* The Russians think you're dead, Eugenjusz. Don't vomit! Corpses don't vomit! Hold back, take your eyes from the grave, think of something else—whatever you do, don't get sick. With a tremendous mental effort I fought down the nausea, but I still trembled violently on the back of the truck, feeling the coldness of death against my flesh.

How could this be happening? Could all the men from Kozelsk have been brought to this forest, murdered, and placed in this and other such vast graves? Were there other graves, equally as large, already covered over? The overpowering odor of rotten flesh in the air suggested that some of the men must have been in the open grave several days.

With today's complement, I realized that more than thirty-five hundred Polish officers could be in this forest, unless the Russians were sparing some or taking them elsewhere for execution. Or perhaps only those few who had tried to escape had been brought here. Perhaps the priests were here. No more than a comparative handful. But no. The massive grave itself told the story.

As I pondered the dimensions of this monstrous act, movement in the grave caught my eye. A man in peasant garb was walking *on top of* the bodies! His arms were folded, and he seemed to be waiting. Then other peasants came into view, strolling on the dead as though on a road! Their gaze shifted between the lodge and the truck.

My mind tried to slip away from the horror of what I was seeing, but suddenly the guard spoke, snapping my mind back to the terrible reality, "Ah, they're coming down again."

Peering through the slats, I saw several forms coming from the lodge: six Polish officers, each with his hands tied behind him and his greatcoat pulled over his head. Rucksacks and food parcels were gone. Two guards followed the officers.

Quietly, as though in a pantomime, the six were lined up

alongside the grave, facing it but not seeing it. The guards came up behind them, prodding and pushing.

For the second time I nearly screamed.

The guard nearest me was a grinning Sergeant Kalanin. Beside him, working diligently at this grisly task, was my friend and confidant: Pavel Borodynsky!

The memory of that next hour is a permanent part of my brain, just as the scrapings of the Ice Age are a permanent part of the earth's surface. I resisted screaming, I resisted vomiting, I resisted weeping, but I could not close my eyes or my mind to what happened.

The six Polish officers were forced to kneel beside the grave. Kalanin took a pistol from his coat pocket. At the same time Pavel Borodynsky produced a similar pistol from the folds of his long coat.

Kalanin bent over behind the first officer in line and placed the barrel of the pistol against the back of the officer's head. Without waiting he pulled the trigger. A shot resounded through the silent forest.

For an instant nothing happened. Then the officer's body slumped, and Kalanin moved on. Borodynsky, meanwhile, planted his foot in the back of the man who had been shot and kicked him into the grave.

Two of the peasants strolled over and pulled the officer across the dead bodies, dragging him by his elbows. A second shot sounded, and another officer was dead. Then he, too, was kicked into the grave by the man who had seemed so kindly, who had wanted only to be with his family in Kiev.

Like well-oiled machines, the two men moved along the line of kneeling officers, shooting them as farmers might shoot pigs. The Russian I had instantly hated and the Russian I had instantly liked and all but trusted worked side by side, efficiently, easily. They clearly had had plenty of experience.

Wanting to scream, I buried my face in the dead man beneath me and tried to force the scene away. But it was no good. The magnetic pull of horror was too powerful. Thus I watched as

Kalanin shot the last man and Borodynsky pushed the dead body into the grave. Then Kalanin exchanged his empty pistol for Borodynsky's loaded gun. Borodynsky calmly wiped the blood from Kalanin's pistol with his bare hands and reloaded it as they walked casually toward the lodge.

At once, they returned with six more men, who were lined up at the grave, forced to kneel, and shot. Six came after them, then six more. The peasants worked swiftly, cramming the now dead into small niches.

All told, I saw fifty-four of my fellow officers shot to death by Kalanin and kicked into the grave by Borodynsky. Kalanin's face revealed his enjoyment of the game. Borodynsky neither smiled nor frowned; he merely performed his job. A Soviet technician, he succeeded better than he expected. Fascinated by his cold-blooded efficiency, I myself became calm, thus preserving my secret: my life.

At last, no more Polish officers came down to the grave. The killers went up the road to the lodge. The peasants sat on the side of the grave, their feet dangling over the silent, unmoving bodies. They chatted, laughed, and smoked. One, puffing on a crooked pipe, turned toward the truck.

"Do they have more Polish pigs for us?" he asked.

"I don't know," the guard replied. "I think they're finished."

"I hope so," the man said, glancing at the dark forms in the grave. "These sons of bitches are heavy, and we're tired. We'd like to go home."

"Here comes Sergeant Kalanin," the guard said. "He's alone, so perhaps you'll get your wish."

Kalanin came into view and glanced at the truck. I closed my eyes and waited.

"Why are you resting?" Kalanin demanded. "It's dark in this damned forest. Unload the truck!"

There was a scuffling of feet as the peasants rose. I prayed that they would not notice that my body was warm. Then a second prayer: that I would be placed on top and not pinned in a coffin of flesh again. The prayers were answered. I was thrown on top of an officer who had been among the last killed. *He* was warm.

When sounds were distant, I opened my eyes slightly. In the dark I saw blood oozing from a gaping wound in a man's forehead. Strange—they had all been shot in the *back* of the head. Once again I almost vomited. The officer had been shot in the back of the head, but the bullet had come out through his forehead, shattering bone and flesh!

Then a prayer that I had not even uttered was answered as Kalanin shouted to the peasants: "Go home. It is too dark to work, and these pigs won't walk away. Cover them with dirt tomorrow."

The peasants chattered and laughed as they climbed from the grave. Once aboard the truck that had brought us, they drove off.

I lay still in the grave as the rot of old and new death oozed up through the bodies, filling my nostrils with a stench that I can never forget. Cars and trucks started in the distance and drove away. Doors slammed in the lodge. The forest became as quiet as the death that surrounded me.

A chill wind swept over the grave, rippling the hair at the back of my head. I could sense the long rows of death all around me, and I shuddered at the thought of so many dead men beneath me.

The darkness shut out the sight of the men who lay with me, head to toe, but it could not blot out the images that ravaged my mind. Again and again my mind conjured up the gruesome spectacle of the shootings; I could see Kalanin methodically putting the pistol to one head after another, Borodynsky kicking one body after another into the grave. I could see the peasants dragging the men by their elbows. I could see the bloody foreheads of men as the bullets crashed through, ripping open bones and flesh. I could see the blood running into their eyes and down along their noses to their open but silent mouths.

Finally, I felt the full force of the day's activities. I wept. The sky was dark, and *life* was dark and frightening.

In a peculiar way my mind tried to reject reality and the

thoughts of blood and killing. It searched for something pleasant. I saw Antoni's smiling face. I heard his voice, cracking jokes, as though he were right beside me in some happy place.

"I'm going to elope with Dr. Loo," his voice confided in the hollow chasm my mind had created. "We'll have a delightful honeymoon on the Riviera checking each other for hernia."

I began to laugh and knew that I was nearing hysteria. Then came the calm, firm voice of Colonel Dzierzynski: "Don't let these bastards destroy your mind. Fight them, Eugenjusz. You are strong and you can fight them."

But I wasn't strong, and I could not fight. I was only barely alive, and my mind was dying. I heard Rudolf Kochloffel warn that mental suicide is followed by physical death.

I felt the chill wind again on my neck and hands. It no longer carried any warmth from the bodies beside me; warmth was leaving with their souls. I had to do something or die there.

I raised my head carefully, slowly, and peered in the direction of the lodge. It was dark, and there was no sound except those made by crickets and an occasional bird.

I craved sleep but knew that I could not—and should not —sleep. I wanted to leave the reeking grave but was frightened to move. Had they left a guard nearby? At once I knew it was a foolish thought. Why would they guard the dead?

14: The Long Journey "Home"

T he chill of night competed with the chill of death. A creeping dampness in the forest made my flesh quiver. All warmth had left the body of the man beneath me. Pain moved inexorably through my body. How far could I go before death overtook me? Wouldn't it be better to die here with my friends? No, I had to move.

I gazed around in the darkness, then sat up. My head swam with dizziness, and I sat for a long time waiting for the dizziness to go away and—who knows?—for some inner strength and knowledge to guide me. Nothing came. I wanted only to lie back and die.

Again my mind began to slip away from reality. Like an animal wounded by a distant hunter, I instinctively felt the desire to flee, but my mind was lethargic. It threatened to overcome my animal instincts.

Then, as I sat there on one of my former comrades, wanting to be dead, the image of Suzan moved slowly into focus in my mind.

She seemed to be talking to me, as though she knew where I was and what had happened. She was telling me to flee from the grave, from the forest, before the Russians returned. The image grew in my mind until I was certain that Suzan was there with me. I looked around in the darkness, expecting to see her sitting beside me. "Leave this place, Andrei," her voice commanded. "If you care nothing for your own safety, care for me, darling. Leave for me and come to me. I am waiting for you, Andrei. I need you."

Suddenly it became urgent that I get away from the dark forest, away from death. I had to return to Suzan. I was *free*. There were no guards to stop me, only my wounds, my fatigue, and my mental lethargy.

I pushed aside my negative thoughts, and, briefly, my mind became as sharp and clear as the stars in the black sky above. The stars! Remembering the little that Colonel Dzierzynski had taught me about navigating with the stars, I sought out the North Star and began to orient myself. When we had arrived in the woods, the lightest part of the sky had been to the right of the grave, opposite the lodge. The lodge, therefore, was east and the village of Gnezdovo, where the train had stopped, probably south.

I decided, then, to head north and, when I was a safe distance from the execution site, west—toward Poland, toward Grodno and Suzan. With the decision made, I began to crawl to the edge of the grave. Just as I was about to haul myself out of the grave, I remembered my papers. The man at the railway station had said that we were to be buried with our boots and our papers so that no trace of us would ever be found.

I took the leather wallet holding my papers from my tunic pocket—leaving only the two worn, faded letters from Suzan; I couldn't part with them—and shoved it down between the bodies of two officers. If I found myself in danger of being caught, I would destroy the letters, but not until then. I needed them for strength.

The edge of the grave was only a meter above the level of the bodies. Even so, it took great effort to pull myself onto the trampled grass; and when I did get out, I had to lie on the ground for several minutes to recover my strength. Finally, however, I got up and stumbled toward the trees, going away from the lodge. At the end of the grave, I looked back at the black pit. I couldn't distinguish any of the bodies, so I merely mumbled an inept good-bye to Antoni and Leo and Stanislaw and Vincenty and Colonel Dzierzynski—and all the others —then stumbled into the black forest.

I ran into a tree and fell down. A wave of pain swept over me, and I lay for a few minutes groaning. I couldn't stop the tears from gushing from my eyes, yet my mind now was clear on one point. No matter how much pain or difficulty, I must get away and return to Suzan.

With considerable effort I got up—only to run smack into another tree in the darkness. My progress was very labored. Occasionally, I came across a clear spot and was able to see the sky. Each time the stars twinkled back, mocking this fool who had believed in freedom, but each time I found the North Star and set off northward again.

Pine and cedar boughs swept against my face, but other than curse the thick limbs and prickly needles on the trees, I could do nothing—I stretched my left hand out in front of me to ward off tree trunks; my right arm was numb and useless.

I had no idea where I was going, except north, and so was surprised when the woods parted and I found myself on the bank of a very wide river. I sat down to rest and stared at the wide water in the starlight.

I remembered that we had passed through Smolensk while I was in the compartment with my dead friends. The only major river west of Smolensk was the Dnieper. In fact, it ran through the middle of Smolensk on its long, crooked journey to the Black Sea. And this was wide enough to be the Dnieper. In any case, I had to cross the river if I were to travel north.

There were no shoals, and so I gathered strength, got up, and half scrambled, half fell down the bank into the water, which shocked me it was so cold. At least the bottom of the river was sandy, and I moved easily into the current. Then when the river became too deep, I swam slowly using my left arm, dragging my right arm, and kicking sporadically with my left leg. I drifted with the easy current, and it seemed to take an eternity to reach the other side.

On the opposite bank I lay half in the water, panting for breath, waiting for some strength to return. It came slowly, but eventually I was able to pull myself out of the water. I was across! Moreover, the coldness and the wet had served as a balm to the pain of my wounds. And with less pain to hamper me, I felt myself strong enough to move on. I got up and stumbled up the steep bank and into a forest.

As I struggled on, the strange clarity of mind that had aided me in leaving the grave and heading in what I believed was the right direction began to diminish. Several times sweet blackness enveloped me and I slept. Waking was terrible, so I tried to keep my wits sharp and fought the desire for unconsciousness. But awareness meant unbearable pain and cold.

I didn't see the fence in the darkness. I walked right into it, and the barbed wire snared my wet coat. I untangled myself and tried to climb the fence, but my hands soon were bleeding, and I collapsed into a soggy, shivering ball. Even if I could have seen the jagged barbs, I had no strength to climb. Hunger was a monster in my stomach, and I had lost considerable blood.

Sleep—or unconsciousness—came to me as I crouched at the base of the fence.

When I awoke, at dawn, fog lay under the trees. I could see no more than a few meters in any direction. Only muted bird calls pierced the fog. The chill was so total and debilitating that for several minutes I couldn't move.

The fingers of my left hand were the first to move. Blood oozed from long, shallow cuts, kept moist by the damp night. I flexed my aching fingers and moved my arms and legs. Then some primordial instinct spurred me again, and, in spite of the pain, I got up and with grim determination climbed the fence and fell to the ground on the opposite side. I landed on my wounded right side and cried out in pain. The fog muted the cry; it could hardly have been heard more than fifty meters away.

Sleep had done little to restore my strength, but at least my mind still was intent on getting away from the terrible scene near the lodge. I could see the peasants arriving in the clearing near the lodge to cover the bodies of my fellow officers. I shuddered and walked in what I hoped was a northerly direction. The fence, according to my calculations, ran east and west, so I walked directly away from it.

After an hour the mist lifted, and I could see the brightness of the rising sun on my right. I was indeed heading north. Later in the day I turned away from the sun, heading west. Often I fell, breaking the impact, usually, on the wet leaves and rotting branches. Dizziness swept over me, and I knew that I soon would collapse from loss of blood and hunger. Once I lay on my back on the wet forest floor, waiting for death, expecting it. For several terrible minutes I lay still, believing that it was all up. I was too weak to move.

My situation was hopeless. Minimally, I could not have traveled ten kilometers from the gravesite and thus was not out of danger of being picked up. Even if I managed to get going again, I had no idea where I was or how far I had to travel—or in what direction—to reach a farm or a village where I might get food. Of course I would have to steal everything I wanted.

The hopelessness of my position was not lost on me. But simply lying there gave me what I needed to continue: rest. And with rest came determination to reach Grodno, Suzan. With that in mind, my wounds and the distance to Grodno no longer mattered. I was going to get there—as soon as I had enough strength. And to get there I needed dry clothes, a place to sleep, and food—any kind of food.

My mind wandered to Camp Kozelsk, and even the bad times there seemed good to me as I lay, cold and hungry and in pain, on the forest floor. The shabby barracks, the rancid soup, the lies, the propaganda, and the mental and physical abuse did not appear so bad after all—certainly not as cruel as the comfortless forest. I remembered the guards and how well they had treated us in the final days of our captivity. I remembered Pavel Borodynsky and how I had spent hours talking with him on guard duty, eating chocolates and pastries I had bought from the camp store.

Pavel Borodynsky!

My God, could that be the answer? I had been accustomed to carry around a few treats for him somewhere in the deep pockets of my greatcoat or in my tunic. I had lost so much weight that my uniform and coat hung loosely on me. It was possible for me to carry around a grapefruit and not know that I had it on me. Perhaps—just perhaps—some small tidbit was hidden away in a loose pocket.

Groping about in the deep pocket of my greatcoat I brought out a soggy bar of chocolate—bought, I recalled with a guilty smile, against the advice of Dr. Kochloffel. I then searched through the pocket of my ill-fitting tunic. Excitement surged through me as my fingers touched the smooth, cold metal of a small can. I brought it out: a can of herring that I had bought on the camp store's final visit, using some of the small store of money I had not put into the barracks pot.

The irony of the situation amused me, even in my condition. I had kept money back to buy treats for a man who had nearly been one of my killers. And that very act, it seemed, was to save my life—at least for the time being.

I ate the candy ravenously, licking the wrinkled paper clean. There was no key to open the can of herring; we had always opened them with penknives. Scrambling around on the ground, however, I found a rock and smashed it onto the can. The rich food and oil burst out of the can and onto the soggy leaves. I snatched up the whole mess, licking the leaves for the oil, then snaked my tongue around the inside of the broken can to get the last drop of nourishment.

I was still hungry, but the chocolate and fish gave me renewed strength. More than that, they gave me renewed *hope*. I struggled to my feet and looked up at the rays of the sun slanting through the trees. Putting the sun behind me, I limped on through the forest, hoping to find a village—and hoping not to. A village could mean help if I were clever, or it could mean captivity and possible death.

As the sun rose higher, my uniform began to dry. Feeling warmer and therefore better, I pressed on. Suddenly the forest seemed to evaporate, and I found myself at the edge of a small, freshly plowed field. In the center a farmer worked slowly with a plow and an old horse. I watched from the trees until he was at the far end of the field. Then I circled the field until I found a path that I figured would lead to the house. I crept slowly along. In the center of another clearing was a white farmhouse and, beyond it, a huge, unpainted barn. My heart was beating rapidly from a mixture of excitement and fear as I circled this larger clearing to come up to the barn from behind. There was no one outside, but I could not take a chance. In all likelihood the farmer's wife was inside and would see me if I tried to cross the clearing to the barn.

Behind the barn was a small corral in which there was a lone cow trying to eat grass on the other side of the fence. Using the cow for cover, I slid under the fence and wriggled across the ground to the barn.

Inside, the barn was warm from the heat of the spring sun. I waited until my eyes grew accustomed to the dusky light. I took a quick drink from a pail of water near an empty stall; then I saw a ladder leading to the loft, where the thick hay lay invitingly in a huge heap almost to the peaked roof. The barn had a comfortable feeling, comfortable odors. It would be warm, dry, and safe up there, a perfect place to try to treat my wounds. Clearly no vital organs had been hit by the bullet in my side, or I never would have made it this far. And the bullet in my thigh had not broken any bones, or I could not have walked. But I had to clean the wounds somehow.

The loft was a chance, but the ladder was long and high. The alternative was almost certain discovery. So somehow I made it, holding the pail of water in my numb right hand. I took off my greatcoat and draped it across a barrel. My boots I took off, stuffed with hay, and set aside to dry. My trouser leg was stuck to the thigh wound by dried blood, so I splashed water on the leg to loosen it and slipped off my pants. There were two wounds, one in front and one at the outer rear of my leg, in the fleshy part. The bullet had passed completely through my leg, leaving a clean wound. It was already beginning to heal.

Getting out of my tunic involved even more difficulty. Not only had the cloth stuck to the wounds in my side and shoulder, but also I could barely use my right arm to slide the tunic from my shoulders after I had unbuttoned it.

There were two more wounds in the fleshy part of my side. But the bullets had passed completely through my body, and the wounds were clear of infection. My shoulder was another matter. The bullet had struck just beneath the collarbone and lodged somewhere in the joint. The bones had to be chipped or broken, and infection would inevitably set in—if it had not already—if the bullet was not removed.

When I had taken everything off, I washed myself completely and lay back naked in the warm loft while my uniform dried on the ladder. The prickly ends of cut alfalfa jabbed my tender skin. In a few moments I began to feel drowsy, but I fought off sleep. It would be far too dangerous to fall asleep in the barn in the middle of the afternoon. The farmer might come in from the field, or his wife might come out from the house. Perhaps they would get feed from the loft.

Worry about discovery moved me to action. I put my uniform back on, even though it was still slightly damp. Then, as I slipped on my boots, I heard sounds at the back door. Someone was trying to open it! I could hear the latch clink as someone worked at trying to lift it. I held the ladder and leaned over to see who was at the door—then almost burst out laughing.

The cow from the corral had stuck its head through the open

top part of the doorway and was pushing its soft nose against the inside latch trying to open it. I covered the wet spots in the hay with dry hay, took the pail, and climbed laboriously down the ladder. I thought of shooing the cow away, but a much better thought came to me. I was hungry, and the cow meant food. I looked around the barn and saw a wooden bin. I lifted the lid and found, as I suspected, that the bin was full of rich, dry oats. I took a handful of oats and went to the door.

"Come on, cow," I whispered. "Come in for some oats."

The cow backed away at first, then sniffed the oats in my outstretched hand. I opened the door and stepped back. The cow followed me as I led it into a stall. Then I poured some oats into the feed box.

While the cow munched contentedly on the oats, I lay on the floor under it and milked the warm teats, squirting the precious liquid directly into my mouth. Finally, my stomach distended, I felt much better.

The cow was still eating the oats, and since I didn't want to push it out until all the evidence had been eaten, I used the time to rummage around the barn. I had already concluded that I should get rid of my uniform. Soon, I knew, I would be out of the forest and the danger of being seen would be magnified. Thus I became very excited when I discovered an old smock and a pair of baggy trousers hanging from a peg. I rolled them up and tucked them under my arm.

Before leaving, I shooed the cow outside and latched the door again. The farmer might not miss the old clothing, and since they were practically worthless, he might not care even if he *did* notice their absence. However, if I left the cow inside, his suspicions would grow and he might go to the provincial police. I had enough problems without having to worry about them.

On the morning after leaving the barn, I conducted what was to me a sad ceremony.

In the dawn light, before the sun had burned away the mist, I built a fire in a ravine. I took off my uniform and threw it into the fire. Next came my precious boots. Finally, I unfolded the two letters from Suzan, read them a last time, and burned them. When all traces of my identity were gone, I put on the oversized trousers and smock I had stolen, waited until the fire had burned to a smoldering heap, then covered the ashes with dirt and wet leaves to conceal any sign that a fire had been there, and set off again in my bare feet.

For the next several days I traveled slowly. My body was stiff, and I spent many hours each day searching for food. I slept in ravines, under jutting rocks, in barns—once in a small cave. I found wild strawberries and mushrooms in the undergrowth; in barns I chewed on oats and wheat, letting the juices flow down my throat but spitting out the indigestible pulp.

The trek through the forest was a wild mixture of reality and fantasy. Reality came with the pain and the hunger, with the stiffness of muscles, with the bleeding of my feet as I stumbled through briars, stepped on jagged stones, and tripped over fallen branches. To escape pain and hunger, to escape reality, my mind sought fantasy. I found it surprisingly easy to slip into a fantasy world, and I learned to turn it on at will. I didn't realize it then, but the ease with which my mind absorbed and welcomed fantasy to escape reality was one of the first concrete signs I exhibited that I was losing my mind.

The ordeal of Kozelsk had done more damage than I realized. The horror of the executions and the grave in the forest had moved me dangerously close to insanity. The long, arduous flight through the forest was adding to the damage.

One day I found a pair of old boots in a barn and put them on my sore, bleeding feet. The boots hurt, of course, but I called on my fantasy world to bring me relief from the pain. Suddenly, Suzan was with me in the dark old barn, and I could hear lovely music. I began to dance with Suzan—around and around the hard clay floor of the barn, feeling no pain.

A fleeting thought told me that I was going crazy. I didn't care. It was good being crazy. As I danced with Suzan, holding her small waist tightly, as I swung her around to the tempo of a waltz, the old barn became a glittering ballroom in Poznan. The waltz music grew in volume in my brain, and the scene shifted to the high school gymnasium, decorated for a special student event. Handsome young men came up to ask to dance with Suzan. I swirled into the crowd and danced with pretty student girls. The music grew louder and boomed through my brain—until I collapsed from fatigue and the old barn returned, surrounding me with darkness, fear, and pain. Especially pain, which worked up through my legs and spread like a cancer through my body. Then voices and laughter came back to me. Antoni Urban and Stanislaw Kaczmarek were joking. "Did you hear about the Russian soldier who stayed up all night to study for a blood test?" Laughter again, raucous, beautiful. I matched it with maniacal guffaws. The stern, sober voice of Colonel Dzierzynski: "Tomorrow night we'll get the ladder from the barracks loft and go over the wall. We'll fly to freedom, away from these bastards." The others came into the barn and discussed escape. Leo Bednarek told us that he was going because he hated all the fucking Communists. Josef Konopka, his dark eyes twinkling merrily, worried about how fast the Russian planes would fly and compared them with the slowness of the railroads. Through all the voices came the steady, deep-throated chuckle of men in the Club. My flesh quivered in anticipation of the planned escape.

One fantasy disappeared as quickly as it had come, and I suffered a few moments of severe pain before I was swept into another. Or perhaps the fantasies were the product of fever. I slept a great deal during the flight from the forest, so perhaps they were dreams. Mostly, though, I was convinced during my lucid moments that the fantasies were indications that I was going mad.

If I was, my madness was still intermittent. I recovered in the barn and pressed on, finally, days—weeks?—later, coming out of the thick forest and seeing rolling fields and farmhouses stretching far into the distance. Near the treeline was a white, tidy farmhouse and a huge barn. White plank fences surrounded the farmhouse, the barn, and a large pasture where horses and cows grazed in the new grass.

A setting sun glinted across the fields and tidy farms. I stood leaning against a tree and watched the neat farm. There are people in that house, I thought; there are human beings there. I, too, am a human being, although I have lived like a wild animal for days. During my flight from the grave, I had carefully avoided houses and had entered barns only at night. Now, I knew that I needed the help of other human beings if I was to survive.

So, all fear of capture and possible death dissipating in my mind, I walked across a field, climbed the white fence, and went directly up to the porch of the house. I knocked firmly with my left hand and waited. The door opened only a crack.

"Yes, what is it?"

An old man stood in the doorway peering out at me. Seeing only a tottering wreck, he opened the door a bit more. I saw a squat, moon-faced woman standing behind him.

"I am a human being," I said simply. "I'm hurt and I'm starving. I need help."

The woman looked at me suspiciously. Blood from my wounds had soaked through the coarse clothing, and my hair was matted with dirt. My beard was scraggly, and bits of dirt and hay clung to me. I must have looked much like an old scarecrow left too long in the field.

"Please. If you don't help me, I will die."

They argued for an eternity. The man wanted to help; the woman was cautious; but nature was on my side. I tumbled forward into the house. Sweet blackness came to my rescue.

I awoke on a sofa. The woman had a pan of hot water and a sheet. She tore bandages while the old man pulled the smock from my filthy, stinking body. Slowly, the old woman bathed, salved, and bandaged my wounds. She brought me a wooden bowl of hot soup, and I ate it, knowing only that it was very good. I tried to eat the black bread, but my throat rejected it.

"You can sleep in the loft," the woman said as she took away the empty bowl and the bread. "Our son slept there before he got married. Sleep tonight. You must go tomorrow."

I nodded. I could tell by their eyes that they were afraid of me and of having me found in their home, but the old couple helped me up the steep stairs to the loft. The dim light of evening came softly through a small window. The woman turned down a wide bed, and I fell into it.

In spite of my fatigue I slept uneasily, or perhaps I slept uneasily *because* I was so tired. In any case, I awoke at the slightest sound. Thus when the old couple went to bed, possibly an hour later, I awoke and heard the sounds of their nightly preparations below. I heard their voices but could not distinguish their words.

In the middle of the night I was awakened by a squeaking door. The days in the forest had trained my mind well; as soon as I awoke, I was clear of mind, without the usual drowsiness that affects a person just awakening. A horse neighed softly. Next came the jangle of metal and a slapping sound. Someone was putting a saddle on a horse; I had heard that sound too many times during my days in the cavalry to be mistaken.

Quietly, I slipped out of the bed and leaned over the loft railing. There was a lamp burning in the old couple's bedroom, and I could see the bed, empty, with the covers turned down. The old couple were not in the house. Moonlight shone through the windows, and I could see the furniture standing in the parlor. Then I saw that the front door was ajar.

I reached for my old boots and clothes and began to slip them on. Something was going on, and nothing that went on could work to my favor. As I stood up with both boots on, the resonant clatter of horse hooves rang out below the window. The old man, alone, was riding across the yard and down a lane toward a white plank gate. He could only be going for the police!

With infinite care I opened the small window and slipped out onto a slanting roof over the porch. As I closed the window, I heard the old woman come into the house. Stealthily, I moved down the roof, slid down a post to the ground, and limped into the night, hating the old couple for their duplicity yet forgiving them because I knew what fear of the NKVD could do to people.

Several kilometers from the farm I found a barn and climbed far back into a cozy loft. Covering myself with hay, I fell into a deep sleep and did not awaken until late the following afternoon. I had to stay hidden in the loft until dark before renewing my long journey toward home.

As I moved through the alien land that evening, I seemed to gather strength. Although the moments of fantasy became less common, I experienced another phenomenon. I began to have complete lapses of memory, which would last anywhere from a few seconds to several minutes.

Once, when I was walking along through a moonlit night, crossing fields and avoiding houses, villages, and roads, I noticed a great oak tree perhaps fifty meters ahead. Suddenly, the tree was not there. I looked around and saw the tree thirty meters behind me.

I didn't remember having passed it! For those few seconds my mind had blanked out. I stood there in the field and stared back at the tree. How had I gone past it without knowing it? Why hadn't I run into the tree? Suppose it had been a cliff or a deep ditch or a river—would my mind have left me to such danger? If it had been a cliff, would I have walked over it?

The lapses of mind came infrequently, but the danger of them plagued me. They became almost as worrisome as my fatigue, my hunger, and my pain.

Hunger was perhaps the greatest of these worries. I foraged for food in barns, in gardens, and in small woods. The pickings were lean. The spring gardens had tiny green onions, strawberries, and rhubarb. Often the taste of the foods I ate left much to be desired, but at least I survived.

One night, outside a barn, my nostrils caught the scent of meat. I rummaged in the dark barn and literally followed my nose to the door of a smokehouse.

The smokehouse was a godsend. I chewed on salted beef and swallowed the juices until my throat could take the heavy meat. Then I gorged myself so much that I vomited. Finally, I tore off strips from the hanging meat and stuffed them in an old oat sack. I knew the farmer would miss the meat, possibly even report it to the authorities, but my hunger overcame my fear of discovery.

For the next few weeks I moved across rural Russia, walking

only a few kilometers a day, sleeping in barns, patches of woods, and haystacks wet from a winter's exposure—and once in an abandoned railway depot on the edge of a village. I stole food wherever I could, entering small villages at night and breaking into shops. The wounds in my leg and side scabbed over, only to be broken open by the strain of walking. The shoulder wound continuously oozed a yellowish fluid, which soaked the old smock—only to have the sun dry it and make it stick to my shoulder.

I crossed many cold rivers and creeks. Usually I had to swim them because the bridges were located in villages—and I didn't dare go into the villages except at night.

The lapses of memory came more frequently, often involving great danger. Once, on a sunny afternoon, I approached a village intending to swing wide around it. Then my mind went blank. When I regained awareness, I was limping innocently down the village's main street. Panic nearly took hold, but I could not run back. I walked on, ignoring the few peasants and shopkeepers who stood watching me curiously.

I was never aware of actually crossing the border into Poland. However, one day, at dusk—I had been traveling slowly since noon—I heard voices ahead of me in the road. I stopped to listen.

My God, I thought, they're speaking Polish!

A feeling of great warmth, even of triumph, flooded over me as I listened to the familiar language. I was on a small, tree-lined country road and could not see the talkers. Then, rounding a gentle curve, I saw them at the gate of a farmhouse. One was in the yard, the other in the road. I ran toward them shouting: "Am I in Poland? Am I in Poland?"

The men turned, and I saw fear in their eyes. I babbled in Polish, telling about the grave and the murders, and I must have looked like a creature from a horror tale. They responded the way most men would respond to such an apparition. The farmer ran into the house and bolted the door. His friend dashed across the road and disappeared into a field.

But I *knew*! I was in *Poland*! I fell on my face and kissed the dirt.

There was no difference in the land, only a vast difference in my feeling toward it. Even so, the Russians had occupied eastern Poland and I remained in danger of capture. Thus I was afraid to stop at a farmhouse for help or to ask questions. My presence could jeopardize the safety of Polish families who helped me, and there was always the possibility that they would be Polish Russians, in sympathy with the Soviet occupation forces.

I spent the night in a barn farther along the narrow road and moved on in the morning. The stars had helped me to reach this point, but now I needed something more specific to find Grodno. Two days later I received the help I needed. I came to an intersection where a sign was posted: Grodno, 20 kilometers.

Incredibly, I was on the right road. I felt like yelping and leaping about, but I merely plodded, scanning the horizon of the undulating country for a sign of the city. Fatigue overtook me, however, and I slept in a haystack, only to awaken before dawn to hurry on.

I had no food, and I was in too much of a hurry to stop and steal it. Stealing food involved a lot of trouble. I had to watch a village or a farmhouse for hours, then wait for darkness to cover my movements. Even then, I couldn't be certain that I would find food once I broke in.

Finally, on the fourth day after first hearing Polish voices, I came to the rise where the Russian army had stood and looked down on the sprawling farms east of Grodno. I had been in the area only once, but I recognized it at once. Even in the dusk, I could see the farm where General Wilczynski had been shot to death.

In that moment, standing on the rise where Russian troops had stood so many months ago, I felt a mixture of love and hate. I wanted to rush on into the city to my beloved Suzan, but my hatred for the old farm couple who had been so disdainful of the Poles and so ingratiating to the Russians was growing to monstrous proportions.

The events of that day in September came to me clearly as I stood looking down at the farmhouse. I did not really blame the old couple for General Wilczynski's death, but the farmer and his wife were inextricably connected with everything that had happened to me during the past eight months. My mind needed someone or something to blame, something to avenge myself on, for all the ignominies, cruelty, hunger, and pain that I had experienced at the hands of the Russians.

And the old couple *were* Russians, even though they had been born in Poland. They were Russians in looks, in temperament, and in sympathies. They had been gracious to the Russian invaders and rude to their countrymen on that September day. They had shown open pleasure at the brutal murder of the general.

However, as I walked down the hill, passed the red barn, and came to the well where we had drunk water on that hot day, I did not know what I was going to do.

"Good evening," I said pleasantly when the old man opened the door and peered at me. The aroma of cooking food wafted out, and I felt dizzy. "I'm a major in the Polish Army Reserves. I need . . . "

The old man tried to slam the door, but I shoved the door open, lurched inside, and slammed the door behind me. I looked terrible, and the old man seemed to wither.

"What is it? What's going on here?" It was the sharp, biting voice of his wife. She came in from the kitchen and stared at me. Her expression seemed haughty and disdainful, as it had on that day in September.

The old man spoke to her in Russian, supposing that I wouldn't understand: "He's a pig of a Polish officer."

"Get out!" the woman shouted in Polish. "You're not wanted!"

I responded in Russian: "Ah, but you make the Soviets welcome."

The old man took a step backward. But the woman, obviously the more aggressive of the two, turned on me again. "I told you to get out," she snarled. "If you don't, we will see that the Russians make a special welcome for you."

"You are Polish," I said, holding back the rage that was growing in me, trying to avoid doing what it commanded me to do. "I am Polish, and I need help. I need food and clothing. I'm going to Grodno and . . . "

"Go!" the old woman screeched. "Get the hell out of here!"

"Yes," the old man echoed, gaining courage from his wife. "Go away!"

I felt my fingers flexing. The fingers of my right hand, which had been weak and almost useless during my long journey, were surprisingly strong. The adrenalin of hatred, which had poured through my muscles the night I had attacked Kalanin, was flowing again. Hunger and fear left me; I felt strong and full of hate. And yet I tried to hold back my rage.

"Please, just give me some food and a decent set of clothes. I must go to Grodno, and I have no papers. They ask for papers, don't they? They must. Please. Only food and clothing and perhaps a ride into the city on your hay wagon. It's not so much to . . . "

They drowned me out with their yelling and screaming. The old woman rushed to the kitchen and returned with a broom. She waved it close and screamed at me. "I'll beat you unless you go! Get out of our house!"

"You idiots!" I screamed back. "I'm Polish! I need help! I don't want to hurt you!" And yet, I did want to hurt them. I wanted to kick them, to beat them, to submit them to all the cruelties to which I had been submitted during my captivity. I wanted revenge for those humiliations and for the deaths of my friends.

The old woman whacked me on the left shoulder with the broom, and rage, pure, insane rage, took control, the same brand of insanity that had overcome me when Kalanin had attacked Colonel Dzierzynski. With a roar that I hardly realized came from me, I leaped upon the old man, who had moved close to me with his borrowed courage.

I seized him by the throat and began to squeeze. Pain jolted my right shoulder, but I welcomed the pain. It made the task of murder more justifiable—I was repaying this man for my pain.

The broom rose and fell on my back, and the old woman's

hoarse screams rattled against my eardrums. I hardly felt the blows from the broomstick, and the screams heightened my rage and excitement. I felt exhilarated as my fingers pressed more deeply into the old man's throat, glorying in the sight of his bulging eyes and open mouth.

Finally, the old man slumped to the ground. His eyes rolled back into his head, and then the fat lids closed. His mouth was open, and his tongue, stilled and thick, lolled over his lips. I let him go and turned to the woman.

"God! God! God!" The woman screamed, as though she were calling for help. The broom now was idle in her hands, and her face was a portrait of terror. I caught her in the kitchen doorway and whirled her around. She was still shouting "No, no, no!" as my fingers closed on her throat.

The broom clattered to the floor, and the woman's eyes pleaded with me to stop. Her pudgy hands gripped my arms, but I hardly felt them. Her mouth flew open, and she made low gagging sounds deep in her throat. I choked her harder, feeling exhilarated anew. Toward the end, a kind of cool detachment came over me, and the woman became an impersonal object—I might as well have been choking her broom.

My God, I wondered later, was this how Pavel Borodynsky had felt as he kicked dead Polish officers into the grave? Were they nothing more to him than a stone he might kick out of his path? Had he felt no remorse, no sorrow for the human lives he was helping to take?

I tried to rationalize my lack of feelings. The killing of the old couple, I told myself, was a kind of vicarious execution of everyone who had harmed me, payment for the war that had destroyed Poland. But the insanity was still a part of me. I smelled the food, and it removed all feelings of remorse. Coldly, methodically, I dumped the old man's body behind a chair and dropped the old woman on a couch in a dark corner. Then, with a gesture quite out of keeping with my feelings, I folded her arms across her chest.

As I turned from the dead bodies, I felt a sudden shudder of revulsion. But again the aroma of food aroused me, and I went into the kitchen. The old woman had prepared a stew with beef, potatoes, carrots, and onions; and I fell upon it ravenously, ladling down spoonfuls of the burning mixture, gulping from a pitcher of cold milk that stood on the table. Fortunately I didn't throw it all up. At last, exhaustion overcame me. My strength was sapped, and my right shoulder felt as though someone was squeezing it in a vise. Somehow remembering to extinguish the lamp, I fell into the bed, thoroughly spent.

When I awoke, I knew instantly that the bodies of the old couple lay in the parlor, only a few feet away. I tried to steel my emotions against them, to feel the same hatred that I had felt the night before. But I could not. My mind was clear and sharp and, at last, full of remorse.

Of course, it did not matter any longer. I did what I knew I must do. I rummaged through the house and found the old man's papers. Next I took a drab suit from the clothes press. Even when I let down the wide cuffs of the trousers, they were not long enough, but the suit would make me look more respectable than the filthy, bloodsoaked garments I was wearing.

Finally, I tore up the sheet on the bed and made bandages. I carefully washed myself in the kitchen, and, using a black salve I found in a cupboard, I dressed my wounds, which had partially opened during my fury of the night before. I put on a set of the old man's underwear, a shirt, the suit, and a pair of boots—luckily, close to my size. I ate the rest of the stew—now cold—and left the house.

There was no house near the farm, and I vaguely hoped that the bodies would not be discovered for some time. But my mind was mostly occupied with the problem of getting into the city without being arrested. The Russians were certain to have guards at the main roads leading into Grodno, and I would have to stop and show some papers—the old farmer's papers.

Fortunately, I now looked nearly as old as the farmer, and I hoped that my scraggly beard would help to conceal any facial differences. In any case, there was nothing to be done, having come so far—I must go on.

I circled the village where I had been held prisoner in the town hall and found the main road leading to Grodno, Krasinski Boulevard. At the city limits I encountered the guardhouse I had expected. My heart was going berserk. Trying not to trip, I walked up to the guard on duty and handed him the farmer's papers. The guard took the papers, opened them, and glanced up at me.

"Stefan Lazinsky. That your name?" He spoke in Polish.

"Yes," I replied in Polish. "Stefan Lazinsky."

"D'you speak Russian?" he asked, pointing to the line which indicated that Lazinsky's parents were from Russia.

"I try to speak it as well as possible," I replied—in Russian.

The guard smiled and gave me back the farmer's papers. "And you succeed, Comrade. Enjoy your day in the city."

I thanked him and went on down the familiar boulevard. The buildings had not changed much since my departure in the autumn. They seemed shabbier, but perhaps that was because there was virtually no traffic on the boulevard, no people out in the yards or on the side streets. In fact, thousands of people from Grodno had been taken to Siberia. Many of those who remained were old and frightened, or they were tradesmen and officials who had agreed to work for and with the Soviet occupation forces. And the children. The Soviets were training the children in special schools around the city—and all around the country —to teach them the concepts of communism.

This sort of detail I was to learn much later, but on that sunny day I felt only a mounting and single-minded excitement. Soon I would be with Suzan! I had not given much thought about how we would escape from Grodno, but I suspected that we would be able to sneak out of the city at night. The Russians had guards only at the major roads, so we could travel on a secondary road until we were clear of the city. I had decided during my long journey from the grave that we would have to try to wait out the war in Rumania.

Our street had not changed. There were the same apartment buildings, the same shady trees, now full of new leaves. There was rubble from the shelling, but it was the rubble I had seen before I left—it had come from the initial attack by the Germans. The Russian assault on Grodno apparently had not touched our quiet suburban street.

When I came to our building, I was exultant. I glanced up at the windows, hoping that Suzan would not look out and see me. I wanted to surprise her at the door. I had conveniently forgotten the sadness and despair in her last letter to me; in my mind she was well and happy, waiting only for me to come home. I could see her sitting in a chair in our small parlor, her hands folded neatly in her lap, waiting patiently for her Andrei.

I turned up the walk and gazed happily at the familiar entrance. Momentarily, I was depressed at the thought that next door Antoni Urban also spent his last free hours—and now he was gone forever. But the thought passed. I was not dead. I *had* come home, as I had promised.

I climbed the stairs slowly, savoring the magic of familiar surroundings. Suzan had climbed these stairs every day since I had been away. I could almost see her gliding down the steps to go to the market or perhaps to a job in the city. I could almost hear her soft footsteps. I stopped and leaned down to touch a step; perhaps Suzan's foot had been there.

At the door of our apartment I paused and straightened the farmer's clothes on my sparse frame, like a schoolboy calling for his first date. My knees began to tremble. I wished that I had shaved; perhaps Suzan would not even recognize me, perhaps I would frighten her. I had lost considerable weight and grown considerably older. But my eyes had not changed. I would tell her with my eyes that I was still her husband.

I knocked softly and waited, controlling my quivering knees by leaning against the door frame. It was about ten o'clock, so I guessed that she might still be sleeping. I knocked again. My heart began to beat erratically, and my face flushed.

The door opened—but instead of the image of Suzan I had conjured, I faced a well-fed, well-manicured man in a green silk robe. He was pudgy, and his face was bright and clean, as though he had just shaved. The odor of cologne and soap filled the corridor. I glanced at the door number. Had I come to the wrong apartment? It was our number. Or had I forgotten it?

"Yes, what is it?" the man asked in Polish.

He ran his smooth nails over his robe and stared at me as though I should be arrested for daring to enter such an apartment building. I glanced down at my short, baggy suit and felt self-conscious.

"I'm sorry," I blurted. "I wanted the Komorowski apartment. Perhaps it's the next one."

He raised his head so that he could look down his short nose at me. "The Skymanskis live there. Who're you looking for?"

"Komorowski," I repeated. "I've been away, and I'm looking for . . ."

Grinning, he snorted derisively, "Oh, you must mean the crazy woman."

"I beg your pardon."

He laughed outright. "If you're looking for that blonde woman, the Russian whore . . ."

"Where is Suzan?" I demanded, pushing into the apartment. I reached the window where I had sat smoking the night the Russian lieutenant came for me. The man's eyes were large, round, and frightened; his haughty look was gone. I must have looked and acted like a maniac.

"Who are you?" he asked, his voice shaky.

"Where is Suzan?"

"Look here," he said, coming toward me. "You must leave. Are you from the Underground?"

"No."

"My God, the military! Please, you *must* leave. I do good business with the Russians, and it would ruin everything if they found you here. My God, suppose they saw you come in. Please, you . . ."

"You bastard," I snarled. "I don't give a fuck about your business with the Russians. Where is the woman who lives here?"

Sensing he personally had nothing much to fear, he became more composed. Then, taking a cigarette from a silver box on an expensive table, he said, almost casually, "If you're talking about the crazy woman, she doesn't live here."

"A pretty woman, with golden hair?"

He laughed. "She's your whore, too, eh? Well, sir, you're wasting your time. The Russians arrested her. She fought them, and they shot her. That whore . . . "

I was on him, roaring with rage and the lust to kill. My fingers sank into his soft neck, and his round eyes expanded. Gurgling sounds came from his throat, and the unlit cigarette fell to the carpet. I kept shouting at him, trying to make him tell me that he was lying about Suzan.

"My God, what are you doing?" a woman's voice screamed from behind. A fat woman in a thin nightgown stood in the bedroom door. Her hair was bleached, and her face was blotched from sleep.

My hands slipped away from the fat neck. Amid her screams, I ran from the apartment and stumbled down the stairs. Doors opened, then slammed, the occupants too frightened to become involved.

I ran as fast as I could, crying Suzan's name, my wounds screaming in protest. Finally, exhausted, I stumbled into a gutted building and crawled through the rubble to the cellar. In a dark corner I hunched down and cried. I had no spirit to go on.

Suzan was dead, a crazy woman shot for fighting the Russians. A crazy woman! That was how she was remembered. The delicate flower that was my soul, my reason for existing, the woman I had come through the hell of Russia to be with—she was gone without a trace. Only those words: The crazy woman.

Desperately, as if my life depended upon it—my reason probably did—I tried to figure out what must have happened to her. What had the fat man in the green silk robe meant when he called her a Russian whore? Had soldiers raped her? For that, had her own people branded her a whore? And who had shot her? Russian soldiers? No, he said "they" had arrested her, so they must have been guards, sent there to arrest her. Why? What was she doing that they would send someone to arrest her?

My God, my mind cried, why did it happen? What a terrible irony that I, who was scheduled to be executed, should survive while Suzan, left behind in Grodno to live, was killed!

At first I refused to accept the fact of her death, and I thought of going back to the apartment to beg the fat man for an explanation. But slowly the full realization of her death came to me; it was final. The man had recognized the name. There was no mistake. If I pursued the matter, they would get me also. Somewhere in Grodno, Suzan lay in a lonely grave, her voice stilled forever, her smile fixed in death, her delight for all the world's good things crushed into oblivion.

But with the realization and acceptance of her death, there was no reason for me to live anymore. I cowered in the corner of the ruined basement and cried silently. I hoped that death would erase the terrible, gnawing grief that washed over me.

15: In the Land of Babel

SLEEP came fitfully, in brief, horrifying snatches, bringing nightmares and a grotesque parade of my recent life.

Colonel Dzierzynski marched with a jagged, bloody hole in his forehead. In his hand was the severed arm of an NKVD guard, and I knew, as one knows in dreams, that he had torn it from Kalanin at the moment of his own death.

Next came Leo Bednarek, his massive arms withered. He tried to smile, but his mouth was a black hole from which snakes and lizards crawled.

Antoni entered with a clot of blood for an eye and a running sore for a mouth. This monstrous apparition cracked: "Jesus Christ, all I wanted was a checkup for hernia!" His left eye glittered mischievously.

Vincenty Jankowski appeared. His frail body danced foolishly while his head bobbled like the head of a broken doll. After him came Rudolf Kochloffel, who had no eyes—merely sockets from which blood oozed incessantly. Stanislaw Kaczmarek's blond hair was crimson from his own blood, his face a death's head. There was Henryk Jagiello and Hugo Mijakowski and Josef Konopka, all of them bursting pyrotechnically, spraying flesh and blood everywhere.

And I marched in the dream. My uniform, soaked in blood, hung in tatters from my limping body, and I trailed skulls behind me. They fell from my pockets like seeds from a planter's hand.

Suzan ran toward our grisly ranks, her golden hair bleached to an ugly bluish white and her delicate features turned to prune-like wrinkles. She cackled like a shrew, and yellow fluid poured from her mouth, eyes, nose, and ears. Her face and head became lovely again, but only for an instant. A huge gun went off, and the shell tore her head from her shoulders and sent it flying into my waiting hands.

I caught the bloody head and woke up screaming!

All my good fortunes came from the dead! The phrase rushed through my mind and tormented my soul. I regretted ever thinking it. In the darkness of the bombed cellar my mind rephrased it: All I touch is death, and everything I touch dies.

Time stopped.

Later, much later, but perhaps only at dawn of the second day after entering the basement, I started to come to myself again, prodded by physical need, so often the thing that brought me back to reality. I had no conscious will to live, but a subconscious will to live could not be suppressed. I was *hungry*, really hungry.

So in the early morning I climbed out of the shattered basement into the quiet street. Finding my way back to my old haunts was easy; and once I was there, I remembered that a small grocer's was located on a corner two blocks from my apartment building. Circling to the back of the store, I broke a window and entered. I filled my pockets with food and snatched up smoked meats, which I immediately stuffed into my mouth, as I stumbled around the store in the half-light.

I left the store with every intention of going back to the

basement, but the sound of an approaching motor sent me to cover. I really was alive—I had my wits about me. I lay behind a fence and watched as a Russian military vehicle went past. In the back seat were two soldiers with machine guns. They hung out the windows, scanning the street and sidewalks. I was convinced that they were looking for me.

When the vehicle was gone, I lay on the ground, trembling. It was early, and the residents were not up yet, but I had to move on because they soon would be arising. In particular, the grocer would soon discover my crime.

But where was I to go? If the Russians had found the dead farm couple—Stefan Lazinsky and his wife—and were out looking for someone, they would have learned that a Stefan Lazinsky had come past the guardhouse on Krasinski Boulevard how long ago—two mornings? Perhaps they had already talked to the fat man and woman in my former apartment.

My will to live became conscious. I wanted to live, why I didn't really know. My country was gone; my friends were gone; and my wife was gone. I was wounded and in pain. The Russians were looking for me, probably, and they would kill me if they caught me.

Perhaps that was it. My fear told me that I had had enough Russian torture. But to escape the Russians, I would have to leave Grodno—and Poland.

And with the idea that I had to leave Poland—somehow —came a real, if hazily defined, incentive. Outside Poland, I might have a chance to avenge Suzan's death. How I would avenge her, I did not know, but I certainly could do nothing with Russians all around me, searching for me.

As I had done in the forest, I took stock of my position. Grodno lay four hundred kilometers south of the Baltic, and the Baltic's southern and eastern shores were controlled by the Germans and the Russians. Rumania lay more than seven hundred kilometers to the south, but it was, as far as I knew, still a free nation. Perhaps, after Rumania, I would go to Paris, where I knew that the Polish government had fled.

In Paris I could tell of what had happened at Kozelsk and in the Katyn Forest. That would be a real revenge if no one knew about it. And as I thought back over the precautions the Russians had taken to conceal their purposes, I doubted anyone did.

One way to get to Paris was to make the long journey south into Rumania and then across Yugoslavia to the Mediterranean. With luck I could find an Allied ship to take me to France. Or I could cross into Hungary and work my way to Switzerland. Surely, the Germans had not taken that mountain country.

I was not sufficiently recovered to be able to plan an itinerary, but I did decide on Rumania. In fact I was about to start when the Russian military car came back up the street. This time it slowed as it came closer. I bowed my head onto my chest and waited for it to pass. The motor labored and hummed as the car idled past. Sweat beading up on my forehead, I fully expected to hear the chatter of a machine gun, once again to feel bullets smashing into my body. But the engine roared louder, and the car moved on up the street.

I began to breathe easier, but then a door opened and slammed in a building behind me, and I became extremely apprehensive again. I looked around and saw no one, but I could hear footsteps on a stairway. I *had* to move. Quickly I climbed the fence to the sidewalk and struck off southward, with my cache of food bumping up and down in my pockets.

Six blocks farther on, I found another partly demolished building. Crawling into the dark basement, I waited out the long day, fearful of every movement outside, certain that every motor vehicle that went past was filled with Russian soldiers looking for me.

When darkness came, my desire to escape had not diminished. The day in the basement had strengthened it, as had the food from the grocery. The quiet street was empty and dark; the Russians had not turned the streetlights back on since the Germans had knocked out the power. Not a vehicle or a person moved along the street.

I was not very familiar with the neighborhood. Suzan and I

had lived in the apartment for less than two weeks when the Russians came. We had been to the grocer's and had taken walks in the evenings, but we had not explored the area. However, I pressed on.

At an intersection my ears, keen from my long trek through the forest, caught the distant sound of a motor. Turning, I saw the approaching headlights of a vehicle. By the slitted guards over the lights I could tell that it was a military vehicle, so I moved swiftly out of the intersection and across a small lawn in front of a house. As the motor became louder, I crawled into the shrubs next to the foundation of the house.

There was a squeal of brakes as the car stopped at the intersection. I felt my heart thumping in my throat. I peered out through the shrubs and saw the slitted headlights and the domed shape of Russian helmets. There were four men in the car.

Suddenly, a bright spotlight shot out from the side of the car. It swung up and down the street, swept across the fronts of houses and onto lawns, moved slowly across the shrubs hiding me. I had the distinct feeling that the Russians knew I was there, but the light went out as suddenly as it had blazed on, leaving the street in darkness again. I heard one of the soldiers speak, but I could not distinguish his words. In any case, the vehicle moved off toward the east. I waited at least ten minutes before coming out of the shrubs to continue my journey.

Perhaps the Russians made regular patrols every night and flashed their spotlight down quiet streets, but I believed that they were searching for something or someone in particular. I was convinced that I was the object of their search. So I moved on with even greater caution, perking my ears for every sound, peering up every cross street before entering an intersection, but all the time pressing on toward the south.

I could not, of course, move very fast. My right leg was stiff, and I still experienced considerable pain in my shoulder. I shuffled along, but I could not keep my oversized boots from clomping loudly in the quiet night.

About an hour after the Russian patrol had passed me, I

neared the southern edge of the city. In the distance was a small house, marked by a dim yellow light in a single window. Beyond that was the blackness of open country. Even though I suspected that the Russians maintained guard posts only on main roads, I took no chances, leaving the street, which had become a narrow dirt road, and took to the fields. I came out only when I had entered a woods and had left the lights of the city far behind me.

Hundreds of kilometers and innumerable dangers lay ahead of me in the night; yet I had resolved to find freedom, and so I went on. Thus began an incredible journey that would, in retrospect, dwarf my flight from Gnezdovo. Luckily, I was not able to review the potential difficulties and danger that clearly. I merely had a compelling desire to reach Paris, to tell my story to Polish officials there.

Almost at once I began to experience periods of unreason. My mind increasingly slipped away from me, and I moved almost entirely in response to fear and instinct. Perhaps that was my salvation. Madness protected me, for I moved, inexorably, onward.

Time passed without notice. I slept when I was tired and limped through fields and woods when I could sleep no more. I stole food when I was hungry and wept when the pain grew too intense.

Thoughts were so jumbled in my head that I usually could not sort them out. When I tried to think clearly, my mind refused, and I often wound up with a splitting headache. So I stopped trying to force my mind to think clearly. When lucid thoughts came, I welcomed them and acted on them. When they didn't, I retreated to a barn or a woods and waited for my mind to function properly. When it still refused, I moved by instinct, shuffling ever southward. I avoided farmhouses and spoke to no human being—Poland seemed as much an alien land as Russia had been.

Thus it was only with great difficulty that, days later, I approached a remote farm in southern Poland. For days I had seen road signs indicating that I was not far from the Rumanian border. Only the day before I had seen a sign pointing south that indicated that the border was less than twenty kilometers away, and I knew I had to find out what the situation was before I committed myself irrevocably to any Rumanian experiences. At least in my bouts with insanity my instincts for self-preservation never deserted me.

When I decided to stop at the farmhouse, I planned to tell the Polish family everything I could remember of my ordeal. But I had not reckoned with the mental damage I had suffered during that ordeal or during the weeks of walking and hiding since leaving Grodno. In those weeks I had not spoken to a single human being; I had not even knowingly talked to myself. And, indeed, I remembered my intentions when I stepped onto the porch of the house and knocked on the door. But when the door opened and a man came out with a kerosene lantern, all I could say was: "Paris."

The farmer, fortunately, was a kindly man, so he simply called his wife and daughter and son and then led me inside. They at once sat me down at the kitchen table, and I ate ravenously. Then in the flickering lamplight, I tried again to talk.

"Paris."

"You want to go to Paris?" the woman asked.

"Paris has fallen," the man said. "All France has fallen to the Nazis. An armistice was signed last month. You can't go to Paris. If you want to escape the Russians"—was it that obvious, I wondered?—"you can go into Rumania and stay, but not to Paris."

I tried to tell him that he was wrong, but my words didn't fit together in a coherent way. They only stared at me.

"Listen," the farmer said. "You need help. You need a doctor. You can't travel anymore. And you certainly can't go to Paris."

"Paris!" It was almost a demand.

The man sent the young people to bed, and the woman treated my wounds, tearing up sheets for bandages. I slept that night and most of the following day. When I awakened, I lay in bed until someone entered the room. It was the pretty, dark-haired daughter. I pointed at a calendar, and she nodded. "It's Friday, July 12," she said. Her eyes met mine and then dropped shyly to her lap. "Can you talk to us now?"

"Paris," I said.

Though I was touched by her concern—the first really human feeling I had experienced in months—I still could not make her understand. In the evening, the father and his son returned from the fields, and again we ate. When darkness came, I got up, showing them that I was going to leave.

"You must stay," the woman pleaded. "We can have the doctor from the village look at your wounds. If you go, you'll die."

"Paris."

The man sighed. He put a hand on my shoulder and spoke gently. "If you must go," he repeated, "you must forget Paris and go to Rumania. It is only twelve kilometers away."

They gave me food and directions for crossing the border in a small woods. As I walked away, I looked back and said: "Paris."

The forest was dark, but somehow I managed not to slam into any trees. I came out on a knoll overlooking a long, gentle valley. Farmhouses dotted the slopes. I was in Rumania!

It had taken only five hours to limp the twelve kilometers, but I felt as though I had traveled a thousand hours. I was already exhausted, so I returned to the woods and found a soft nest between three trees and slept. When dawn came, I went down the hill and stopped at an old stone house. A pleasant-faced woman opened the door.

I didn't know much Rumanian, but I knew enough to get along, and I was very relieved to find that I could again communicate—not that it had much effect. The woman closed the door, and I was ready to move on when it was opened again by a man with a pipe.

"What is it?" he asked. His voice was friendly.

"I need help," I said with an effort. "I'm going to Paris."

He looked at me for a long time, then took the pipe from his mouth and burst into laughter. "You are either crazy or brave," he said in Polish. "You certainly aren't German, and only Germans are welcome in Paris these days."

They took me into the house. Over breakfast they filled me in on the progress of the war, so far as they knew the details. One thing was certain. Paris was out of the question.

"Where in the world have you been?" the man asked me at last.

I tried to remember, but the past was fuzzy. "Prison," I said at last, deliberately. "Russian prison."

"Ah," he said, leaning back in his chair. "And you escaped?"

I nodded and tried to remember. Only vague images of buildings at Kozelsk flashed through my mind, then the forest and bumping into trees.

"Where will you go?"

"Paris."

"Holy Mother, you *can't* go to Paris! The Germans are there."

"Oh, yes."

"You must go south, my friend," he said. "Reach the Mediterranean and find a ship going to London. That's where the Poles have gone, and no place on the continent is safe for you."

I remembered my dreams of the Vistula and the small river villages I had conjured while studying the crack in the barracks wall.

"Switzerland," I mumbled. "Are the Germans in Switzerland?"

"Not even Hitler is mad enough to fight in those hills," he laughed. "But the Germans are all around Switzerland. You can't go unless you're an airplane."

Antoni's promise to grow wings if it would win him Janina flashed through my mind, and I laughed. The couple exchanged glances.

"You will go to the Mediterranean?" the man finally asked.

"No. To Switzerland."

Reluctantly, the Rumanian farmer gave me directions on how to begin my journey to Switzerland. I was to go into the city and catch a freight train heading south, to Ploesti. There, I would switch to an east–west line going, through Belgrade, to the

Italian border. I would have to cross a part of Italy to reach Switzerland.

Before I was out of sight, my mind became muddled and I forgot. I set off in a northwesterly direction, which would take me through Czechoslovakia, providing the Germans didn't kill me first.

As I traveled across Rumania, there were no fantasies to tax my energies and make me fearful, only the subtle realization that I was losing my mind and my memory. I felt it was my duty now to save what I could of my body.

Buried deep within me was the desire to tell my story to free people, and fragments of that story came to me as I walked along roads, fields, and railroad tracks. However, when I stopped at the homes of farmers for food and directions to Czechoslovakia, I found that I could not relate what had happened to me—not even the fragments of memories could I put into words.

At one point, I recall, memories of my childhood and of the entire ordeal at Kozelsk and Katyn Forest became crystal clear. But in time all of those memories died, and I was alone in a world that I could not trust, a world that apparently had no place for me.

Weeks later I arrived at a large rail yard in western Rumania. Beyond lay Hungary. Although the two countries were friendly, I circled the yards and entered Hungary in a remote area.

Crossing Hungary took days, weeks, but was uneventful, and I finally arrived at the Czechoslovakian border. Across the border I saw German sentries and Czech policemen, and fear returned instantly. I thought of going back to Rumania, but quickly realizing that the Germans would soon be there, too, I left the road and crossed the border at a point far away from the sentries.

In Czechoslovakia I again took to traveling at night and hiding by day. This time, however, I risked riding trains, and when I couldn't find an open door on a freight car, I climbed onto the metal rods that ran underneath the length of the cars.

In fact, I was so successful at riding the rods that I became a trifle careless—and once with nearly fatal results. Relaxing underneath a train headed southwest, toward Austria, I fell asleep.

I awoke only when the train stopped near a large city. I was cramped and stiff, but I didn't dare leave the train. Then as I lay still, I heard the sharp chatter of a machine gun. The bullets clanged in the night. Why? Who were they firing at? I also heard German voices. But I could see nothing. Another burst erupted. Then, with a start, I realized that the guards were flushing out riders by walking alongside the train and firing up into the rods.

Sweat filled my palms, and my body turned clammy. The roar of the machine gun was getting closer. Bullets rang out against the rods in the still night. Then came laughter and the crunch of heavy boots on gravel. During the next burst I tumbled off the rods and onto the ties below. I was in darkness, but they might have flashlights.

With pain shooting through my body, I rolled over onto the opposite track and down the bank into the weeds. The gun fired again. Bits of dirt, rust, and metal showered me.

The Germans laughed, muttered obscenities, and moved on. When they were several car-lengths away, I scrambled back onto the rods. The train turned north toward Germany. When it slowed on a hill, I dropped between the tracks and let the train run over and past me.

The incredible part of my journey across Czechoslovakia was not what happened to me—it was what did *not* happen. I should have been shot by a farmer, a shop owner, or the Germans—at least I should have been captured. But I was not even pursued.

My mind seemed to dissolve, and I felt no fear. I had lost even the normal instincts of self-preservation. Once, I broke a butcher's window in broad daylight. On another occasion, I stopped a small boy in a large village and babbled at him, begging for food. He carried a basket, and I was certain it contained food. The child ran screaming down the street.

I walked past German soldiers, wandered about villages, and

made no attempt to hide. I caught trains in the daytime and even rode on top. My method of travel didn't change when I entered Austria, an integral part of Germany. I crossed the country easily and reached the Swiss border.

I had forgotten virtually everything by then. Rambling through my mind were mere fragments of memories. I knew that I was a major in the Polish Army Reserves and that I had been in prison—I guessed that it had been a Russian prison. I also knew that I could not communicate even this fragmentary information to anyone, in any language.

The night air was warm and the sky was brilliant with stars when I crossed the border. I had left a freight train five kilometers back and had threaded across trickling mountain streams. I walked through the starlit night, my right leg throbbing in pain, my right shoulder and arm numb and useless.

At dawn I came to a hilltop and looked down on a large town. I went slowly down the hill and found a road. I walked along it boldly, though hardly briskly. I had reached freedom, and that was all that mattered. Ahead was a sign: CHUR, Population, 12,543.

Accosting people on the main street, I tried to ask if there were any Poles in Chur, but I only babbled in a mixture of German, French, and Polish. They looked at me quizzically and scratched their heads. A pot-bellied policeman arrived when I attracted a crowd. I understood his German perfectly.

"Oh, another refugee from the Nazis," he said as if it was an everyday occurrence.

I told him that I was a Polish officer from a Russian prison camp. He repeated his statement, and I knew that he hadn't understood me. When he took my arm, I thought I was going to jail. I didn't mind. I was sick of running, and I was convinced that my babbling stemmed from a fever. Even in jail the Swiss would help me.

The policeman led me through the town to a large building I had seen from the hilltop. "I've got another one for you," he said to a woman in a crisp white uniform. "I think this one is Polish. Good luck."

The woman smiled sympathetically and led me to an immaculate white examining room. As she helped me onto a high bed, a red-faced doctor entered with a fat nurse. They cut off my clothing, and when I kept babbling impatiently to make them understand, the doctor nodded to the nurse. She gave me a shot in my lean buttocks. The world became fuzzy and then disappeared—there were not even any nightmares to haunt me.

I awoke with sharp pains in my shoulder, side, and leg. I was in a comfortable bed with a soft pillow, and I could feel large bandages on various parts of my body. But most of all, I was ravenously hungry.

A plump, attractive nurse brought a tray of food. I babbled, trying to find out what had happened, but she only smiled. She fed me soft eggs, bread soaked in milk, and hot tea—I promptly threw it all up.

The doctor came later and listened to my chest with a cold stethoscope. He shushed me when I tried to tell him what I remembered. Then, with a kindly smile, he explained why I was in pain.

"We opened your wounds, treated them, and stitched them up again. You have broken bones in your shoulder, and we took out fragments of a bullet. Were you shot by Germans? Just nod or shake your head."

I shook my head.

"Are you Polish?"

I nodded.

"The wounds are old. Do you know how long ago you were shot?"

I shook my head. I simply could not remember.

"We have notified the Polish authorities," he said. "Rest a few days and perhaps you can learn to talk. And you also must eat. You are suffering from acute malnutrition."

As day followed day, I tried to converse with the doctor and the nurses. They merely stared at me and walked away. I soon stopped trying.

In the third week two men in Polish army uniforms arrived. The interview was brief and inconclusive. I managed to convey only that I was a cavalry major in the reserves, that I had fought in Poznan, that I had been captured by the Russians, and that I had escaped. They believed everything except the capture and escape. Russia was far away, beyond enemy territory. They chose to believe that I had escaped from a German camp. It was much easier for them, and I was simply too tired to argue. It didn't seem to matter.

The officers came once each week for two months, but they learned nothing. The doctor told them, in my hearing, that I required psychiatric help. The hospital had no psychiatrist, and since Switzerland was full of refugees, many with deep psychological problems, it would be difficult to obtain one from Zurich. But the doctor would put in a request.

Weeks turned into months. No psychiatrist came, and the Polish officers called less frequently. I was allowed out of bed in November and told that I would walk with a limp for the rest of my life; my right arm would never again function properly. I had lost, I learned, fifty-six pounds.

Near Christmas, the Polish officers came to discuss the papers I had taken from the Polish farmer after killing him and his wife.

"Are you Stefan Lazinsky?" one officer asked.

I shook my head.

"You're not a farmer from near Grodno?"

I shook my head again.

"You still say that you were a major in the cavalry and fought in Poznan?" It had taken a great deal of labor and ingenuity on my part to convey even that much information.

I nodded.

"Can you explain how you happened to be carrying the papers of a Polish farmer named Stefan Lazinsky?"

I merely stared, and the officer sighed. I could not explain anything; nor can I now explain why I was unable to speak. No psychiatric examinations were made of me during my stay at the hospital in Chur, but I do know that my mind was free of the fears that had troubled me since my escape. I could not remember details of my past, and I could not speak. My emotions were easily aroused, like a child's, and I wept easily—sometimes without provocation. I was most upset by the Polish officers' questioning. Once, when their questioning was particularly intense, the fat nurse threw them both out.

She, above everyone else, realized what effect the questioning was having on me. In response I fell in love with her and cried when they came to take me away from the hospital.

It was a cold, windy, bitter day in January when I left with the two Polish officers. We went directly to an airport, where the International Red Cross had arranged to fly me to London. I imagined that my people wanted me questioned by a Polish psychiatrist. Perhaps they were fearful that I might divulge something vital to the safety of the Polish government in exile.

I can offer no other explanation. I was an unknown entity. As far as Polish Intelligence was concerned, I could have been a high-ranking officer carrying important information, or I could have been a spy for the Nazis. There was no way of telling without psychiatric help, and my people wanted that psychiatrist to be Polish, a man they could trust.

The plane was untouched by the *Luftwaffe*. The huge red cross on the side was honored.

In London, I was placed in a military hospital, where several other Polish soldiers were interned with mental and physical disorders. For the first few days I was kept in a private room; then I was moved onto a ward. During my stay in the private room, I was visited daily by Polish Intelligence officers and a Polish-speaking psychiatrist who bombarded me with questions and gave me a number of simple manipulation tests—all of which I apparently failed.

The questioning had the effect of driving me deeper into my amnesia, and I soon forgot even the fragments that I had remembered in Switzerland. I could no longer respond affirmatively to the question of my rank. Without knowing it —without caring—I slipped into a complete state of amnesia.

In the spring of 1941 a Polish general came to the hospital to talk with me. The purpose of his visit was to promote me, officially, to lieutenant colonel. Psychiatrists at the hospital, eager to try any therapy that might arouse me from lethargy, had suggested the promotion in the hope that it might help.

The promotion was conducted with great solemnity. The general made a short speech, presented me with the insignia of a lieutenant colonel, and shook my hand. But it meant nothing. I sat with the insignia in my hands, unaware of their significance, staring out the window at the dark, drab buildings near the hospital.

I have no recollection of the other men on my ward. There were no more emotions to disturb me; I had no fear of anything. Nothing could touch me, and my world was one of blankness.

Paradoxically, I could hear and see everything that went on around me on the ward. I could hear men speaking in Polish and could see them walking around or sitting in their robes and pajamas. Many of them played cards, and some of them laughed and joked in spite of their problems from the war.

Psychiatrists in the hospital apparently considered my case hopeless or decreed that I needed a change of scenery and a new set of psychiatrists to work on my problem. Perhaps they merely wanted me off their hands. In any event, shortly after my promotion to lieutenant colonel, a young Polish lieutenant came to the hospital to take me away. The lieutenant, a cheerful man (and that is all that I can remember about him), took me by train to Edinburgh, Scotland, where I was turned over to the medical staff of a psychiatric clinic, where I was registered as Lieutenant Colonel John Zamoyski. The name of one of Poland's most famous patriots had been given to me by authorities in London, the way the name "John Doe" is given to Americans who cannot remember their names.

I must have been reasonably happy at the hospital in Scotland. Although I could not communicate with others—and had nothing to communicate anyway—I enjoyed hearing others talk. I sat for hours listening to students, doctors, nurses, other patients, understanding them in a veiled and pleasant way.

In the first months a number of staff psychiatrists came to see me, to question me, to give me tests similar to those given to me in London. Then suddenly the doctors stopped coming around.

I seemed to have become a kind of case study for the medical students at the university. However, by the late summer of 1941, I could no longer make sense out of the things that were said around me. Words became a jumble of nonsense sounds; even the songs of birds were strange and alien.

I lived in a vacuum, in the midst of Babel.

16: END OF THE DREAM

T HE first sensation was warmth—the sun. And then reality opened its door a bit wider, and I saw grass and a large leafy tree full of green leaves. A young man in a white smock sat beside me on a hard bench, reading a book. Around us were buildings; people—some were old, most wearing pajamas and robes—were entering and leaving. Curiously, I, too, was in pajamas and robe.

I touched the young man's arm and pointed to the tree. "*Drzewo?*"

He leaped as though I had exploded a firecracker.

"What did you say? John, did you say something?"

"*Drzewo,*" I repeated, pointing to the tree. "Tree."

"Lord, to be sure," he said excitedly. "You can *talk*. Look, look down there. What is that?"

"Grass. Any idiot would know that." · ·

He laughed and clapped his hands. "And that?"

"The sky! What are you so excited about?"

"You, John." His hands were on my arms, his eyes fixed on

225

mine. "I've spent months talking to you and haven't got a response before. Dozens of students and doctors have tried. Lord, man, don't you know how long you've been here?"

I shook my head and asked: "Where are we? Who are you?"

"You're in a hospital in Scotland," he explained. "My name is Drewery, and I'm a medical student in training here. Tell me your name, John."

"Isn't it 'John'?"

He laughed again. "Tell me, John, what do you remember?"

"I don't understand."

"Look here, man," he went on. "You haven't spoken in years. Now, you can say 'tree' and 'grass' and 'sky.' Do you remember other words, other things?"

I gazed around and named everything in sight.

"Wonderful," he cried. "Now tell me your name."

I was puzzled. Was he a new breed of medical student, dedicated to driving men crazy? I tried to remember, but the past was a blank. There was only the present, and it was confusing.

"Come on," he said, leaping up. "Let's go see the doctor."

Suddenly I was afraid to go, though I didn't know why. I clearly was safe and in good hands. But fear nagged me, and I shuddered violently.

"What's wrong, John?" Drewery asked when I did not get up.

As suddenly as it had come, the fear subsided, and instead I felt bewildered. I looked down and saw his book on the lush, green grass.

"You forgot your book," I said, getting up to go with him.

The doctor assigned to my case was a short man. He had thin hair and thick glasses and the largest hands I had ever seen. Drewery rattled on about the "phenomenon."

"Colonel Zamoyski," the doctor said in a soft voice thick with a Scottish accent, "this is an incredible phenomenon. Do you feel up to a few questions?"

"Yes, sir, but why is it incredible?"

"You mean you don't even know how long you've been here?"

the doctor asked. "Don't you realize that you've been here seven years?" He opened a file. On it was the name: Lieutenant Colonel John Zamoyski, Polish Army. "You came here on April 22, 1941. It is now May 19, *1948*."

The fear returned, in furious, lashing waves. *Seven years!*

I fought back the waves of non-understanding. I had to know more. "Where was I before that?" I asked.

The doctor leaned forward. "We were hoping *you* could tell *us*."

I tried to remember, but a galloping headache prevented all thought. Irritated, I simply said: "Perhaps I dropped from the moon!"

The doctor did not react to my gibe. Instead he consulted the file again. "You were sent by the Polish Army headquarters. Psychiatrists in London considered your case hopeless. So did we."

A flash of remembrance sped through my mind. I saw a young lieutenant staring out of a train window. I was beside him, and we were rushing across flat countryside. I saw a general put something in my hand, shake my hand, and call me lieutenant colonel. I saw doctors and Polish officers and heard questions —always questions.

"You came to London from Switzerland," the doctor continued, "but we don't know where you were before that. The Polish authorities in Bern said you claimed to have been a prisoner of the Russians but concluded that you were captured by the Germans at Poznan. You were shot and escaped."

More fleeting images came. I saw a plump, pretty nurse, then a lovely, golden-haired woman with delicate features. I saw myself speeding on a horse, shouting and firing a pistol. I was in a hot staff car with two men. One was a general. The headache grew.

As the doctor read from the file, for no apparent reason I began to cry. He closed the folder and smiled. "Forgive me, Colonel Zamoyski. But you see, we've been puzzled about you for a very long time. Mr. Drewery, please take the colonel to his room. We can talk another time. All right?"

"No," I said abruptly. The fear had passed again. I had to know more. "Tell me about the seven years."

"There really isn't much to tell. We haven't been able to communicate with you. You have said nothing in all those years."

"What about other things? What has gone on in the world?"

"Do you remember the war?"

Vague impressions assaulted me. I saw troops and horses, I saw men fall, heard horses scream in pain.

"The war," I mumbled. "We fought the Germans. We lost, and the Russians came. But . . . "

"We can talk later," he said. "We must let nature take the helm now. When you are ready, we'll talk."

"What happened? Is the war still going on?" I had to know, to grasp any fact that would tie me to this new reality.

The doctor took off his thick glasses. He glanced at Drewery, then rested a steady gaze on me. "It ended in 1945. The Allies won," he said simply.

I felt a lump of elation in my throat, although I didn't know why. Gradually, it came to me. "Poland is free," I sighed. "The Germans were beaten. Poland is free."

"We'll talk more tomorrow," the doctor said.

"No. Please. Tell me about it."

The doctor sighed and went on, slowly, choosing his words carefully. He told of how Germany had invaded Russia, of how the United States had entered the war, of the invasion of Europe, of how the four powers had divided Germany.

"And the Russians?"

"They have East Germany." He lowered his eyes. Again he said: "I believe we should wait for another time."

"There's more? Yes, of course there is. Tell me."

He discussed the Yalta agreement and how Yugoslavia, Hungary, Rumania, Czechoslovakia, and Bulgaria had become communist nations.

"And Poland? What of Poland?"

"Your country," he said, spreading his hands on the desk, "has been divided. The Russians took the eastern part."

"And the rest? What has happened to it?"

He studied his hands, and young Drewery shifted nervously. The fear edged back into my mind, and I did not want to hear. But I would have the truth. I would not let them off. "What of the rest of Poland?"

"It is a communist country, a satellite of Russia."

"Oh, God!"

I leaned forward and put my hands over my face. Somehow, though I did not know why I felt this, I knew the worst had happened. I felt like weeping, but I didn't weep. I felt a tremendous grief for the loss of my country, and I felt an overwhelming loneliness.

The doctor gently—this time successfully—urged me to return to my room.

In the ensuing days memories flooded into my mind so swiftly that I often was unable to comprehend or tolerate them without crying. The pattern was strange. I remembered my life until the day that I went to meet the Russians. I remembered Radjiga and Suzan and my parents and my grandfather, even my friends in school and some of my students at Poznan.

But I did not remember my name or their names. I did not remember anything from the time of my riding in the staff car until my appearance in Switzerland—and had only vague recollections of the Swiss hospital and of my stay in London. And *all* memory was shrouded in a mist that kept me from recalling anything with clarity.

My lapses were far more worrying to me than they were to the medical authorities. As the doctor explained it: "You suffered a deep psychological wound during your internment, something so unspeakable that your mind rejects it. That's why you remember nothing of that period and why memories of other parts of your life are so sketchy. When you no longer fear what happened, memory probably will be restored."

I gazed out at the bright spring day. People walked about in sunlight; the world seemed safe. But deep in my mind lurked unknown, and therefore particularly horrifying, fears, and I knew that when they surfaced, either I would be free or I would be their prisoner for the remainder of my life.

Young Drewery was a great source of information, filling me in briefly on the passage of events. Most importantly, I learned that the Free Polish government functioned in London, without diplomatic recognition. I also learned that the Polish military still existed and planned, at some elusive future date, to try to liberate Poland.

This all was reassuring, but the corollaries were not. The advent of distrust in the West for Russia meant that Russian spies were everywhere—even more in my imagination than in fact —and I became phobic with fear and distrust. Things got so bad that I stopped revealing any additional recollections to Drewery or the doctor. When I remembered Suzan's name, during a moment of quiet one night, I told no one. I merely lay in bed, savoring the memory of her fragile beauty and immense warmth.

On June 11, 1948, I was returned to duty with the Free Polish army in London.

"We shall miss you, Colonel Zamoyski," the doctor said. "I'm sorry we haven't opened all the doors, but your people feel that you'll recover more quickly with them. Perhaps they're right."

Drewery and two other students took me to the train station. As we said good-bye, Drewery clasped my hand. "You're always welcome in Scotland, John," he said. "If you ever need sanctuary, come back."

It was such a genuine expression of personal affection that, as usual when confronted with such frankness, I was embarrassed. All I could say was: "Thank you. My bad memory will certainly remember that."

Drewery smiled at my joke, and I climbed aboard the train, which moved into a drizzling rain. As the train raced over Scotland and northern England, my thoughts turned inward, examining each fragment of memory, trying to pierce the veil. Each time I thought of Suzan, a cold melancholy tempered my happiness. I could see her face clearly, then the image suddenly shattered. I thought of Poland in the hands of Communists and could not bear the thought. Now, what did that mean? Why the unbearable nature of this piece of information? Why the sense of urgent fear?

I realized, of course, that my fears were part of my condition. Perhaps they stemmed from what had happened between September 19, 1939, and August, 1940. I did not know, but the fears were very real, and they were getting worse the closer I got to London.

Suddenly, I realized that I was afraid of mingling with my own people. It took some time for me to analyze my feelings, but eventually I had it all figured out.

If Poland was communist controlled, Communists must have infiltrated the ranks of the Free Poles in London. Communist ideology required communist infiltration of all free societies, and it would be particularly derelict of them not to infiltrate the ranks of Free Poles wherever they existed. The trouble was, analyzing this fear only made me feel worse. The certainty of any danger only increased my apprehension, and my fears were instantly crystallized as a name flashed through my mind. The name came out of nowhere and matched the rhythm of the clacking wheels. I knew it was my own: Komorowski, Komorowski, *Komorowski*! I didn't know how I could bear the knowledge.

As I left the train, two men approached. One was young and tall, with raven hair, dark eyes, a handsome face, and wide shoulders. He reminded me of someone—who? The second man was short, fat, balding, and considerably older.

"Colonel Zamoyski?" the young man said, smiling widely.

I was wearing a new suit the hospital had given me; my uniform was packed in an old suitcase—also a gift.

"Yes," I replied.

Both men flipped open their wallets, but I had no time to read

their names. I saw only the Polish White Eagle on their
identification cards.

"Polish Intelligence," the younger man said. "We were sent to
meet you."

They both looked up and down the platform, but there were
only people getting off the train and other people meeting them.

"What's wrong?" I asked. "What's up?"

The young man placed his hand on my arm. "Nothing for you
to worry about, Colonel. We've simply been trying to keep your
arrival—ah, under wraps, as they say."

"Why?"

"If you don't mind," he said as we moved out of the station
and into a waiting taxi, "we'll discuss it in a more private
place."

Rain streaked the streets of London, and we rode in silence.
The older man kept screwing his head around, surveying the
street behind. Suddenly, I blurted out: "What the hell are you
looking for?"

"Who knows?" the young man answered.

It was too enigmatic an answer for me. I demanded more
information. "Are there Communists in our group here?" It was
a stab in the dark, but to my horror it struck home.

"We can't prove anything yet," the younger agent went on,
"but we suspect it."

Nothing more was said, and finally the taxi stopped at an old
hotel near Belgrave Square. I had expected to be taken to some
military installation, so I hesitated before getting out.

"It's all right, sir," the young man said. "Colonel Frankowski
wants you to stay here for a time."

"Colonel Frankowski?"

"Yes, sir. Your commanding officer."

They had already registered me at the hotel, so I was whisked
through the tiny lobby and onto an elevator. The room was small
but comfortable. I stared out into the rain, wishing the men
would leave, then hoping that they would stay. I was afraid of
them, but I also was afraid of being alone.

"Colonel Zamoyski," the older man said, speaking for the first time. "Please sit down. We must ask a few questions."

Were one or both Russian agents? I possessed no information of value either to the Free Poles or to the Russians, and these intelligence men were turning my arrival into a silly intrigue. It was small comfort to realize that probably all intelligence men—and secret police—behaved this way.

When we were settled—I in a small chair beside the big bed —they began again.

"According to your file," the young man said, "you told the authorities in Switzerland—Chur, I believe—that you had been captured by the Russians in September, 1939. Is this true?"

What was this? I asked myself. A new game. They knew perfectly well what was in my file. Well, two could play. "Yes. I mean, I believe I told them that."

"The Polish Intelligence agents who interviewed you at that time," the old man added, "said they believed you had been captured and shot by the Germans. At one point in the testimony you agree to this. Now, which was it, Colonel Zamoyski—the Germans or the Russians?"

"I don't understand. I don't remember ever saying that I had been captured by the Germans."

"Who captured you?" the young man asked. His manner was brisk but not unfriendly.

"I don't know. I remember leaving Grodno to meet the Red Army."

"When was this?"

"I don't know. I don't remember. Sometime in September."

"What happened then?" It was the old man, speaking from the window where he occasionally stole a glance outside from behind the curtain. They were like a couple of actors in a bad Russian movie.

"I don't know."

The young man, who was sitting on the side of the bed, leaned forward and touched my knee. "Do you remember your real name?"

"No." I wasn't going to give anything away until I knew where I stood.

The questions rained on me: Where was I born? Did I have a family? If so, what were their names? When was I called to active duty? What was my rank then? What was my brigade? Was I in the cavalry or infantry? Who was my commanding officer? Where did I serve during the war? Where and when was I captured? Who captured me? Who shot me? Where was I interned? How did I escape?

Perhaps they were trying to help me, perhaps not. It didn't make any difference. I wasn't going to answer even when I knew the answers. Until I learned whom I could and could not trust —if I ever learned it—I would keep my few valued recollections to myself.

"Were you married?" the old man asked.

"Yes. I mean, I believe so."

"What was your wife's name?"

"I don't know. Even if I did, how would that help?"

The young man said: "If we knew her name, especially her maiden name, we could find yours."

"But the records are in Poland," I reminded him.

They smiled. The old man spoke: "We could find out. We have ways."

I shook my head, which was splitting. I wished the men would leave me alone. I felt trapped in the old hotel, and there was something grossly unpleasant about the interrogation. These were meant to be friends. (Were they?) I wanted to scream at them to stop, but instead I sat placidly, waiting for them to finish. I had learned a lot since 1939.

"We will assume that you were a prisoner of the Russians," the young man was saying. His voice reached through the protective shell my mind constantly was fabricating to protect myself. "Do you have any recollection of where they took you, where they kept you prisoner?"

"No."

The two men looked at each other, and it was as if a decision had been made. The young man looked more resolute. "Are you aware, Colonel Zamoyski," the young man went on, "that more than fifteen thousand Polish officers were captured by the Russians and have never been seen or heard from again?"

"I was not aware of that." The news meant nothing to me, and I could not see what it had to do with my case.

"Have you ever heard of Katyn Forest?" the older man asked, whirling from his station at the window.

"I don't know. I might have read about a forest by that name in eastern Poland, but I don't know."

The two agents questioned me for several hours, asking the same questions over and over again, though they did not mention Katyn or the missing officers again. In their careful way they clearly were trying to spark some memory that would lead to specific recollections—later it became clear that they were interested only in the missing officers, though of course I did not know that at the time.

We got closer to the truth when, suddenly, I burst out: "You're just like the goddamn Russians! Don't you know when to stop?"

The older man walked over from the window and leaned toward me. "Tell me, Colonel Zamoyski, how do you know what the Russians are like?" His voice was soft and low, almost friendly.

"I don't understand."

"You said we were just like the Russians," he said in the same gentle tone. "What do you know about the Russians? Have you been interrogated by them?"

My mind began to buzz with frightening and unintelligible images and thoughts gleaned from the hours of interrogation by the NKVD. I began to feel, again, that I was on the verge of another discovery and that I was out of my depth.

"I don't know," I said calmly, swallowing back my growing fear.

My head throbbed. I longed for sleep. I stopped answering their questions, and they finally left.

I was kept in the drab hotel for a month. Every few days, relays of agents came to ask questions; I suspected that they knew that within me I carried vitally important information. From my own memories and the drift of the questioning, I knew it involved the Russians—perhaps even the fifteen thousand officers—but I didn't know any more. Usually, they were the same questions. Occasionally, a reference would be made to the missing fifteen thousand officers, though the Katyn Forest was not mentioned again, and I doubt that I helped them in their investigation.

During that long, dreary time, I was confined to the room, almost a prisoner. I was assured that it was for my own protection, and I didn't care to speculate about the dangers. Still, I wanted to get out and away from the hotel. It was very depressing, being secluded.

Then, on the morning of June 14, a Monday, two agents arrived while I was having breakfast in my room. All my meals were brought to the room by bellboys or Intelligence agents.

"Good news," one of the men said. "We are finished with our questions. You're to return to active duty today."

"Doing what?" I asked, astounded at the sudden change in events.

"We don't know. Our orders are to present you to Colonel Frankowski. He's in charge of military records, administration, and archives. I hear you'll have something to do with our official newspaper, but I don't know. It will be up to Colonel Frankowski."

I was elated. Just to leave the drab room would be a pleasure, and any job would be better than remaining idle. In addition, I somehow felt that I would be happy dealing with records and archives. In my talks with the doctors in Edinburgh, I had shown a great interest in history—perhaps that is why I received the assignment in Colonel Frankowski's unit, I speculated—and if I was to get the job the agent mentioned, I thought I might enjoy it.

As we were leaving the hotel, one of the agents turned to me and asked: "By the way, Colonel Zamoyski, do you know General Wilczynski?"

The question touched a sensitive chord in my mind, setting off a tremor of fear. A quick image of the general flashed through my mind. His face was bloody. Why? And why had the man asked the question?

"I don't know him," I replied softly. "Why d'you ask?"

The man shrugged. "General Wilczynski was commander of the Grodno Military District when the Russians invaded. He was murdered by the Russians. It was just an idle question."

But it had not been an idle question. The agent had been watching my face closely for my reaction. I tried to remain outwardly calm, although vivid memories were stirring in my mind. Then, as we rode to the garrison in a taxi, I suddenly knew who General Wilczynski was. I had been with him in the staff car that day in September when we had gone out to meet the Russians. I had already remembered that there were three men in the back seat, one in the front. I had been one of those in the back, and another, I suddenly recalled, was the general. The identity of the third man in the back seat remained a blank, and I couldn't remember exactly where we were going or what happened. I knew, though, that it would come to me, and I dreaded learning the truth.

Colonel Frankowski's office, located in a building near the Horse Guard Barracks, was large, drafty, and depressing. I sat alone in it on a wooden chair, my old uniform smelling of mothballs and pinching me in the crotch, armpits, and stomach. I had not yet been issued a new uniform and was wearing the one given me in London seven years before. Since then I had not only regained my previous weight but also added twenty more pounds.

Suddenly the door burst open, and a small, ugly colonel charged into the gloomy office. His uniform was loose, and his left elbow jutted, giving the impression of his arm being perpetually akimbo. His dark eyes were small and searching, and his voice offset his physical shortcomings and the sloppiness of his loose uniform.

"Good morning, Colonel Zamoyski," he said brightly. He

grasped my hand. "By God, it's time they let you out of that rabbit warren. Please sit down and make yourself comfortable. Cigar?"

He darted nimbly behind an ancient desk and fished cigars from an old humidor. I had been briefed on Colonel Frankowski by the Polish Intelligence agents. A brilliant artilleryman, he had been shot in the left elbow by the Germans. He was a prisoner of war from early September, 1939, until March, 1944. I had expected a giant, not a midget with a crooked arm. But he was nonetheless impressive, exuding a genial authority.

"What's my assignment?" I asked, puffing on the cigar as the colonel held a match for me.

He ran his hand through slicked-down black hair and looked me over carefully. "Excellent question," he said. "Christ, I wish I had asked that when they put me here. I might have turned it down."

He explained our role. The Germans and Russians had virtually destroyed the Polish ego. Free Poles were homeless and were in danger of losing touch with Polish culture. The Communists were rewriting Polish history, destroying Polish thought, Polish nationalism, and Polish individualism. All signs of the old Poland were being erased. We were a counter-propaganda team, with instructions to bolster Polish morale and to fortify it with the truth.

"You will have many duties," the colonel said, wreathing himself in a cloud of cigar smoke. "I hear you have a good feel for history. We need someone with a love of history—true history. I hope your memory will improve as time goes on and that you'll be of great service in this area."

"In what area?" I asked.

"One of our jobs is to do research for articles in *Dziennik Polski*, the official government newspaper. We don't write the articles, of course, unless we find that someone—you?—has journalistic talent, but we help writers from the newspaper find what they want in our records. We'll start you on that job. I will arrange to have you issued a special identification card giving you access to the archives," he went on.

"What about other duties, military duties?"

The colonel sighed and leaned back in his chair. "Although we call ourselves a military organization, we have no battles to fight in the military sense. We provide information to journalists; we provide reports to our government; and we do our best to make certain that the truth of what happened to Poland does not become distorted through communist lies. We are guardians of the truth, in effect. Your duties aren't overly taxing, but I don't think you'll find them unpleasant."

Dziennik Polski, or *Polish Thought*, was sold to Poles in England and distributed through mysterious channels into communist Poland—even the eastern part now absorbed by Russia.

"We keep Poland alive," Colonel Frankowski said. Then with increased animation, he added: "Jesus, we'll show those fucking Communists yet! They can capture our bodies, but not our minds."

His words evoked fragments of memories. He sounded like someone I had known—like several people I had known.

"Colonel Zamoyski," he said, resting his crooked elbow on the desk top, "someday there will be a revolution in Poland. When it comes, we'll move in and throw the Russians the hell off our land."

"What about the Allies? Wouldn't an attack be a violation of Allied treaties with Russia?"

"Good question. If I had asked that three years ago, I would be out making a good living for my family. I say this: Fuck the Allies. They made agreements while we were on our backs. We're not bound by them. We were sold down the river, as the Americans say, but we will paddle back. Nobody can stop us."

His enthusiasm was contagious, and together we began to get excited about the possibilities, for the present and the future, both of which time periods we discussed animatedly for nearly a half hour—until, that is, the colonel pressed a buzzer, and two officers entered the office.

"Ah, good," the colonel said effusively. "Colonel Horowicz, Captain Pietriekowski, this is Colonel Zamoyski, our mystery man from Scotland. Watch these men, John. If you have secrets." he joked, "they will pull them the hell out of you." I suspected that he was joking, but suddenly things didn't seem so funny.

They were big men. Colonel Zygmund Horowicz had dark hair and eyes, massive shoulders, and a look of constant bemusement. But a facade of diffidence masked a keen sense of humor, I learned soon enough. Captain Marian Pietriekowski was fair skinned and smiling. His dynamic personality seemed to leap out at you even when he stood still. After they welcomed me to London, we chatted about small details, and then I went with them to the officers' quarters on the top floor.

"These are your sumptuous quarters," Colonel Horowicz said with a wry smile, mocking the spartan room.

"Don't look so sad," Captain Pietriekowski said as I entered. "Mine is smaller and has one less chair. This is a palace by comparison."

The room boasted a cot, a desk, a metal dresser with a cracked mirror, a desk chair, two lamps, and two small armchairs. The window looked out on a solid brick wall.

"It's fine," I said. "I'll be quite comfortable here."

"You'd better be," Marian said, laughing. "Colonel Frankowski insists that we be comfortable—or else."

In the following months, I began to feel at ease in the drab military complex on Whitehall. Hovering about me, though, was an aura of distrust, inexplicable fear, and impending doom. I worried that, at any moment, my past would come rushing into my brain and flood me with the horror that I suspected lay hidden behind the shield that my mind barely maintained.

My job was not unpleasant, as Colonel Frankowski had predicted, but it was not very satisfying because it clearly was of little importance. My work was mostly clerical, the type that any man or woman with a semblance of intelligence could handle. I had no responsibilities befitting the rank of lieutenant colonel. In fact, I was little more than an office manager for an immense store of files, although I was called the garrison historical researcher.

My office, smaller than Colonel Frankowski's but equally as drab, was in the basement among the files, many of which had been spirited out of Poland when the government and military headquarters fled from the Germans. Some had been sent out later by the Polish Underground, and some had been accumulated in the years following the war. The files included everything from early reports of military movements to activities of the Polish Intelligence and the Underground to financial reports on the operation of the government and the military. There also were files for government and military personnel, but I was unable to find my own among them. I searched, surreptitiously, for the name Komorowski. I found many, but few were officers and none was me.

In addition to files, we had history books, scientific journals, medical books, diaries, biographies, law books, ancient and modern literature, encyclopedias, and military, government, and embassy reports—all proof that the Polish could think, write, and act.

My assistant was a small man named Lieutenant Alexi Janovic. He was fifty, but he looked older. He spoke with a soft, almost inaudible voice and, when not needed, faded into the dusty archives. He worked like an automaton, gathering up massive armloads of files and poring over them like a scholar.

For diversion I went out frequently with Captain Pietriekowski. Occasionally, Colonel Horowicz would come along. Sometimes—not often—we got drunk to escape the dreariness of our existence.

Although I remembered London from my summers of study, I carefully avoided the places I had frequented, fearful that someone would recognize me. I was not certain who I was—I didn't want to be certain. Once, out of nostalgic affection, I rode a bus past the Bexley Institute, where I had studied, but I did not get off.

Work took up most of my time. We constantly received requests from the editors of *Dziennik Polski* for material for a variety of stories on Polish subjects, especially on Poland's role during the war. Lieutenant Janovic and I would dig out the material, and one of us would deliver it to the newspaper office. Much of the material was classified, so files were sent through a maze of bureaucratic channels before they appeared in print. It was very discouraging that often only 10 percent of our material was used.

When I wasn't working or going about town, I caught up on recent literature or sat in the small recreation room with other officers. We talked of Poland's days of freedom and glory. Infrequently, Colonel Frankowski appeared in his characteristic cloud of cigar smoke to take part.

"God," he said one night in November, 1949, "it may take us years to accomplish our aim, but Poland will be free again."

"Hear, hear," several men muttered. But there was a certain solemnity in their approval, a sadness that revealed doubt.

By the time I had been with the garrison a year, I had heard hundreds of similar statements and claims. All were made with a grim lack of enthusiasm, and usually such subjects were dropped immediately by tacit agreement. On this occasion, however, the conversation turned to something that made me sit up and take notice.

"If Churchill had not stopped us," Pietriekowski said, "we would have cleared up the Katyn mess. I don't like the Nazis, but I know the Russians were responsible for that. I *know* it!"

"The only man who could have helped," Colonel Frankowski said through cigar smoke, "was that poor bastard from Gnezdovo, but of course we didn't use him properly."

"Gnezdovo?" I asked, a tingling starting in my brain. "Where's that?"

"A village near Smolensk," Colonel Horowicz said. "You know, where the Katyn Forest massacre took place."

Katyn? I remembered that the Polish Intelligence officers had mentioned Katyn, but they had said nothing about a massacre. I must have looked blank. Several of the men laughed.

"Christ," Colonel Frankowski said with amusement. "Our historical researcher doesn't know about Katyn!"

"What about the man from Gnezdovo?" I asked, not to be put off. "Who's he?"

"A Russian," Colonel Maranovicz offered. "I don't remember his real name, but he came here as Michael Laboda. Our people questioned him, then got him a job. Churchill wouldn't let us publish his story in 1944. We could use it now, but we don't have him anymore."

Pain spread through my head and into my neck and shoulders. I felt the room sway with my own dizziness.

"What happened to him?"

"The NKVD hanged him," Marian said.

"And the fucking British called it suicide," Colonel Frankowski snapped. "Jesus, how can a man hang himself in an empty shack. Suicide!"

"But why?" I asked, somehow fearing the answer.

"The killings." Colonel Maranovicz said. "What else?"

Tiny sparks of memory ignited in my mind, revealing a grotesque face with a glob of blood for an eye and a mass of flesh, bone, and teeth for a mouth. Somehow, I kept from screaming, but when the pain intensified beyond endurance, I went to my small room and fell across the cot. My head pounded like a million hammers and a familiar voice boomed: "Komorowski, we're coming to get you! You can't hide from us!"

I put a name with the voice: Kalanin!

17: THE RETURN OF TERROR

T HE trembling was so violent that the broken mirror over my bureau rattled and the shade flapped against the sill. A tide of nausea rose; my head throbbed viciously; and grisly images flashed into my mind.

Bloody fangs snapped at me, and a slant-eyed man in a uniform threatened me with a hell beyond comprehension. The stocky body of a general jerked spasmodically against a barn door as bullets tore into it, then it tumbled over onto its bloody neck, its head gone. A Russian voice questioned, threatened, placated, intimidated. Bodies lay in an open grave. A Polish officer knelt and had his brains blown out through his forehead.

I was on a train, packed like a herring among bodies. The man above had a gaping hole in his face and blood poured out, warming me. There was the clacking of wheels, the hissing of steam, the tug of power as we sped along toward a grave.

I didn't realize that I was screaming until the door opened and two men entered. I tried to look at them, but my eyes seemed permanently focused on the terrible images raging in my head.

"I thought he looked awfully sick," a soft voice said. "You know his history, don't you, doctor?"

"Something of it."

The doctor loosened my necktie. I had not bothered to undress; I had simply fallen across the bed, a ripe victim for the horror locked in my brain. A bright light probed my right eye, and I felt the doctor's warm hands on my face.

"It could be a heart attack," the doctor said in Polish. At least he was a Polish doctor.

"No," I protested, trying to control my trembling. "I'm all right."

"Good," the doctor said. "Just let me check." He put a stethoscope to my chest. "Strong, but fast. Do you have any chest pains?"

"No pains. Please, just go and leave me alone."

The doctor went to the doorway and whispered to someone. I heard the word "hospital."

"No hospital!" I yelled. "It was only a nightmare; it was nothing."

But it was not a nightmare. It was reality pouring out of memory that my brain had kept locked for seven years. The gruesome images distilled my latent fears into a crushing wall of terror.

After the doctor had given me a shot to calm my nerves, everyone left. It was a small consolation. I lay in the darkness and waited for the return of the images. They didn't disappoint me. I saw starving men in cattle cars and emaciated corpses left to the buzzards in nearby fields. A panorama of horror assaulted me, and I bit the pillow to keep from screaming again. Woven through the ghastly tableau was the evil face of an NKVD sergeant. His name echoed in my mind: *Kalanin.*

Who was Kalanin? Who were those bloody, emaciated

Polish officers? Who was the stocky general whose head was chewed to bits? I didn't know the answers, and I prayed not to know. I prayed for sleep. But, instead, I lay sweating, listening to voices of the past, seeing past suffering, sleeping only in short, troubled snatches.

Finally, dawn came. I dressed and showered hurriedly and headed at once for the basement, hoping to lose myself in dull routine. Virtually everyone in the building was watching me. I worked listlessly, gathering facts to be brought to life by the editors of *Dziennik Polski*. So it went for several days.

"Jesus, you had us scared," Colonel Frankowski said one evening as we sat in the cramped dining room. "You're all right now?"

"I'm fine," I lied. "Surely you've had nightmares?"

Although Marian Pietriekowski had been the one to bring the doctor to my room, it was Zygmund Horowicz who seemed most sensitive about what was going on inside my mind. He spent a great deal of time with me in the ensuing days, and, quite often, I found him looking at me in a kindly way. He seemed always on the verge of beginning something, but he always held back. Then, one evening in my room, he could hold back no longer.

"You always said you were captured by the Russians, John, and we were talking about the Katyn massacre when you had that little spell, as you call it. Do you know anything about Katyn?"

"No. Nothing at all. How many died there?"

"Reports vary," he said. "Perhaps forty-five hundred, perhaps five thousand."

"My God! And this Russian from Gnezdovo saw all those killings?"

Colonel Horowicz, his dark face growing sad, leaned back in the small armchair. "That's what they say."

"Forty-five hundred?"

"They killed more than fifteen thousand," he said without emotion. "Only the graves of forty-five hundred were found."

"What happened to the others?"

"Nobody knows. They disappeared. Oh, there are theories, of course. They've been traced to certain points in Russia, but the trail always died. And there are rumors. One is that about five thousand officers were taken in barges out into the Baltic and sunk by naval guns.

"You should know about all this," he went on with a smile. "As Colonel Frankowski says, you're our historical researcher. You should know about Starobelsk and Ostashkov and Kozelsk."

"Kozelsk." The name seemed to fit my tongue. "Where's that?"

"It's a village in the middle of nowhere. The men from Katyn were kept at a monastery near Kozelsk. The whole file is locked up in the library, you know."

"I suppose I should see that file."

"Yes," he said, looking at me strangely. "I think you should."

The following day I went to see Colonel Frankowski. "Everyone thinks I should know more about Katyn," I said flatly.

"Everyone?" he asked. "Do *you* think so?" He waved his cigar about, creating a thin circle of smoke.

"Yes, sir, I do."

"Just to amuse yourself?"

"No, sir. I've checked, and *Dziennik Polski* has not written about it since 1947, after the British lifted their ban. I'd like to see another story in the newspaper about Katyn."

"Why?" He took the wet stub of his cigar from his mouth, inspected it with disgust, and crushed it into an ashtray.

"I know what you're thinking, sir," I said, with a thin smile, "but hearing about Katyn didn't bring on these nightmares. I have them frequently."

"So you are merely curious about it?" He lit another cigar.

"More than that. When I came here, you told me that our job was to keep our people from going soft on communism.

We should repeat the story about the massacre and the ten thousand missing officers. They should be reminded of just how far the Russians will go to accomplish their aims."

"All right," he said, but without his usual emphatic enthusiasm. "I'll have the files opened to you. But just one thing, John."

"Yes, sir?"

"Be careful. There is grisly material in those files. Don't start believing things that don't apply to you."

"Sir?"

He blew smoke, and a draft swirled it to the ceiling. "God knows where you were before you arrived in Switzerland, and I'm no psychiatrist, but I know that the mind plays tricks. You don't know where you were, and the mind needs to know about its past. Your mind could identify with events that didn't really happen to you."

"You mean that my mind might put me at Katyn, even if I wasn't there?"

"I mean precisely that."

"I'll be careful. I think I can separate fact from fantasy."

"I hope so, John. I truly hope so."

In early January, I began my research into Katyn. The librarian, a homely, brooding man, led me to a small reading room and stacked twenty-five thick manila envelopes on an old desk. My hands shook as I waited for him to leave, so I kept them behind my back.

My fear of the unknown was growing. But it had not killed my curiosity, and, locking the door, I opened the first envelope. Then for an entire month, I pored over the files. It was a month of agony. Innumerable times I wanted to stop, and, since then, I have wished that I *had* stopped. But I also wanted to go on. I could not stop.

The photographs were the most horrifying. The Germans who had discovered the graves in early 1943 had photographically chronicled *everything*. There were photos of men separating bodies with picks, shovels, and hooks, of doctors performing autopsies. There were closeups showing tiny holes in the backs of heads and jagged, gaping wounds in front. Some photographs showed how the prisoners' hands had been tied so tightly that the cord had cut through the flesh.

There were eight mass graves in the forest, each covered by fairly new evergreen trees. Some of the bodies, stacked twelve deep, were stuck together by chemical decomposition. They found the bodies of General Minkiewicz and General Smorawinski in separate graves, their hands tied behind their backs, their arms broken. General Bohaterewicz, Admiral Czernicki, and a number of other senior officers were found in a common grave.

General Wolkowicki had survived, and the files contained a statement made by him in 1943. He had served in the Russian navy during the Russo-Japanese War and had objected to the surrender of his ship by the captain. For this old loyalty, he presumed, his life had been spared. He had been taken from Kozelsk to the Smolensk prison. (This fact explained, later, in part, why the general had not been invited to the farewell dinner at Kozelsk; there was no explanation as to why Admiral Czernicki had been excluded.)

Other graves not far from the mass graves contained the bodies of several Russians in peasant garb. Some were in prison clothing. The presumption was that these men had been the grave diggers.

One bulky file contained the papers of many of the men buried at Katyn. They were all photostats. Among them were papers and letters of a woman, Janina Lewandowski, and of a Father Ziolkowski.

The files contained the rest of the sad story of Katyn—and also explained why Polish Intelligence was so interested in my story. They would be interested in anyone who might throw light on the subject because the Russians had effectively thrown all blame for the massacre onto the Germans.

The politics of the affair were easy to understand, if the morality was not. In 1943 the Soviet Union was bitterly at war with Germany, as were Great Britain and the United States. And while every shred of evidence pointed to the Russians as being responsible—from the report of the international commission of investigation immediately appointed by the Germans to the personal investigators of many senior and responsible officers, including that of the U.S. Minister to the Balkans, to the calculated and patently impossible lies and obstructionism of the Russians—the British and American high commands rigidly adhered to the Russian story. Indeed, Churchill and Roosevelt both intervened to prevent the truth's getting out.

In short, so far as the world was aware in 1950, the murderers of Katyn were the Germans. Yet in 1950, too, the Russians, the real perpetrators of the crimes, controlled Poland, and Polish Intelligence therefore had a double incentive to arrive at the truth—to accuse the true criminals and to draw the world's attention and sympathy to the plight of the victims' country, Poland.

All this became clear as I studied the file: the guilt of Russia, the enormity of the crime, the political necessity for arriving at the truth and for parading that truth.

But of far more importance to me was what I realized about myself. I *recognized* the pictures of Janina Lewandowski and of Father Ziolkowski. Yet I had never seen them before, as far as I could remember, so I could only have seen them at Kozelsk. This was the first inkling I had of the truth, but soon I was caught up, helplessly, in an avalanche of horror.

Rationally, I found it extremely difficult to believe that the Soviets could so effectively sweep a major war crime under the international carpet. Somewhere in the world, there was justice. Somehow, some day, the world would demand to know the truth.

More deeply in my mind, I endured gory nightmares from which I would awaken, suffocating, gasping, sweating profusely. I would get up, turn on the light, and sit staring at my trembling hands and at my face in the broken mirror of my bureau.

In those moments real memories came sharply. I recalled General Wilczynski's murder and my last night with Suzan. I remembered the seemingly endless week in the town hall while the Russians pounded Grodno. I could almost hear Colonel Dzierzynski's biting sarcasm as he groused about the Russians' not knowing the way to Rumania. I could see Antoni Urban's dark, happy face and hear his cheerful voice find humor in the grimness of our captivity.

When I came across a partial list of the dead—some papers had been destroyed in the grave, from decomposition —memories of my other friends became clear. The names leaped out at me and became real people with smiles, ailments, problems, personalities, and hopes. I saw, in my mind's eye, the homely, pock-marked face of Josef Konopka, the huge head and skeletal frame of Vincenty Jankowski, the quiet and serene expression of Henryk Jagiello. I saw the fair face of Stanislaw Kaczmarek and his head of peach-fuzz blond hair. I saw the strong arms of Leo Bednarek and heard him curse the Communists for taking his family's farm and killing his two brothers.

The calm, plain beauty of Janina Lewandowski grew sharp in my memory, and I saw her sitting with her friends. And I saw the Club, with its glittering old chandelier and thick, faded playing cards. I saw General Minkiewicz in a shabby suit, walking with great dignity between two rows of officers— going to what we thought was freedom.

Final certainty came to me when I saw the face and fragile body of little Father Kantak, whose name was not on the list of the dead found at Katyn, and I remembered how he had hovered over my cot when I had been brought to the barracks after seventy-four hours of interrogation and beatings. This puzzled me.

Then I knew.

The camp at Kozelsk was no longer hazy. I remembered *Kombrig* Zarubin. There was Commissar Koraliev standing on the stoop of the administration building giving a speech. There was Colonel Miranov. I remembered Pavel Borodynsky and his soft blue eyes and kindly voice. And Kalanin! I could see those slanted eyes, those yellow teeth, smell that reeking breath. I remembered flying into a rage and nearly choking him to death.

The images and recollections, both good and gruesome, had found a basis in the files. *I had been at Kozelsk! I had been at Katyn!*

Fortunately, the full impact of Katyn did not crash into my consciousness all at once. It seeped in, tormenting me in small doses, day by day. When I finally remembered Antoni's murdered face, I did not scream. I merely wept silently.

Early in March, two men from Polish Intelligence came to my room at midnight to ask why I was investigating the Katyn affair. One of the men was short and nervous. He reminded me a great deal of Rudolf Kochloffel, except that I took an instant dislike to this man, just as I had taken an instant liking to Rudolf.

I was of course on guard. I now knew practically everything about myself, but, more important to the others, I knew enough about Katyn to place the responsibility where it belonged. And given the pains to which the Russians had gone to conceal their responsibility, I knew that my information could easily be lethal. The only thing that had changed was that now I *knew* I was right to be paranoid.

I decided to play the whole thing down and told them that I was investigating Katyn for a possible story in *Dziennik Polski* and that the assignment had been approved by Colonel Casimir Frankowski, my commanding officer.

The pudgy man with the nervous eyes asked bluntly: "Was this Colonel Frankowski's idea?"

Uneasily I said, "No, it was my idea."

He seemed to be searching for a weakness. "I see," he said. "Why did you want to know so much about Katyn?"

"There's no big mystery," I replied, trying to be casual. "Colonel Frankowski once chided me for not knowing about Katyn. After all, I am supposed to be a historical researcher here. I should know about it, and the colonel had every right to chide me. I decided to learn about it and to obtain material for a newspaper story at the same time."

The agent glanced at his partner, a slim, taciturn young man who didn't appear to understand what he was doing. "I see," he repeated. "But why bother? The case was settled long ago."

"I got just the opposite impression," I retorted. "It appears that nothing was settled."

It was a slip, and the short man caught it. He leaned forward and inspected his fingernails. "In what way, Colonel Zamoyski?" he asked evenly.

Backpedaling, I reviewed what I had learned, mentioning the fact that the Tribunal at Nuremburg had failed to handle the case properly. Another slip.

"Are you a judge? Are you an attorney?"

"I don't know," I said, relieved to find myself on familiar ground. "You must know my history. I don't what what I was before the war."

"You remember nothing of your past?" His question carried a note of skepticism, as though he knew that I was lying. He seemed to be waiting for me to blurt out the truth, but I did not trust him. I began to feel as though I was back at Kozelsk being interrogated by NKVD officers.

The questioning continued for an hour. One minute, the pudgy little man would appear quite hostile; the next, soothing and friendly. I lied about virtually everything. No, I did not remember my real name. No, I had no knowledge of Katyn beyond what I had read in the files. No, I did not remember if I had been captured by the Germans or the Russians. The war years, and the years following it, were still a blank.

After they left, I lay on my cot and let my mind float along on the memories I had retrieved. Following a chronological pattern, my mind unraveled much of that lost period.

And then the final piece clicked into place.

In one blinding, explosive flash, the knowledge of Suzan's death came to me! I saw the fat, pink face of the man in our apartment in Grodno and heard him laugh. He spoke of a crazy woman with golden hair who had fought the Russians and was shot. He called her a whore, a Russian whore! Great sobs wrenched my body, and I cried openly, unashamedly, not caring if anyone heard me through the paper thin walls of my room and thought me crazy. My grief could not be contained; it was as though Suzan had died that very moment!

Memories of her flooded in with the grief. I saw Suzan at the high school in Poznan, laughing, smiling, flirting, exuding the vitality that was her trademark. I saw her in the little tea shop we had frequented after evening classes, her eyes glittering with happiness as we discussed marriage. I heard her breathe those two words that I came to love: "Oh, Andrei!"

There was nothing left. Except me—Eugenjusz Andrei Komorowski, probably the only living eyewitness to one of the war's most barbarous and unnecessary crimes, of use only to the politicians of both sides. Everywhere I turned I saw people waiting to destroy me, the Russians certainly, and even the Poles in their own way.

In the days following the visit by the two Polish Intelligence agents—if they were agents—I went about my duties in London torn between fear and conscience. As an officer in the Polish Army Reserves, even a decimated army living in squalor in a foreign land, it was my clear responsibility to tell the world what I knew of the Katyn massacre. Moreover, I had sworn to do so. That had been the spur that had driven me out of Grodno—that was supposed to have been my revenge on the Russians. But that also had been years ago, before my flight across Europe to Switzerland, before my hospitalization—both periods of life I never fully remembered —and now I felt that all I could do to triumph was to survive. And even that would be difficult.

In my paranoia, I felt I owed no one but myself anything. And to myself I owed life above all else. Moreover, it was *my life* that I was most likely to lose once I revealed what I knew.

The Russians had murdered nearly half the officer corps of the Polish military because Stalin wanted Poland. Those officers, representing the cream of the Polish intelligentsia, were a threat to his designs, and so they had been liquidated. He had achieved his goal, almost without effort—and with the tacit support of the Allies. In spite of massive evidence that the Russians had committed the act, Western powers had chosen to help the Soviets cover up the crime. Only the Germans and the Free Poles wanted the truth to be told.

Even though the Western world was disenchanted with the Russians in 1950, would the people be interested in proof of a Russian war crime? Would they believe the truth, and would they offer sanctuary to the man who provided that proof? What protection had been given to the Russian peasant who called himself Michael Laboda but whose real name was Ivan Krivosertsov, and who had identified himself in a long deposition he made to officers of the Second Polish Army Corps in the fall of 1944 as an eyewitness to the massacre of Polish officers in the Katyn Forest near his home, a man who had tried to hide himself in a quiet suburb of London after confessing all he knew? None. He had "committed suicide."

And if there was no protection for Ivan Krivosertsov, how much would there be for me, whom the Russians would have more reason to get rid of. I was an officer, a Pole, a victim: in short, a far more dangerous witness.

During that agonizing period my nights were full of terrifying nightmares and my days full of fears that some Communist hiding in our ranks would find me out. I was convinced that Communists had infiltrated the Free Polish movement, and I strongly suspected that the Intelligence men who had come to question me at midnight were Soviet agents. I had no proof, of course, but a mind that has something to conceal rarely needs proof; where none exists, the mind manufactures it.

Somehow I had to get away. But how? How much did the Russians know? Surely they would not need proof to act? Strong suspicion would be sufficient justification for them to dispose of me. And what did Polish Intelligence know of me? If they knew very much, surely their information would get back to the Russians. Why had they asked me about Katyn on my arrival in London? Why had one agent asked me about General Wilczynski? Why was I assigned to a unit where I would be in close contact with historical data? Was it to jog my memory? I began to suspect that my fellow officers had deliberately concocted the conversation about Katyn to see if it had any effect on me.

I tried desperately to rid my mind of suspicions. But in mid-May, an event took place that forced me to come to a decision.

On the evening of May 18, I broke a rule I had some time ago adopted for myself by going out alone for a walk. It was a pleasant day in London, and the trees in the parks and along the boulevards were bursting with new green. Flowers blossomed in tiny garden plots, and the city seemed quiet, safe, and inviting. I walked along the Victoria Embankment beside the Thames. Hundreds of people were outdoors, enjoying the fine weather. At dusk, I left the Embankment and headed toward the headquarters building by way of Trafalgar Square. When I reached Charing Cross, a black limousine pulled alongside, and a man jumped out from the back seat.

"Pardon me, sir," he said, "could you please direct us to St. James's Park?"

As I stopped to give him directions, I noticed that the driver of the car also had gotten out and was coming around the car toward me. There were only a few people on the sidewalk, and all at once the man who had asked directions grabbed my arm with a suddenness that startled me.

"Come along," he said in a nervous whisper. "We want to talk to you."

The man and the driver pushed me toward the open door of the car, and one of them forced my head down. Inside, I saw a third man sitting in the far corner of the back seat. The man in the car was the pudgy Polish Intelligence agent who had come to question me in my room!

I grabbed the top of the car and braced myself against the pressure from behind. "Let go!" I shouted. Fear and rage mixed inside me.

The pudgy man in the car looked squarely at me. "Hurry up, Colonel Zamoyski. We have a lot to talk about."

It was, I thought in an instant, another fight for life, and again instinct took over. As the driver took a pistol from his coat pocket, I lashed out, knocking the gun out of his hand. It clattered across the sidewalk. I swung with my left hand and caught the first man in the throat with my fist.

A few people had stopped on the sidewalk to watch, but no one moved to help. I knew I had little time. Slamming the door on the man in the car, I threw myself at the driver, bowling him over, and set off up the street, running as fast as I could in a scuttling, limping, desperate run. Back on the Embankment, I mingled with the strollers as I made my way up toward Westminster Bridge. No cars were allowed on the Embankment in those days, so I knew that the men would have to chase me on foot, if they chased me at all. I climbed the steps to the bridge and looked back along the wide Embankment. The three men were not in sight; there were only people strolling in the warm evening along the silently flowing Thames.

Slackening my pace, I disappeared into the crowds again. I passed Westminster Abbey and worked my way, circuitously, down narrow alleys until I came to the headquarters building. Entering the back door, I went immediately to my room, where I pulled the shade and locked the door. Safe! The pudgy man and his companions would hardly try to grab me in my quarters unless they really were Polish Intelligence agents.

All the terror and uncertainty of Kozelsk returned to me; it all seemed clear. If Intelligence wanted to talk to me, they had only to come to my room or send a message. Therefore, the man in the car *was* a communist counteragent. If so, it meant that the Communists were on to me, and if they were, they certainly would try again. The first effort had been bungled. I would hardly be so lucky the second time.

I decided to go it alone. Specifically, I decided not to tell anyone about the incident, not even Colonel Frankowski. I trusted the colonel, but what could he do to protect me from future assaults? And how would I explain why I had been accosted without giving away my story? The decision was reinforced the following day. In the files I ran across another, and more recent, Russian crime, one almost as blatant as Katyn, that the world had chosen to ignore.

In a seeming effort to bring about a peaceful settlement of the differences between the Soviets and the Free Poles, Soviet Marshal Zhukov, in 1945, invited Polish Vice Premier Jan Jankowski, who was serving in the Polish Government-in-Exile in London, to come to Moscow for talks. He was asked to bring twenty-six members of the Free Polish movement with him. The twenty-six associates just happened to have been former leaders in the Polish Underground. The visit was highly publicized in the London press as a good will gesture on the part of the Soviets. A plane was sent to London to fly the delegation to Moscow, but the plane carrying the vice premier and his party did not land at either of Moscow's two main passenger airports. It landed some distance from the city, and the delegation was met not by Marshal Zhukov but by a contingent of NKVD guards.

According to news stories in Russian and British newspapers, the twenty-seven men were taken directly to Lubianka Prison, and the Kremlin announced that the men would stand trial for "reactionary crimes against the People's Republic of Poland." In spite of protests from the British and American governments, the men were tried, found guilty, and executed by the Russians.

If the Soviets could commit such an open act of murder, with the whole world looking on, what chance did I have? First Krivosertsov/Laboda, then the twenty-seven leading Poles. And I would be safe? And if I were to be next, what good would it do my corpse even if my eventual execution was protested by the Britsh and the Americans?

The more I thought about it, the more convinced I became that I was a loose end; and the Russians did not leave loose ends lying around. There would be other attempts to kidnap me, and one, eventually, would succeed. Then I, too, would die.

The only course of action, in my mind, was to leave London, to leave England, Europe. I thought of going to Switzerland, where I might find peace and safety in a remote mountain village. And I thought of returning to Scotland, remembering the medical student's invitation to come back at anytime. But I discarded both ideas. I felt that no place in or near Europe was safe—I needed to put more space between me and the Communists.

I finally decided that I would go to the United States. Of course there was no country in the world where I would feel perfectly safe. There were Communists in America, I knew, but I didn't believe they could be as extreme as those infesting Europe. In any case, I subscribed to the idea that America was the land of opportunity, safety, and freedom. For me, America was the least of all evils.

During the night of May 20, 1951, I made my decision. In the morning, I went directly to Colonel Frankowski's office to execute my plan.

"I've been wanting to talk to you," the colonel began, waving a dead cigar. "When are they going to print the Katyn story?"

"I don't think they will, sir. The editors felt that there was no new information to justify a story now."

"Too goddamn bad. You spent a long time on that."

"Yes, sir, a long time. I probably should have checked with the editors before I started the research."

"Anyway," he said, holding a match to the stub of a cigar, 'you wanted to speak with me?"

"Only to ask if I might take a leave of absence."

He gazed at me curiously, his crooked elbow resting on the scarred old desk, his stubby cigar clamped between his teeth.

"Jesus, you *are* feeling better. Our little sparrow wishes to leave the nest, eh?"

I shrugged nonchalantly. I had learned something from the Russians. "I've saved my back pay," I told him. "It's burning holes in my pocket and I've always wanted to visit America."

"So have I," the colonel said. "I wish I could go with you, but I don't have any money burning holes in my pocket. I'll get you the leave, John. I can't think of anyone who deserves it more."

The wheels of bureaucracy turned slowly. It was three weeks before I was able to obtain a visa for a ten-day visit to the United States. During that time, I stayed in the headquarters building and slept with my shade pulled. I was constantly on the alert, distrusting even Lieutenant Janovic, and my nerves became raw.

The time finally came, however. And on the morning of June 21, Captain Marian Pietriekowski and Colonel Zygmund Horowicz accompanied me to the train station. I was to sail from Southampton the following day aboard the S.S. *Île de France*.

"I still say you should fly," Marian said as we walked

through the concourse to the train gate. He was carrying my old suitcase, which contained my worldly possessions, including three thousand dollars. I had left my uniform in my room and had bought a new suit.

"Airplanes crash," I said.

"Ships sink," he replied, grinning.

"But not as often—or as quickly."

"I'm on your side, John," Colonel Horowicz said. "I'd certainly go by boat. You have a better chance of getting there in one piece."

"Or at all," I said. I wasn't joking.

We stood at the gate, and people filed through to the train. Zygmund Horowicz gripped my hand, then embraced me.

"We'll miss you, John, but it's good to see you smiling and laughing. And you're not even drunk. Have a good trip and come back safely."

"We'll keep your room ready," Marian said.

I was tempted to tell them that I would not return. But I said nothing. Just as once I had seemed destined to reap good fortune from the dead, I now seemed destined to lose good friends through misfortune.

In Southampton there was no easing of the fear. I spent the night in a cheap hotel, where I wrote a letter of resignation to Colonel Frankowski. In the letter, I told him that I could not continue living in the vacuum that was my life, that I would seek a new identity in America and, I hoped, find happiness, at least safety and security. I asked him, as a friend, to keep my letter confidential until I was safely on shore in America. The letter was highly emotional, and I counted heavily on the colonel's compassion to give me the opportunity that I sought, that I needed.

I mailed the letter near the docks and boarded the ship just before noon. I stood at the railing for a while and waved to anonymous faces on the dock, looking constantly for the pudgy man, but even before the ship departed, I went to my stateroom and locked the door. In my paranoia I was reasonably sure that certain passengers on the ship were Russian agents, waiting to toss me overboard, so I seldom went out.

An additional worry concerned Colonel Frankowski. Would he turn my letter over to higher authorities in London? I had every right to resign, but if Polish Intelligence wanted me and learned where I was, a message could be sent by radio to the ship or to the authorities in New York. I would be taken into custody, perhaps even returned to London. All this could happen, but I counted on the fact that there was nothing amiss in what I was doing, and that therefore the colonel would do nothing. In any case, as the fears for my personal safety grew, my concern about the letter lessened.

It was, to say the least, a dismal voyage.

18: LAND OF FREEDOM, LAND OF FEAR

THERE is no prison as impregnable as that contrived by the mind. Thus even as the *Île de France* cut the calm waters of New York harbor, the cold steel bars of my mental prison kept me from the soaring liberty that America traditionally promised.

There was no doubt in my mind that the Russians, or their agents, strongly suspected that I knew something about Katyn. The questions I could find no answers to were: How much did the Russians and the Polish Communists know of me? Had they kept abreast of my activities during my last two months in London? Did they know that I had come to America on a ten-day visa? Were communist agents aboard the ship? But there were no answers—only fear.

All I hoped for was a place in the vast city to hide, to become anonymous. I planned to find out where most of the Polish immigrants stayed and to live in that section of the city, disappearing into their ranks.

263

When the ship docked, I waited until almost everyone had
gone ashore. Then I took my battered suitcase and went up
to the deck to disembark. I stood at the rail for several minutes, watching the crowd on the dock, before descending
the gaily decorated gangway.

As I walked along the pier, I glanced cautiously about,
fearful that someone would leap out of the crowd—in broad
daylight—and shoot me in the head. I sighed deeply with relief when I reached the street and got into the back seat of a
taxi.

The driver looked at me in the rearview mirror, then
asked: "Where to, buddy?"

"A hotel," I replied. "A very cheap hotel."

He grunted and flipped down the meter flag. He drove
along West Avenue. I didn't think we were being followed.

Since the Russians would be looking for a man who limped
from an old wound, who spoke good English, who knew history, and who was well educated, I had already decided that
the moment I hit New York I would be none of those. I was
a poor Polish immigrant who knew little. Only the limp gave
me trouble.

The taxi jolted northward and turned down Thirty-fourth
Street. After we had gone four blocks, I told the driver to
stop.

"There's no cheap hotel here, buddy," he said, disgruntled.

"No matter. I want out here."

He stopped so abruptly that I lurched forward. I gave him
a dollar and got out. He squealed his tires as he drove off.

To be at the corner of Thirty-fourth Street and Seventh
Avenue in the middle of the afternoon is to be in crowds. In
fact, that is what I'd noticed and why I'd gotten out. Keeping
up with the masses, I crossed Thirty-fourth and walked south
on Seventh, frequently glancing behind me to see if I was
being followed. It was impossible to tell, but to be sure I was
safe, at the next corner I turned west to Ninth Avenue, then
south to Twenty-third. Finally I came out near the docks at

Twenty-sixth Street. A small neon hotel sign hung on the front
of a dilapidated brick building, a likely looking place. Looking
up and down the street to make sure that nobody was watching
me, I ducked inside and registered under the name of John
Pulaski. It was the first name that came to mind.

At least the hotel was cheap. I paid a grimy-looking clerk
sixteen dollars for a week and walked up three flights to my
room, which overlooked the docks and the Hudson River. I
spent hours at that window, watching the street below and
listening to traffic roar past above me on the elevated West
Side Highway.

I stayed there only three nights. Each day I walked around
and, by asking people on the streets, finally located a Polish
section in Manhattan. There were Poles in other parts of the
city, I learned, but I wanted to stay in Manhattan, where
there were more people. I still felt that safety lay in numbers,
in spite of what had happened at Kozelsk.

On the fourth day, I found an apartment on the second
floor of a shabby old building on Third Avenue near Fourteenth Street. I gave the name Abraham Switzky, a name I had
found in the obituary column of the *New York Times*. The
apartment consisted of a tiny parlor, a bedroom, and a
curtained-off section for cooking. I was to share the bath
down the corridor with the other tenants on the floor.

If it had not been for sharing the bathroom, my fear might
have made me a hermit. But within a week of being in the
apartment, I had met the others on the floor. I found them
to be quite friendly, even though I was reluctant to make
friends. To make friends was to make myself vulnerable. So I
hid myself from them, speaking broken English, trying to
sound like many of the Poles I had met in London who had
not learned the language before leaving Poland, covering my
tracks.

Nevertheless, I made friends. My first acquaintances were
Lothar Rikinian, a retired hotel doorman who had fled
Rumania in 1946, and Alfred Kruk, an old Lithuanian who

had been a construction worker in New York for many years. Although I was forty-nine and they were in their late sixties, we appeared to be the same age. My hair was thoroughly gray.

Lothar was a small, wistful man who said little and never complained. Alfred, who was large, with broad shoulders, loved to boast about climbing the bare girders of New York's skyscrapers. We played cards, mostly in Alfred's room, when Alfred wasn't bragging about his prowess as a builder of skyscrapers and walker of girders.

I began to experience real pleasure when I met the Czerniakowskis, one of four Polish families in the building. The meeting came about in an unusual manner and frightened me half out of my wits. Early on a Saturday morning a small, almost inaudible knock sounded on the door. Inevitably, I jumped to the conclusion that the Communists had come for me. I grabbed an old oak cane I had bought to help me eliminate my limp and held it at the ready behind the door.

"Who is it?" I demanded.

The knock came again, but this time so tenuously that I began to wonder. Foolishly lowering the heavy cane, I opened the door a crack. Standing in the hallway was a tiny blonde girl with fragile, beautiful features. My God, I thought, a miniature Suzan!

"Hello," the little girl said. "My name is Bettina. Do you have any stories to tell?"

I was so relieved that I tossed the cane on the bed and opened the door wider. Trembling, I touched her shoulder.

"You're shaking," she said. "Why are you shaking?"

I was shaking as much from the appearance of the child —so much like Suzan's—as I was from the recent bout of fear. But I smiled and explained that I always trembled in the presence of pretty girls.

"You silly," she said. "Do you have any stories to tell me? Mr. Kruk tells wonderful stories about climbing over skyscrapers."

"I've lots of stories to tell you, Bettina," I said. I was unable to take my eyes from her face. "Not today, though. Today, I must look for a job." I had been living on my savings, which I had spread under the old carpet in the parlor, and I knew three thousand dollars wouldn't go far.

"Papa says you must be rich," she said. She had an enchanting, tinkling voice. "Rich people don't have to look for jobs, do they?"

Apparently, my idleness during the two weeks I had been in the apartment had been noticed. In this poor neighborhood virtually everyone worked. Even Alfred and Lothar had part-time jobs as custodians in nearby office buildings.

"Who is your papa?" I asked.

"His name is Stanley and he has a big belly like this." She swung thin, pink arms, indicating a huge stomach. "Mama says he drinks too much beer, but I think he's going to have a baby. What do you think?"

"I think you're too young to know about such things."

"I'm four years old!" she said indignantly.

"Oh, excuse me. I didn't realize you were so old."

She cocked her pretty head at me; her golden hair bounced on her slim shoulders. "You're old," she said. "Are you a hundred?"

A door opened down the corridor, and a man with a potbelly came toward us. He was short and stout, with a round face that was almost beet red.

"Bettina," he scolded, "I told you not to bother people."

I looked up. "It's nothing," I said in my deliberately fractured English. "It's good to have such pretty visitor. You are her papa?"

He extended his large, meaty hand. He was younger than he looked at first, possibly thirty. "Stanley Czerniakowski," he said.

"Abraham Switzky." There was no hesitation. I practiced the name virtually in my sleep, frightened half out of my wits that I might make a slip and use my real name.

"We teach our children not to bother other people in the building," Stanley apologized. "We're the only people here with children, and they can be a nuisance."

"Not to me. She reminds me of . . . of one of my children."

He laughed an easy, throaty laugh, that old Polish chuckle. His round face beamed, and I instantly liked Stanley Czerniakowski. He put his meaty hands on his daughter's fragile shoulders and squeezed them affectionately. "We call her B-24," he said, laughing. "She's a regular little bomber."

"I wouldn't bomb anybody," Bettina protested. "Bombs are nasty."

"You're right," I said. "Bombs are very nasty, but little bombers with golden hair are quite pretty. Here, I got something for you, little bomber."

I kept a supply of candy in my bureau because my taste for sugar had not diminished since my days at Kozelsk. I brought Bettina a Hershey bar. She looked up at her father, and he nodded. Snatching the candy, she ran down the corridor, squealing delightedly.

"That was a mistake," Stanley said amiably. "Now her sister and brother will be pestering you for candy."

"I have plenty," I said. I gave him candy for his other two children; he apologized again and then left.

The Czerniakowskis lived in the shabby, dreary building while Stanley worked as a stevedore and saved money to buy a house in the Bronx. His wife, Olga, was attractive, even in dresses that made her look matronly. Their son, Stanley, Jr., was small and puny-looking; he had suffered a childhood disease, which they never discussed. Their eldest child, Dorothy, was a direct contrast: a husky child of eight who used her strength and cunning to protect her puny brother. Dorothy had the disconcerting habit of hiding until boys on the street made Stanley cry, then of swooping down like the eagle of death to pummel them into submission.

I was constantly on guard against a slip, even with my new

friends. To throw everyone off any scent they might detect, I made vague hints about having lived in another section of the state and about having a wife who had recently died. When asked a direct question, I made it clear that I did not wish to speak of my past. The questions soon stopped; few people in America, I soon found out, cared to press too hard for answers. Perhaps everyone had things to hide.

Of course, I still was convinced that the NKVD would find me, even in this nondescript building on the edge of New York's Greenwich Village. But hours of street-watching from my window turned up nothing suspicious. Indeed, things became *better*—I found a quiet job as a dishwasher in a small restaurant on Fourteenth Street. The pay was abominable —barely enough to let me eke out an existence—but the conditions were ideal. I worked in a tiny kitchen, out of public view.

The only problem with the job was the hours: four in the afternoon until midnight. I was deathly afraid of being on the streets after dark. Each night, as I walked home from the restaurant, I peered into loading docks, fully expecting a whole squadron of NKVD men and dogs to leap out at me. If someone happened to be dawdling on the street when I walked by, I circled the block, even went several blocks out of my way, to be sure that I had lost him before going to my apartment.

Nights were always the worst. Each time a car stopped, each time I heard footsteps on the stairs, I felt that they had come. Sweat bathed my body and soaked my sheets. Sleep brought little respite.

Any knock on the door sent me into a frenzy of fear. I kept the oak cane leaning against the wall beside my bed. In time I learned to recognize the most common knocks, those of Stanley Czerniakowski or Alfred Kruk or Lothar Rikinian. There was no mistaking the light knock of little Bettina Czerniakowski. But others came, salesmen, the landlord, messengers from the restaurant who came to fetch me when the daytime dishwasher called in sick and I was wanted to take his place. The strain was difficult to live with, especially at first.

Fortunately, in time, the routine of living dulled my fears. Within a year, I no longer jumped when someone knocked on the door or when a car stopped outside the building. I even stopped sitting beside the window watching for NKVD agents, and my nightmares became less intense and horrifying.

A great aid to my condition was the Czerniakowski children. They visited often, and I told them wild stories and gave them candy.

Another help was Stanley Czerniakowski, a man who had the strong, thick arms of Leo Bednarek and the thick neck of Colonel Dzierzynski. A jovial man without an overt problem in the world, Stanley belonged to a Polish-American Club in the Bronx, and he insisted that I go there with him each week.

Most of all, I loved hearing the tenuous knock on my door and rushing to see the little bomber, Bettina Czerniakowski.

"Will you tell me another story? One just for me?"

"Do you want a story about good people or bad people?"

She would ponder a moment, then announce her decision: "Good people. I'm not in the mood for bad people today."

"Neither am I. Bring Dorothy and little Stanley and we have a story about good people. We also have some candy."

She would pout because she always wanted a story just for herself. But the candy would persuade her, and she would run off to fetch her brother and sister.

I always placed the stories in America, in cities I had heard of but never visited, although the people were modeled after those I had known during happy days in Poland. There were many stories about Suzan and Antoni.

Infrequently, I was invited to have dinner with the family, and I began to trust them. At Christmas that first year I had a basket of fruit delivered to their door. I almost signed the card: Eugenjusz Komorowski.

During my trips to the Bronx with Stanley I became acquainted with New York's complex subway system, which frightened me to death at first, and got my first exposure to television.

Television fascinated me. And the chief news subject had a large effect on me. There was a great deal of talk about the threat of communism in America, and Senator Joseph McCarthy claimed repeatedly that Communists had infiltrated all levels of American life—from local American Legion posts to the administration of the President of the United States. I did not need any convincing, of course. But assertions that there was a Communist in every woodpile only helped to intensify my fears. If the Communists did in fact take over, it would surely be an easy matter for them to find and murder me.

Stanley Czerniakowski, typically, took all the talk of communism lightly. In fact, I found a kind of safety in his attitude. It was like learning that someone else does not believe in the horrors of purgatory or hell, that someone else shares your hopeful feelings about those places of terror.

"That crazy bastard McCarthy will have us all in jail as Commies," Stanley groused one night as we sat drinking beer at the club bar. I drank very little beer then, and no whisky, fearful that I might overindulge and say things about my past that I wanted kept secret.

The bartender leaned over the bar. "And you, Stanley Czerniakowski, will be one of the first to wind up in the can."

"Why should I go to jail?"

The bartender laughed. "For calling the senator a crazy bastard."

"Well, he is," Stanley said gruffly. He drained his glass and ordered two more beers. I was still sipping on my first one. "Come on, Abe," he said to me, "let's go downstairs and bowl a couple of games."

He knew that I couldn't bowl. My right arm was crooked, and the weight of the bowling ball made my shoulder hurt terribly. But he always asked me, and I always wound up sitting back and watching him fire the black missile down the hardwood alleys to scatter pins all over the place. He was a furious and fairly accurate bowler.

I suppose I was settling down. The talk of communism, the McCarthy hearings, which I followed on the radio, and the general paranoia did not have the effect on me that I had expected. Perhaps it was simply that in New York, having experienced nothing untoward, I was learning that there was more to life than I had known for more than ten years.

I played cards frequently with Lothar Rikinian and Alfred Kruk. I also read paperback books, bought at a newsstand near the restaurant where I worked, and told endless stories to the Czerniakowski children. The hurt of the war and the sordid memories of Kozelsk and the Katyn graves were disappearing. Even my grief over Suzan was lessening. I enjoyed being Abraham Switzky, dishwasher. I still was on guard. Always careful, I exercised an hour each day in the privacy of my apartment. If the NKVD came for me, I wanted to be ready for them physically.

In the autumn of 1951 I needed my wits. Everything suddenly changed.

In August the newspapers had announced that the House of Representatives was establishing a select committee to investigate the Katyn Forest massacre. News of the impending investigation was like the opening of an old wound. Fear returned to me with overwhelming force. Compounding my fear was the knowledge that the select committee would be searching the world for witnesses to the events leading up to and following the crime. So far, no investigative body had found a witness to the crime itself.

I was that witness, and the powerful House of Representatives would be doing everything possible to turn up an eyewitness. The Communists, too, would be searching, and they, unlike the committee, knew that I was an eyewitness to the crime—or at least I thought they knew. They had found me in London; they could find me in the United States.

It would be especially easy to find me if I volunteered my information to the committee, and I was not about to point the finger at myself, especially since I had come to the conclusion that Americans really did not care who had murdered the more than fifteen thousand Polish officers. They were too concerned with their own problems. In short, what would telling my story accomplish? And what help could a Polish dishwasher named Abraham Switzky expect? Probably he would be killed, at least deported as an illegal immigrant.

Of course, I battled with my conscience, as I had in London. After all, these were to be congressional hearings, not the sham of Nuremburg, where the Russians had called the plays. And this was America, where a large and powerful Polish community demanded a true rendering of the story and where truth was held to be the foundation of the state. But in the end, feelings of self-preservation and a healthy respect for public apathy, whatever its intentions, kept me quiet.

Unfortunately, my decision did not allay my increasing fears. I dreaded the time when the hearings would convene, sure that though I had decided to remain silent, the Communists would not know this and would have redoubled their efforts to find me. I was a threat to them; I would remain a threat as long as I lived.

Shortly after midnight on October 17, 1951, my worst fears were realized. Walking home from my job, I heard shuffling footsteps as I passed a dark loading dock. Two forms moved in the darkness, and I felt a cold rush of fear in my throat.

Two men appeared from the darkness. One approached me while the second man moved along the front of a building so that he was behind me. Convinced that I was near death, I waited, my hands closing into fists.

The first man, a short, wiry individual with dark skin, walked boldly up to me. "Got a match, Pops," he said. It was not a question. He had no cigarette in his hand.

I moved so that I was facing both of them. He repeated his question. "I don't have any matches," I said, waiting.

"How about money?" the second man asked, taking a step toward me. "You got any money?"

I gave him two dollars, all I had with me. They looked at the bills and snorted.

"You got more than that, Pops," the little man said. "Do you have it stashed away in your apartment over on Third?"

These men knew where I lived! "What you want?" I demanded, trying to hide my fear. "You have my money. Go away and leave me alone."

The men exchanged glances, and the second man reached into his pocket. I waited to see if he had a gun, but he kept his hand there. The wiry man held out his hands, placatingly.

"Look, Pops, some friends of yours want to talk to you. They would have come themselves, but the heat is on. Look, we're only trying to make a few extra bucks on the side. Now, why don't you cooperate and . . . "

"What you want?" I repeated. I knew the answer. I felt my anger rising.

"Come on," the second man said irritably. "Let's go to your place, then we can bullshit about what to do next."

As he talked, he drew a gun from his pocket and moved toward me. My fear changed swiftly to rage. God damn it, I was not going to go without a fight. I leaped at the man and grabbed his wrist, forcing the gun into the air. I slammed my fist into his stomach and heard the pistol clatter on the pavement. The second man came at me, and I smashed him in the face.

The fight lasted only a few minutes. At the end the men lay crumpled on the sidewalk. The street was empty, quiet.

Then I ran, stumbling, to my apartment. Quickly, I collected my money from beneath the rug, packed my few belongings, and took the subway to the Pennsylvania Station, mentally thanking Stanley Czerniakowski for teaching me how to use the complex transportation system. In the back of my fear-stricken mind was the thought that I would go to Milwaukee. I had no reason to go there, except that I remembered that Colonel Dzierzynski had worn a wristwatch made in Milwaukee. It was as good a place as any.

Perhaps I could find sanctuary there.

The morning was bright, the air crisp. I rode a taxi from the station to a small hotel in south Chicago, registered as Stanley Kaminski, and hid there for three days, once again peering from behind dirty curtains, waiting for the Russians to come.

On the fourth day I boarded a train for Milwaukee and changed my name to Andrew Kowalski. As I waited for the train to move, a big man with a brilliant smile and unruly black hair bustled aboard. He tossed a huge canvas bag on the luggage rack above me.

"Halloo," he said effusively. "This is the last seat. Jesus, there's not a pretty woman on this whole fucking train."

The man, who spoke with a thick French accent, fell into the seat beside me and immediately launched into a friendly conversation. Within minutes, I knew that his name was Louis Fontaine—"call me Louie"—that he had sailed the Great Lakes for several years, and that he loved women almost as much as sailing. He had vivid blue eyes—sharp and full of the devil—raven hair, curly and thick, and muscled arms covered with an assortment of tattoos.

Louis Fontaine was burly, raucous, loud, and thoroughly likable.

"You a sailor?" he asked as the train moved out.

"No."

"Goddamn pity. Everybody should be a sailor. I try to get boat out of Chicago, but nothing goes this time of year. Fuck Chicago. I go to work on ferry to Michigan until goddamn lake freeze. You want to be sailor, white hair?"

"I hadn't thought about it."

"How old are you? You too old to be sailor?"

"I'm fifty," I told him. "I just look older."

He scrutinized me carefully. "Too fucking bad you not think to be sailor. You make one fine sailor."

"Why do you say that?"

"Big shoulders for pulling lines," he said, his face a kaleidoscope of merriment. "Long legs for good balance. And that face. Jesus, bet you drive women crazy with rugged face and gray hair, white hair."

It suddenly struck me that I had not slept with a woman in twelve years! Once in London, Marian Pietriekowski and I had gotten drunk and picked up two whores in a bar. But I had fallen asleep on her. And here was a wild French sailor telling me that I must drive women crazy!

"I never been on ship," I lied to him.

"No matter," he said, peering out the train window. He laughed at something outside. "You got a job?"

"No."

"What will you do in Milwaukee?"

"Work for watch company."

"Which watch company?"

"I don't know. They have one, don't they?"

"Damn if I know. Holy Jesus, why work for a fucking watch company when you can be sailor? You come with me in Milwaukee. I fix it so you get sailing papers. Most lake sailors already go to ocean because weather soon cold. I got friends, so I fix it for you. Ferries need men bad."

Louis Fontaine chattered, laughed, and bragged all the way to Milwaukee. In his way he was as engaging as Antoni Urban. He was good medicine, and he gave me little time to worry about the Russians.

"Tell me, Louis," I said once, interrupting his rhapsody of the life of a sailor, "you have been to Paris?"

"Why do you ask such question?"

"You're French, aren't you?"

He roared. "How you tell that? You reader of minds? Sure

I am French and sure to hell I been to Paris. Everybody been
to Paris."

"I haven't," I said. "Once, I was to meet some friends
there."

"What happened, Kowalski? Why you not go to Paris to
meet with friends?"

I gazed at his sparkling blue eyes and knew that he would
not understand the sadness I felt.

"Something happen on way to Paris," I told him. "Something which keep us all from meeting there."

"Too fucking bad. You would have liked Paris."

As soon as we entered the rambling old boarding house near
the Kinnickinnic River, I knew that it was a whorehouse. A
plump woman with bleached hair squealed, "Louie!" and ran
into the sailor's arms. Several pretty girls lined up to kiss him.

"I have good friend to stay tonight," Louie told the plump
woman. "You have room for him, eh?"

"Of course," the woman said, smiling at me. "Come on,
doll. I'll show you the second-best room in the joint. Louie
has the best."

By any standards it was a strange whorehouse. There were
rooms for the girls and, in a separate wing, rooms for boarders.
The boarders could be customers or they could keep to themselves. Most were customers.

My room was a small garret overlooking the river. The
next day Louis Fontaine came up to my room with a bottle of
whisky, and we toasted our new friendship and my new
career as a budding seaman. The man simply was unable to
accept refusal. I told him a hundred times that I didn't want
to be a sailor, but he just told me a hundred times that I had
the shoulders and legs for the job. I was going to become a
sailor!

As we got delightfully drunk, Louie decided that we
needed love. He bounded downstairs, three steps at a time,
and returned with two women. One was young and pretty,

with delicate white skin. The other was a heavy and robust middle-aged Swedish woman. She, obviously, was for me.

We talked, laughed, and drank until early in the morning—fortunately, my tongue didn't loosen, and nobody discovered that my name was not Andrew Kowalski—and then Louie diplomatically left me alone with the buxom Swede. I looked at her through a veil of whisky.

"You don't want me, do you? she said thickly, her heavy lips pouting. "You'd rather have the young, skinny one."

Somewhere in my drunk mind was the memory of a young and vibrant girl who had been the core of my existence, a girl who still lived in my mind, fresh and uncrushable. Yet even in my drunkenness I realized that life had moved on, that the wheel of history had altered everything. I was no longer young, and Suzan was gone forever.

I reached out and closed my fingers on the soft, golden hair of the plump whore.

"Suzan?" I said softly.

"If you like," she replied with rare understanding. "My name is Gert, but I'll be Suzan for you. For tonight."

The huge, cumbersome ferry eased away from the Municipal Pier of Milwaukee and passed into the cold, choppy waters of Lake Michigan. Only a few passengers were aboard for the trip to Muskegon, Michigan. The day was bright, but a cool breeze kept the passengers inside the large, central salon.

Louie was not aboard. He had purchased seaman's papers for me and had refused any money. I knew that the papers had cost him dearly in bribes, but he said only that "friends" owed him a favor.

"I'm going on a fucking old scow to Ludington," he had said when we had parted. "Holy Jesus, I hope it floats. It is long on service, short on luck. See you in a few days, eh, my friend?"

"Yes. A few days."

"You go see Gert when you come back to Milwaukee. She is good in bed, right?"

"Yes. Very good."

He clapped me on the shoulder and smiled brightly. *"Bon voyage, mon ami."*

"Good-bye, Louis."

"Holy Jesus, when you learn to call me Louie?"

And that was the last I saw of Louis Fontaine, as he walked away, swaggering, with his enormous sea bag on his broad shoulders.

Away from Louie, my fear returned. I surveyed the faces of the passengers, watching for a sign that one of them might know me. I had come a long distance from New York, but my fear had come with me. I knew that I could not slacken my vigilance.

Aboard my boat were a number of foreign seamen, among them two young Russians. On my second trip I overheard them speaking in their native tongue. They stood at the railing, talking in low, confidential voices. I eased close to listen. They were discussing the war in Korea and the uproar in America about Communists. Then I heard them mention the Katyn Forest massacre and the upcoming congressional investigation.

In their opinion, the hearings would be a farce. The Germans had obviously killed the Poles at Katyn. Even if they hadn't, the Russian seamen laughed, what difference did it make who had killed a bunch of Polish pigs?

I looked up and down the deck. It was empty. I could easily have taken them by surprise and thrown them overboard, and I very nearly did it. But the rage subsided, and fear returned. Perhaps these men were not seamen, any more than I was a seaman. Perhaps they had been sent to follow me. Perhaps, during this voyage, or the next, they would catch me by surprise and throw *me* overboard.

When the ferry docked at Muskegon, I left it and took a taxi to the train station, watching behind me to see if the

Russians were following. I boarded the first train to Chicago, changed my name to Ignace Pitkowski, and found a room in Hammond, Indiana, just over the Illinois state line. I found a job as a janitor in a steel mill where, because of my deliberately thick accent, the personnel office did not insist on my previous employment record or even a Social Security number. As far as they knew, I had just arrived from the old country, and they were being kind to me by giving me a job sweeping floors. When they later insisted that I provide a number, I gave a fake one, and they never found out that it was fake.

During the summer of 1952 I followed the progress of the investigation by the select committee of the House of Representatives into the Katyn massacre.

The committee interviewed scores of witnesses, took hundreds of depositions, viewed hundreds of exhibits. Hearings were held in Washington, Chicago, London, Frankfurt, Berlin, and Naples. And in August, 1952, the committee announced the findings of its special Katyn investigation:

The Russians, using the NKVD secret police as their instrument, had murdered about forty-five hundred Polish officers in the Katyn Forest in the spring of 1940, several months before Nazi Germany invaded Russia.

The committee called the act "one of the most barbarous international crimes in world history" and claimed that Russia had ordered the executions as a part of its plan for the "complete communization of Europe and eventually the entire free world, including the United States."

In the final analysis the select committee recommended that the United Nations seek action in the World Court of Justice against the Soviet Union. If the United Nations did not act, the committee said, the president should seek an international commission to sit as a jury, with Russia as the defendant in the Katyn affair.

The committee's recommendations caused a great stir among America's Polish community and became a prime topic of conversation and argument at the Polish-American Club in Hammond. But nothing came of the report or of the committee's recommendations. The matter was never brought to the floor of the House of Representatives for a vote, and the United Nations never acted on the first phase of the recommendations. The committee's report simply died, and nothing was done about it—then or since.

I, for one, was glad to see the matter ended. The more talk there was about Katyn, the more frightened I was that the NKVD would send someone to find me and to eliminate me. Instead, I continued to live quietly.

In 1953 I was fired from the steel mill when business slumped. Because I had spent so much time at the Polish-American Club and knew the manager well, I was able to get a job sweeping out after the club closed for the night and stocking the bar when supplies ran low. I also washed windows, cleaned the bathrooms, and ran errands. At the age of fifty-two, I gave the appearance of being seventy—and I let people believe I was.

In my spare time I read novels and history books and watched television in my small room in the basement of the club. I needed little money, and the manager paid me in cash. He never asked me for my Social Security number, so I did not have to lie about that.

Many of my old fears of discovery began to fade away, and, as the years passed, memories of Kozelsk and of Katyn slipped into a safe nook in the back of my mind. Even so, I exercised every day in my basement room and, frequently, went to the Hammond YMCA to work out. I realized, even then, that I never would be safe from the NKVD.

My fears proved to be well founded one August evening in 1956. I was sitting at the bar, my duties over until the club closed for the night, sipping beer, when two men entered and looked around the large room. I had never seen them before, but there was something about them that made me suspicious.

The men were wearing raincoats, although it was not raining. Their collars were turned up, and their wide brims were turned down. They walked past empty tables to the bar. Was this a movie?

"Where can we find Ignace Pitkowski?" one of the men asked the bartender. "We understand he might work here."

The bartender shrugged and pretended ignorance, but I turned on my stool and faced the men. I did not want to run again.

"I am Ignace Pitkowski."

The men approached me and flashed their wallets. "We wish to talk to you," one said in flawless Polish.

"All right," I said, sipping my beer and controlling a slight shiver.

"Not here," the second man said. He glanced around the club and then leaned forward, lowering his voice. "We want to talk to you about some missing Polish officers."

I felt my heart pound heavily. "What about them? What makes you think I know anything about missing officers?"

The man grinned. "We have ways."

"Are you from Polish Intelligence?"

"We're from the Alliance for Polish Liberation," the first man interjected. "Please, Mr. Pitkowski, we can't talk here. We want you to come to our headquarters in Gary and make a deposition."

"What kind of deposition?"

"Please. We must not talk here."

I looked around the club. Except for the bartender there were only two old men playing cards at a corner table and a young couple sitting near the jukebox. There was no one to help me. I could refuse to go with them, to force them to play their hand right in the club in front of witnesses, but I followed the men outside. It was dark, but street lamps made the sidewalk bright. Cars, trucks, and buses whizzed past in a steady, rumbling stream, rattling over railroad tracks.

"Our car is just down the street," the first man said pleasantly.

We walked north. There were no people, except those in the passing cars. As we passed an alley, one man pulled me into the semi-darkness of the alley. The second man pulled a revolver from his jacket pocket.

For one breathless moment, I welcomed death. I saw myself helpless at the edge of a vast grave, my hands tied behind my back, my greatcoat pulled over my head to blind me from the cruelty of man. Time stopped, and I waited for the bullet.

But the moment passed, and rage took over. My hands were *not* tied, and I was *not* helpless. I was not like the others who had gone like sheep to their slaughter. Life was too precious to be given away without a struggle.

With striking suddenness, I lashed out at the man with the gun. My fingers closed over the cold steel, and I smashed the gun into his nose. I heard bones crack and felt warm blood.

The second man reached into his pocket, presumably for a revolver. Doubling my fist, I swung from behind me. The blow caught him in the stomach, and he sagged. I brought my knee up into his face, and he whipped back like a sapling and cracked his head against the corner of a building.

Traffic streaked past unaware of the drama at the alley entrance, and I was back in Kozelsk attacking Kalanin, I was in London fighting the men who had tried to pick me up, I was in New York beating up two men who had come to take me to their "friends." I wanted to *live*, as I had wanted to live when I had crawled out of that forest pit.

I grabbed the man who had brought out the gun and smashed his head against the brick building until he fell to the ground. The second man came to his knees, groaning. I kicked him in the face and sent him sprawling into a row of garbage cans.

Finally, I slumped to the ground and put my hands over my face. Tears mixed with the blood on my fingers. I cried for reasons that I didn't comprehend. Questions ran endlessly through my mind. When would the Russians give up? They had murdered more than fifteen thousand of us, so why couldn't they let just one man, just one insignificant Polish officer, escape?

Amid visions of men being pried apart by hooks, picks, and shovels, the answer came. They would never let up. They knew that their grisly plan had not been a total success, and it rankled them. They would keep trying to find me, and when I was too weak to defend myself, they would get me, put a clean end to Kozelsk. Only then would Russian logic and perverted Russian justice be appeased.

I got up slowly, wiped the blood from my hands onto the clothes of one of the beaten men, and stumbled away from the alley. Once more, I would have to disappear. Once again, I would find menial jobs, living in many cities under alien names. I would make new friends, only to depart from them when the Russians found me again.

But life was with me. It would stay as long as I dared to fight for a freedom that I knew deep in my heart that I had earned. And when they finally found me—as they surely would—and put their long overdue bullet into my brain, they would not be killing a helpless and deluded prisoner of an undeclared war.

They would be killing a free man.